# Federalism and nationalism

**Studies in Federalism**, edited by
Murray Forsyth,
Centre for Federal Studies
University of Leicester

# FEDERALISM AND NATIONALISM

*Edited by*
*Murray Forsyth*

**Leicester University Press**,
(A division of Pinter Publishers)
Leicester and London

© Leicester University Press, 1989

First published in Great Britain in 1989 by Leicester University Press
(a division of Pinter Publishers)

*Editorial offices*
Fielding Johnson Building, University of Leicester, University Road,
Leicester, LE1 7RH, England

*Trade and other enquiries*
25 Floral Street, London, WC2E 9DS, England

**British Library Cataloguing in Publication Data**
A CIP catalogue record for this book
is available from the British Library.

ISBN 0-312-03219-6

Typeset by Florencetype Ltd, Kewstoke, Avon
Printed in Great Britain by Biddles of Guildford Limited

# Contents

# Notes on the contributors

**Christopher Binns** is Lecturer in Government at the University of Manchester.

**Audrey Brassloff** is Senior Lecturer in the Department of Modern Languages at the University of Salford.

**Martin Dent** is Senior Lecturer in Politics at the University of Keele.

**Murray Forsyth** is Reader in International Politics at the University of Leicester.

**Alain Gagnon** is Professor of Political Science at Carleton University.

**Alistair Hennessy** is Professor of History at the University of Warwick.

**Richard Jay** is Senior Lecturer in Political Science at the Queen's University, Belfast.

**Peter Savigear** is Senior Lecturer in Politics at the University of Leicester.

**Robert Senelle** is Professor of Law at the University of Ghent.

**David Welsh** is Professor of South African Studies at the University of Cape Town.

## Acknowledgements

This volume of essays grew out of a conference on 'Contemporary applications of federalism' that was held at Leicester University in September 1986. The Editor would like to thank the Nuffield Foundation for providing a grant which enabled this conference to take place. He would also like to thank the following for permission to reproduce material: The US Information Agency for the map on p. 117; Hodder and Stoughton Educational for the map on p. 171; and Greystone Books for the map on p. 211.

# Introduction

*Murray Forsyth*

One of the most striking political developments in recent decades has been the resurgence of ethnic nationalism. Not only in Europe, but in almost every other continent, it has manifested itself as a powerful, disruptive, and sometimes violent force. On the whole, the tendency of the resurgence has been towards the devolution of power away from the level of existing states towards smaller self-governing units. This pressure towards disaggregation has exerted itself at the very time that other processes, particularly economic ones, have tended to impel states in precisely the opposite direction, towards the creation of larger political unities, such as that of the European Community. The purpose of this book is to inquire how far federal structures of government are able to provide a means of reconciling the demands of particularistic ethnic nationalism with the maintenance of the wider unity of the state. Is it appropriate to think of federalism in this context? Can federalism reconcile the simultaneous contemporary pressures in favour of size and of smallness?

The book approaches the subject from three convergent perspectives. First of all it examines the way in which politically mobilised ethnicity – either alone or in conjunction with other forces – has in practice reshaped unitary states and impelled them in a federal direction. Perhaps the best examples of this tendency are provided by Spain and Belgium, both of which have undergone a remarkable constitutional mutation in recent years. What is particularly noteworthy about the developments in these two countries is that the new constitutional structures that have emerged, and which have pronounced federal characteristics, have been the outcome, not of some consciously pursued federal 'grand design', but rather of the action and reaction of various, concrete political demands. *On s'engage et puis on voit* – the dictum cited by Audrey Brassloff in her contribution to the present study, sums up the tendency well. This is not to say that federal ideas have not played

1

a role in each instance. They may well – as the wish to 'tidy up' what has spontaneously emerged becomes stronger – play a bigger one in the future. But they were not the prime determinants at the outset. While it would be rash to prejudge the direction in which either Spain or Belgium will develop in the future, it may be suggested that federal structures which emerge in this way, from the immediate push and pull of political forces, have the greatest chance of enduring.

The first part of the book is thus devoted chiefly to the Spanish and Belgian examples. Alistair Hennessy places the current developments in Spain in historical perspective, showing how strong and persistent have been the forces and traditions resisting the establishment of a unitary political system in that country. On the ideological plane, he draws attention to the ideas of Pi y Margall, the disciple of Proudhon and the 'founding father' of Spanish federal theory. He also describes the historical background of the rise of sub-state nationalism in Catalonia and the Basque Country. Audrey Brassloff concentrates on more recent developments, examining in detail the decentralised constitutional structure that has emerged since Franco's death, and surveying the mixture of forces that have produced and taken advantage of it. Like Hennessy and many of the other contributors, she underlines the intimate connection between movements in favour of national autonomy and regional attempts to obtain or to retain economic resources. As she emphasizes, the two can and do overlap, though regional movements need not always have an ethnic dimension.

In the chapter that follows, Robert Senelle unravels the constitutional reforms that have taken place in Belgium since 1970, reforms which represent the culmination of a long process of internal differentiation along linguistic lines. Perhaps the most interesting aspect of the complex institutional structures that are emerging is the painstaking and ingenious attempt that has been made to do justice simultaneously to the 'linguistic and cultural factor' and to the 'regional and economic factor'. Senelle concludes by assessing the distance that Belgium has travelled from its unitary origin, and envisages the eventual transformation of the country into a 'federal monarchy'.

France too, is treated in the first part of the book. Peter Savigear looks at the special provisions that have recently been made for the island of Corsica, not because they demonstrate that France has become significantly federal in structure, but because they show that here, even in this extremely potent example of a unitary state, it has been felt necessary to give some recognition to the autonomy of communities with a strong sense of ethnic identity. Savigear makes plain how limited has been the impact of autonomy on the traditional power structures of Corsica.

The chapters in the second part of the book follow a different line of approach. They examine how existing federal systems that have been deliberately organized to accommodate ethnic groups by giving them political status within the system have worked in practice. To what extent have federal systems of this type been successful in producing a stable body politic, and in peacefully reconciling differing national aspirations? What lessons do they offer?

Here it is worth observing that many, if not most, federal systems, including that of the United States of America, which is perhaps the most widely studied of all, were not constructed with a view to reconciling different ethnic demands. Their constituent states or provinces were not inhabited by people of different language, race and culture, but by people of the same language, race and culture. It is true that when the American federal system was founded there was a large black population in the southern states, but the union was not formed with their participation nor to enable them to have autonomy. Indeed, the constitution actually recognized that they were not full members of the union, but of a subordinate status. When John Jay defended the new constitution in the second of the *Federalist Papers*, he could write that 'Providence has been pleased to give this one connected country to one united people – a people descended from the same ancestors, speaking the same language, professing the same religion, attached to the same principles of government, very similar in their manners and customs . . .'

Similarly, the various German federal systems that succeeded one another from the founding of the German Bund in 1815 up until the present, as well as the old United Provinces of the Netherlands, and the modern federal Commonwealth of Australia were all founded on the basis of an underlying ethnic homogeneity. Even the Swiss experience, which is so often cited as an example of a federal union of different nationalities, has to be treated with some care. The thirteen cantons of the old Swiss Confederation which lasted for some five hundred years, up till 1798, were all of Germanic stock, and the business of the confederal Diet was conducted exclusively in German. Other communities, speaking French and Italian, were allied or subordinated to the Germanic core; they did not have equal status to the cantons. It was not until 1815, after the subordinate French and Italian territories had been emancipated, and when the French-speaking allies were raised to full cantonal status, that the Swiss union became the multi-lingual one with which we are familiar. Even the federal system of 1815 was not instituted or supported primarily because it was a means of uniting different linguistic communities.

The first case in which the decision to create a federal rather than a unitary form of government was determined very powerfully by the wish to accommodate differences based on ethnicity seems to have been the constitution of the Canadian Confederation by the British North

America Act of 1867. This federal constitution was remarkable in that it simultaneously *united* under one common government a number of separate provinces – Canada, Nova Scotia, and New Brunswick – and *divided* the hitherto united province of Canada into two political units, one of which, Ontario, was English-speaking and the other, Quebec, was French-speaking. The division was made in order to resolve the political deadlock that had arisen between the two communities.

If it is to the Canadian Confederation that priority must be accorded in the actual use of federal structures to resolve the political problems caused by deep-rooted ethnic differences, it was during the prolonged efforts to reform the structure of the Austrian Empire, between the years 1848 and 1918, that the idea of federalism as a means of accommodating different ethnic units within one and the same state was first elaborated in a systematic and thorough-going way. The various works of Karl Renner deserve to be mentioned in this context. They are perhaps the nearest equivalent, in this particular field, to the more famous *Federalist Papers* of Madison, Hamilton and Jay. In other words, they examine with classical rigour a problem with which, as we have seen, the Americans were not concerned.

Renner's ideas were, of course, not put into practice in the Habsburg lands, and the Empire fell apart into separate states in 1918. Since that time, however, the idea of using federal structures to reconcile the advantages that derive from political and economic size with the realities of cultural diversity has found expression in various parts of the world. The transformation of the Russian Empire into a federal union was but a token step in this direction, given the intense centralizing drive of the communist government, which only now shows signs of slackening. In Yugoslavia, since the Second World War, federal structures institutionalizing cultural diversity have gradually developed more significance, and in Nigeria and India federal structures have been established which reflect more or less precisely the ethnic diversity of the population.

The older use of federalism to unite people living in different political units, who nevertheless shared a common language and culture, has thus become increasingly complemented in modern times by the use of federalism to unite people who seek the advantages of membership of a common political unit, but differ markedly in descent, language and culture. In the second part of the book three examples of this latter kind of federalism are examined: first the Yugoslavian system, then the Canadian, and finally, within the overall context of Africa, the Nigerian federation. This selection, dictated by limitations of space, is not meant to imply that other examples – such as that of India – are of lesser significance, and it is hoped that it will be possible to do justice to those federal systems that have not been included, in subsequent volumes in this series.

As the examples of Canada, Yugoslavia and Nigeria demonstrate, it would be foolish to imagine that federalism provides some simple technique which can automatically conjure harmony out of ethnic differences. Alain Gagnon, surveying what has been undoubtedly the most successful of the three examples chosen, Canada, makes the pertinent point that it is misleading to think of a federal structure 'resolving' an issue like that of the cleavage between the Francophone and Anglophone citizenry. Federal structures do not 'resolve' such problems; at best, they enable them to be 'managed'. This distinction would seem to be crucial. Christopher Binns, looking at Yugoslavia, shows that the 'ethnic federalism' that was established there after the Second World War remained largely a dead letter until the 1960s, when an upsurge of sub-state nationalism, generated by a number of factors, breathed unexpected life into it. Now the problem is that the centrifugal tendencies have developed to such an extent that it is difficult for effective policies to be implemented at the centre. To this is added the problem that the constitutent territorial units of the Yugoslavian system were expressly intended to be distinct nation states, but in fact they do not correspond exactly to homogeneous ethnic communities. There is a gap between the proclaimed goal and the reality, and this has generated unrest. Here again is an important lesson.

Martin Dent, who contributes the chapter on Nigeria, gives a vivid account of the tremendous strains to which the federal system there has been subject since it was established in 1960. In spite of civil war, the collapse of two constitutions, and several bouts of 'corrective government' applied by military leaders, Dent believes that federalism has become a fixed feature of the Nigerian political landscape and that the prospects for its successful operation have improved rather than worsened. He points to a number of lessons that have been learnt. Not the least important of these is that in the Third World context it is not enough for powers at the centre and state level of a federal system to be effectively organized, it is equally vital that local or municipal government is strong and free from corruption. This conclusion complements and reinforces an observation made by Hennessy in connection with Spain: 'A successful federal system presupposes a strong associative element rooted in a democratic political culture. It is not sufficient for this to be expressed in aspiration alone, it must be embodied in practical experience of local government.' (p. 2)

The third part of the book turns from the working of existing federal systems and adopts a more speculative approach. It asks whether federal structures might help, if not – *pace* Gagnon – to 'resolve' the problems posed by ethnic cleavages, at least to make them manageable, in certain problematic areas of the world. Two particularly intransigent issues are examined: those of Northern Ireland and of South Africa. Richard Jay, after describing the background of the former problem, sifts through the various alternative proposals that have been made to break the impasse in Ulster, and comes to the conclusion that the conditions and attitudes there are not favourable at the present time for the creation of federal structures. More modest, pragmatic steps building on the existing, if imperfect Anglo-Irish Agreement, seem to him to offer the most realistic hope for the future. In other words, the moral seems to be once again: *on s'engage et puis on voit.*

Lastly, David Welsh traces the thin but by no means negligible tradition of federal ideas and sentiments that has existed in South Africa, while emphasizing that the dominant trend in the country, since the Union was founded in 1910, has been that of centralization, and the dominant political ethos has come to be that of 'winner takes all'. Given this tendency and this ethos, Welsh believes that the protagonists of some kind of federal reordering of South Africa face an uphill task, though he does not dismiss their alternative completely. As his last words suggest, possibly the experience of a long and barren political deadlock offers the best chance for a modification of the stultifying 'winner takes all' mentality.

This collection of essays, then, does not offer any panaceas. What it shows is that federal structures can and have grown out of deep ethnic differences within states and can help to manage these differences. At the same time it shows that the growth and the effectiveness of federal structures depend on a wide range of conditions. The depth of ethnic passion; the number of competing groups in question; their relative size and strength; the depth of the economic and educational disparities between them; the presence of a will to unity; the reality of the concrete benefits to be derived from unity; the readiness to distribute the benefits of union equitably; the political traditions of the people concerned; the presence or absence of democracy at the local level; the links between groups within and beyond the borders of the state; the external situation in general – these would seem to be the factors upon which the healthy development of federalism depends when it is viewed as a remedy for this particular kind of problem.

In conclusion it may be added that although the studies in this book are not directly related to European integration, they are indirectly of relevance to it. The European Community, even in its present form, has several of the hallmarks of a confederation or union of states, albeit one limited to economic matters. It is likely, though not inevitable, that this confederation will deepen and strengthen in the future. However, it will always differ in kind from the federal system of the United States of America, because of the immense depth of the ethnic differences between its various members states. Moreover the development of closer European integration, by lessening the significance of existing state boundary lines, and by creating an alternative focus of political loyalty beyond the level of the existing states, is likely to give an added impetus to sub-state ethnic nationalism in Europe. This is because the smaller ethnic units will see – and to some extent have already seen, as the statements of their spokesmen make clear – an opportunity of stepping out of the shadows of the states in which they are currently blended, and of establishing direct, unmediated contact with the new political authority at the European level.

For both these reasons federal systems which have been formed on the basis of ethnic heterogeneity, like the ones discussed in this book, have considerable relevance to the future development of European integration.

*Part One*

# The unitary state under pressure

# 1 The renaissance of federal ideas in contemporary Spain

*Alistair Hennessy*

The history of the last hundred and fifty years both within and outside Europe is littered with the wrecks of federal experiments, and none greater than that of the first Spanish Republic of 1873. Spanish Republicanism has been synonymous with decentralization, but the attempt to embody this in federal form in the nineteenth century was a disastrous failure, and it was not until the Second Republic of 1931–6 that federal tendencies began to re-emerge only to be submerged again during the Franco period. Since Franco's death in 1975, however, the federal idea has resurfaced as a solution to the recurring Spanish problem of regional assertiveness and although the present state cannot be described as federal it has the constitutional potentiality to become one.

Spanish federalism is inseparable from the ideas and career of Francisco Pi y Margall (1824–1901) its major theoretician and practitioner. A founder of the Republican Party which by definition in the nineteenth century was federalist, he was a Catalan by birth, a lawyer by training and a practising politician for most of his life after 1868, becoming President for four of the eleven months of the short-lived First Republic in 1873. Apart from an early work *La Reacción y la Revolución* of 1854 which foreshadowed later anarchist ideas, he was the leading Spanish disciple of Proudhon, whose *Du Principe Fédératif* he translated while in exile in France in 1868. His own federal credo *Las Nacionalidades* was published in 1876.

It is interesting to note how Pi did not regard federal republicanism after the revolution of 1868 as solely a Spanish phenomenon but as part of a wider revival of European republicanism. In his Hegelian style of reasoning he argued that federalism was the synthesis towards which all European powers were progressing. This is not so fanciful as first appears. We have been so brain-washed by an interpretation of European history which regards German unification and the Italian

11

Risorgimento as inevitable and desirable that it is easy to overlook the considerable canvassing of federal and confederal solutions to the nationality problem in the 1850s and 1860s. Pi was to argue that nations as they had existed and as they were emerging were 'false nations' created by wars and secret diplomacy. They were creations *'arriba-abajo'* not *'abajo-arriba'*, that is they were created from above by monarchical fiat rather than from below by the will of the people, and implicitly encouraged militarism, so condemning Europe to endless wars. Federalism was not only proposed as the solution to Spain's domestic politics but also to conflicts between European states. Federalism, republicanism and pacifism were inseparably linked.

In the 1860s federal solutions to ethnic, social and economic problems seemed to have brighter prospects in Europe than in the Americas where it had its widest application but where, except for the example of the Canadian Confederation of 1867, federalism was not a successful model to imitate – least of all the United States which had just been torn apart in a devastating civil war over the issue of states' rights. Latin America was even less promising with the Argentinian conflicts between *federales* and *unitarios*, the fiasco of the Venezuelan federal republic of 1812 and Mexican civil conflicts. The stablest Latin American country was the centralized monarchy of Brazil, from which Spanish republicans predictably averted their gaze. In Europe, on the other hand, the *Ausgleich* of 1867 had met most Hungarian demands although at the expense of the other nationalities, and Pi could even see in Imperial Germany a confirmation of his views, printing the German constitution as an appendix to his 1876 book, missing the point that it was a 'mock federal' state, giving predominance to Prussia – in much the same way as Mexico and Argentina, and the Brazilian Republic after 1889 were to be federal states in name only.

## Spanish Centralization and Decentralization

Pi exemplified in his fervent, overrigid federal beliefs the view that Spain, through its history, geography and culture has been, in essence, a federal state. His interpretation of Spanish history, the stock-in-trade of the radical tradition, was that the Spanish Liberal state in the nineteenth century was an artificial creation, the heir of Bourbon and French Revolutionary inspired centralization both of which were alien to the essence of the national spirit in which loyalty to the *'patria chica'* (the 'little fatherland') eclipsed wider loyalties. Spain had been the first of the 'New Monarchies' in the fifteenth century, stemming from the marriage of Ferdinand and Isabella in 1469 which united the two major kingdoms of Castile and Aragón. This, followed by the Conquest of Granada in 1492 was the culmination of the 700 years *Reconquista* in which the Moors had been gradually pushed south by a relentless campaign waged by the small Christian states of northern Spain which were eventually unified under the crown of Castile. The Crown made no attempt to enforce administrative uniformity and the Basques, Navarrese, Aragonese and Catalans, as well as Castilian towns, were permitted to keep separate legal codes (*fueros*) in return for their support. The ensuing relationship was thus a contractual one. It has been accepted by most historians that the expansionist period of Spanish history lasted for so long as this contractual nature of the state was observed, and that it was the gradual erosion of these privileges which signalled and foreshadowed Spanish decline. In this interpretation Philip II, Olivares and the Bourbons after 1701 with their French influenced policies were the great betrayers of the constitutional tradition. The War of Independence was adduced as the example which vindicated this interpretation. Under the impact of Napoleonic invasion, the central state collapsed and resistance was organized in juntas, at the village level – the *guerrilla* – when in Pi's words 'Spain was virtually a federal republic'. At the end of the war the Bourbons were restored and began to reassert centralized control but the collapse of the centralized state had weakened its legitimacy.

Opposition was first expressed in the Liberal Revolution of 1820 which introduced two elements into Spanish history which were to be constants over the next hundred years: the intervention of the military into politics through the *pronunciamiento*, and anti-clericalism. When Ferdinand VII died in 1833, leaving a disputed succession, the Carlist pretender was able to rally Catholic opinion. Faced with the Carlist revolt the Liberals, lacking mass support in a traditional population still largely Catholic, could only survive by relying on its military contacts. After a seven-year civil war the military came to dominate politics and from then until the present have never been far from the centre of politics. As politics fragmented, the military claimed to represent the general will against the particularist will of personalist factions.

Carlism was the response of a traditional, predominantly rural society to the modernizing, centralist and secularizing trends of foreign imported liberal ideas. Carlism's main strength lay in the Basque provinces where religion combined with defence of traditional privileges threatened by Madrid fuelled a resistance which was to last six years. Carlism represented the first and most persistent of the centrifugal tendencies which had been given new life by the junta tradition of the War of Independence. In order to overcome these tendencies the Liberals strengthened their control by imposing administrative uniformity in the re-organization of the country into the 39 provinces which still exist, and by abolishing the *fueros* at the end of the war in 1839, bequeathing a legacy which is at the root of the Basque problem today.

## Pi y Margall's federal ideas

The mainspring of Pi's federal ideas must be sought in Spanish historical development, buttressed and legitimated by Spanish constitutional law and the '*fuero*' tradition, in Hegelian dialectics and in Proudhonian federalism. In modern jargon Pi's views might be described as 'participatory democracy' with its emphasis on 'natural' units such as the family and the '*pueblo*'.[1] The nation in his view would be a federation of self-governing communities spun together in a web of explicit contractual relationships, in contrast to the 'artificial' and 'unnatural' nations of contemporary Europe created by wars, power politics and dynastic alliances. Although the case of the United States and Switzerland were cited, the influence of their example was limited. Nevertheless, Pi's views paralleled those of the anti-Federalists of the United States who maintained that true republicanism was dependent on the political vitality of local communities. Only in this way could public interest be maintained in public matters. The more limited the gathering the easier it would be for the individual to equate private interest with larger group interests. Powerful, distant centralized government was inimical to true freedom. Power, in Pi's view must be divided and subdivided wherever it appeared. It is easy to see why, taken with his austere moralism, he was regarded by the anarchists as one of their precursors.

The Liberal response to this type of argument was that it played into the hands of local elites and that it was the centralized state's function to break the power of these elites through a centrally appointed bureaucracy supported, if necessary, by military power. Convincing though this might appear in terms of breaking the political stranglehold and economic backwardness of local vested interests it ran counter both to the lessons of Spanish history and to the realities of power in the Liberal state itself which was sustained by a network of clientelist relationships (*caciquismo*) whereby local notables ran elections in conjunction with centrally appointed bureaucrats in return for pay-offs and privileges.

A major federal critique of the Liberal state was that it was an *empleocracia* nourishing the *empleomania* of an impoverished middle class. But so far from destroying *empleomania* one of the main appeals of the Federals to their underemployed lower-middle-class followers was the prospect of numerous openings in the states of the new federation while for lawyers there would be endless pickings from conflicts between them. The main support for federalism thus came from frustrated local elites excluded from the *caciquismo* system and from mass opposition to the hated military conscription system.

Although Pi's views articulated local and popular grievances they were out of touch with political and economic realities. Spain's poverty could not support an expensive federal system and there was insufficient complementarity of interests between the components of his federation to cement them into a coherent national state structure. Rationalist views derived from Hegelian premises and based on a dogmatic anti-clericalism (an integral feature of the republican tradition) were no consensus to replace the Catholic beliefs and Liberal policy which still engaged the loyalty of most Spaniards.

The Liberal state survived the federal challenge and in 1876 the Bourbons, the symbol of that state, were restored. But a far more serious threat now came from the growth of peripheral capitalism in Catalonia and the Basque Provinces which Pi rightly saw as a threat to his idea of a federal state where no region or regions would predominate. Regionalism, burgeoning into nationalism, feeding on real and imagined grievances, was the antithesis to his conception of federalism.

## The Peripheral Challenge

The impact of industrialization on Catalonia and the Basque provinces took different forms. In Catalonia, industrialization was primarily, but not exclusively, based on textile manufacturing in Barcelona and its satellite towns. Because of *laissez-faire* policies adopted by the Madrid government, removing import controls on cheap English textiles, the internal market was limited. Catalan manufacturers therefore became increasingly dependent on a protected colonial market which became the *sine qua non* of Catalan prosperity – hence the close links with Cuba which was virtually a Catalan colony in the nineteenth century. Not only did Catalan textiles enjoy preferential treatment in Cuba but repatriated profits financed economic growth in Catalonia itself. The loss of Cuba and its opening to United States' manufacturers therefore provoked a deep structural crisis in Catalonia and exacerbated social tensions which were to turn Barcelona into the Belfast of Spain in the early decades of the twentieth century.

Catalanism, already divided between industrialized Barcelona and its hinterland and a clerical traditionalist rural interior became even more fragmented as the upper bourgeoisie were inhibited from pursuing outright nationalist policies by the constraints of a militant working class, largely anarchist in orientation. A high percentage of this working class consisted of immigrants from the impoverished south who had little sympathy with the nationalist concerns of their employers.

In the Basque provinces industrialization came much later in the 1880s and was based on mining iron ore, metallurgy and shipbuilding. An old established commercial bourgeoisie which had acted as factors for Castilian wheat and sheep exporters and merchants trading with the

Americas was replaced by an industrial Spanish and Basque bourgeoisie. In contrast to Catalonia, Basque economic expansion was not linked to a colonial market but to European industrial growth, particularly in South Wales with which a symbiotic relationship developed. Under this stimulus the Basque provinces experienced one of the fastest rates of economic growth in Europe with consequent social stresses as the population trebled in the twenty years before 1900. Bilbao had the highest death rate of any city in Europe and the highest crime rate of any Spanish city. Social conditions provoked the first general strike in 1890. The socialist party and the UGT had their origins in Bilbao. The disorienting effects of this experience and the swamping of the indigenous Basque population provoked a Bilbao lawyer, Sabana Arana, to found the Basque Nationalist Party (PNV) in 1895.

Both Catalans and Basques resorted to racist ideas to justify their feeling of superiority over Spaniards. Catalans flirted with the idea of craniometry and traded abuse with Madrid accusing the government of neglect in riposte to accusations of selfishness. Arana's ideology flourished on stark antinomies. Intermarriage between Basques and Spaniards was to be forbidden. *Abertzales* (patriots) were contrasted to *españolistas* (hispanicizers). Spaniards were effeminate, lazy, blasphemous and immoral; Basques were moral, abstemious, hardworking and were racially purer – a deduction from the longevity of the Basque language. Arana attacked both the '*maketos*' the Spanish immigrants, and the Liberal industrialists whom he held responsible for importing immorality with industrialization.

Industrialization was the central problem: 'If Vizcaya were poor and only had fields and livestock, then we would be patriots and happy'. Fiercely Catholic and immersed in the '*fuero*' tradition, the motto for the PNV was 'God and the Old Law'. After Arana's death a younger generation of Basque speakers launched a cultural offensive to win the support of peasants kept monolingual by priests to insulate them against the corrupting influence of Spanish. The prosperity of the First World War hastened the process of deruralization at the same time as it brought the PNV support among the previously apolitical peasantry. However, Basques were split between those prepared to form electoral alliances with non-nationalist parties and those who argued for complete independence. With the advent of the Second Republic the deeply divided Basque provinces were less successful than Catalonia in pressing their claims for an Autonomy Statute. The Right representing the industrial bourgeoisie were against autonomy in any form; the socialists and republicans who were in favour of autonomy were hostile to the PNV's confessionalism, and finally the PNV itself was hostile to the Republic's secularizing policies. It was only after the Civil War had started that the Basques gained their autonomy from a republican government anxious to ensure their support. With the Basque collapse in 1937 a government in exile was established but within the Basque provinces a younger generation founded ETA in 1959 to pursue a more activist policy. It was their vanguard opposition to Franco, climaxed in the Burgos trial and assassination of Admiral Carrero Blanco in 1973, which gave ETA a pre-emptive claim to the leadership of Basque aspirations. But on Franco's death opposition to Madrid did not finish. Socialism was added to nationalism and the doctrine of internal colonialism provided legitimation for continued resistance even after the granting of autonomous status in 1979.

The people of Galicia, the third of the historic nationalities, never developed a nationalist dynamic comparable to either Basques or Catalans mainly because it lacked the economic clout to challenge Madrid. The region was characterized by a *minifundio* (smallholding) landowning pattern with a highly dispersed and impoverished rural population. Galicia had the highest percentage of its population in the primary sector and the lowest index of productivity (the Basques have the highest). Unlike Catalans and Basques the Gallegans are perennial migrants. Although independent sentiment was expressed as early as the War of Independence when Galicia virtually acted as a separate kingdom, it was not until the early twentieth century that a political party with a regional base, *Solidaridad Gallega*, was formed. The *Rexurdimentio*, was a pallid echo of the Catalan *Renaixenca*, an affair of provincial intellectuals who only fomented a linguistic revival as late as 1916. During the second Republic Galicianism found expression in the *Partido Galleguista* and in a plebiscite on the eve of the Civil War four-fifths of the population voted for autonomy, which they finally achieved by the granting of an Autonomy Statute in 1980.

Apart from these three cases, other regions with more attenuated claims to distinctiveness have also been assertive. The most important of these has been Andalusia which is the largest region (a sixth of the national electorate) and has a distinctive culture derived from its Moorish antecedents. It has claimed autonomous status with the mass support of a rural population which, in spite of massive emigration, still remains among the poorest in Spain.

The achievement of autonomous status by six regions via the 'quick route' of Article 151 in the Constitution (see below) would seem to presage a process which could finally turn Spain into a federal state. Among the remaining eleven regions there are differing degrees of support for autonomy, from Valencia with its linguistic claims similar to the Balearics to the Canary Islands with its independence movement. However, a major obstacle to implementing a fully blown federal solution to what the Catalan historian Vicens described as 'The Spains in their pluralistic unity', is the imbalance between economically developed and economically retarded regions. This is not a feature peculiar to Spain and may be found in established federal states but the historic experience of Spanish federalism suggests caution, particularly during the sensitive transition from dictatorship to democracy.

## The post-Franco period

It was inevitable that Franco's authoritarian, centralizing policy, with the ruthless crushing of all expressions of regionalist opinion including the use of languages other than Spanish, should have provoked a violent reaction and ensured that any successor regime would be decentralist.

There could, therefore, be little question that the new regime, albeit a monarchy, would revive the republican decentralist tradition. What was in question was the form which decentralization would take. Would the new state structure be a thorough-going federal one, or one with lesser degrees of autonomy? The structure finally enshrined in the Constitution of 1978 was a compromise, two-tier solution allowing for degrees of autonomy. Article 2 refers to 'the indissoluble unity of the Spanish Nation, the common and indivisible fatherland of all Spaniards, and recognizes and guarantees the right to autonomy of the nationalities and regions'. The Constitution was a radical departure from both the Francoist and nineteenth-century Liberal models of the centralist state. Although not defining the state as federal the Constitution embodies powerful federalizing tendencies.

A distinction is made between 'nationalities' and 'regions', between the 'historical' nationalities, Catalonia, Euzkadi (the Basque Provinces) and Galicia, and those regions which had not, in the past, articulated regionalist demands for autonomy. Nevertheless, it was recognized that where regional assertiveness was weaker there could be resentment against those regions whose economic power enabled them to force concessions from Madrid. The Constitution therefore recognizes two levels of autonomy. One, designed to meet the reiterated demands of the historic nationalities is met by Article 151 under which Catalonia and the Basque Provinces acquired autonomy in 1979 and Galicia in 1980. The only other region to be granted similar powers under this clause is Andalusia. In order to avoid accusations of preferential treatment, to recognize decentralist aspirations as well as to offset the influence of the recognized Autonomous Regions, Article 143 allows for the granting of autonomous status to other regions after a period of five years in which at least two-thirds of local provincial councils show a clear majority in favour.

The powers of the Autonomous Communities vary according to whether autonomy is granted under Article 151 or 143. If under the former, powers up to the limit prescribed in Article 149 can be assumed. If under the latter, powers are confined to those outlined in Article 148 where the State's powers are enumerated. The actual powers granted are determined by the Autonomous Statutes and by political agreement between the State and the Autonomous Community as well as by the Constitutional Court. The role of the Court is crucial in resolving conflicts between State and Communities as it is able either to enlarge or restrict the decision-making capacity of State or Community. It will contribute decisively towards the future shape of the state structure. Although Spain is not yet a federal state it has the potential to become one and has been described as 'federizable'.

Whether it will in fact realize this potential is dependent on the balance of political forces and working within the constraints imposed by the transition from dictatorship to democracy. A major constraint has been the attitude of the military which was a mainstay of both the Liberal and Francoist state. A key tenet of military ideology under Franco was that the rising in 1936 and the subsequent Civil War had saved Spain, not only from communism, but also from political fragmentation. The military has been traditionally anti-regionalist and under Franco was the visible symbol of '*España Una y Grande*'. The military did not perceive Catalonia to be the major problem as in the pre-Franco period, partly due to the remarkable young socialist mayor who deliberately wooed the military and under whom, as Minister of Defence later, the military establishment was to be pruned without any drastic consequences.

After the '*Tejerazo*', the failed coup by the Civil Guard Lieutenant Colonel Tejero Molina in February 1981, military susceptibilities about the consequences of a too rapid progress towards regional autonomy were smoothed by LOAPA (the Organic Law for the Harmonization of the Autonomy Process) in September 1981, which attempted to emasculate concessions to the regions.

The Basque provinces were a different matter as they provided the main threat to the integrity of the Spanish state. It is difficult to avoid the conclusion that ETA's provocative terrorism is designed to provoke a military coup and so polarize public opinion and rally support for Basque nationalism, not only among those in the Basque provinces who are lukewarm towards it but in the rest of Spain where support for Basque nationalism is minimal.

The period since Franco's death has been a remarkable decade with developments for which there have been no precedents in Spanish history. There has been the independence, skill and democratic conviction of King Juan Carlos, whose grooming by Franco would seem not to have predisposed him to become a democratic monarch; the virtual demise of anarchism as a dominating political movement; the political debility of the communists who during the Franco period seemed destined to emerge as the strongest successor party; the extraordinary competence and political skill of the most youthful government in Europe; the acceptance by the military of a non-political role; the moderation of regionalist demands – with the exception of ETA.

Contemporary Spain is unrecognizable to those who knew it a generation ago. It has experienced an industrial revolution which has not been confined to the old industrial heartlands of Catalonia and the Basque Provinces (and which owed more perhaps to Franco than his opponents care to admit); working-class leaders talk with a moderation incomprehensible to ageing militants; the political and spiritual hold of the Catholic Church has been broken; there has been a revolution in sexual morality; the press, television and cinema are among the most uninhibited in Europe. Spaniards are now 'European' in a way they have never been before; millions have travelled abroad – whether as migrant labourers to France, Germany and Switzerland or as tourists benefiting from a consumer boom. The once idyllic Mediterranean coast has been ravaged by the excesses of a speculative building boom which has no parallel in Europe.

The extent to which these changes have weakened loyalties to the 'patria chica' is still open to question. The gap between Spain and Europe has narrowed so that both share the same inanities, enjoy comparable freedoms, suffer from similar problems – terrorism, pollution, drug abuse – both share similar tastes arising from the homogenizing tendencies of mass culture. As social and geographical mobility increase as a consequence of these tendencies it may be argued that the desire to find recognizable identity in more restricted loyalties and the urge to recapture a vanishing sense of community increases. It may be too early to speak of a disappearance of the national community and the emergence of a nation of small communities comprising small, participatory groups such as family, ethnic and voluntary associations, but if trends in the United States are a reliable indication the time when Spain will be a federation of smaller communities enjoying Pi y Margall's sense of 'unity in variety' may not be that far off.

## Conclusion

1.  Contemporary trends must be seen in the context of a fragile transitional period from dictatorship to democracy in which an inevitable reaction against the centralization of the Francoist state has re-opened tension between the State and peripheral nationalisms which in their turn have raised expectations for greater devolution in other regions. The two-tier system of Autonomous Communities is the response.

2.   A successful federal system presupposes a strong associative element rooted in a democratic political culture. It is not sufficient for this to be expressed in aspiration alone, it must be embodied in practical experience of local government. Historically, Spanish municipalities have enjoyed wide liberties and powers but control by centrally appointed administrators, the *jefes políticos* – and the operation of clientelist networks have weakened them to a point where a conscious desire to re-create local self-governing institutions is needed. A comparison from the Americas shows how federalism in the US was built on the town councils of the 13 colonies – especially New England – whereas the failures of federalism in Spanish America may be largely attributed to the weakness of the *cabildos* (town councils).

3.   Where there are wide economic imbalances there has to be a high degree of self-denial on the part of the economically favoured if the funds to reduce disparities are to be channelled to the economically weak. There are also economic imbalances within regions (for example the impoverished rural interiors in Andalusia and Galicia contrasted with dynamic economic coastal regions). Both in 1931 and 1975 the transition to democracy occurred during a world economic crisis. Political reorganization, therefore, occurred at the same time as economic reorganization and that exacerbated imbalances both between and within the regions, increasing the difficulties of implementing federal solutions.

4.   The legacy of Civil War was violence – the violence of state oppression and the violence of the resistance – although it is easy to exaggerate this. In comparison with Ulster or the Middle East the victims of terrorism were fewer – 70 in 1979 and 130 in 1980 with right-wing terrorism accounting for 40 in the Basque country alone. Some of this penchant for violence can be attributed to generational factors – to the fact that a younger generation had not been subdued by the memories of the violence of the Civil War. But terrorism has played into the hands of Madrid, and the presence of the Civil Guard throughout Spain – a hated symbol of centralism ever since its foundation in the 1840s – reflects the way in which the coercive power of the state is still perceived to be a reality in the regions.

5.   There would seem to be a point where nationalist movements reach a point of no return. The problem is how to prevent regionalism turning into nationalism feeding on real and imaginary grievances (nations like individuals can suffer from corrosive moods of self-pity).

6.   Federal systems are expensive to operate and given other demands – e.g. social security schemes and, in particular, the cost both of

modernizing the army and pensioning off regular officers – key prerequisites for political stability – insufficient funding may endanger federal policies.

7.  One must beware of demonstration effects in proposing federal solutions. The American experience seems to me to be irrelevant to a consideration of federalism elsewhere, being *sui generis* in terms of the peculiar historical conditioning factors of 'new nationhood' – one point, at least, which was recognized by the otherwise impractical Spanish Federals of the nineteenth century.

8.  Federalism must be seen as a social movement in which particular social groups are beneficiaries. In its most extreme form it might be characterized as a 'cock of the dung-hill syndrome'. Federal theorists must not be taken at their face value: ideology can cloud motivation in this as in other political movements. Pi y Margall was right (in the long term at least) but for the wrong reasons.

9.  Finally, the Spanish experience must be placed in the context of the search for a post-imperial consensus. The argument that Spain prospered for so long as the contractual nature of the state was observed, is integral to the radical tradition which is now finding expression in the contemporary state structure. Counter-arguments that Spain and its empire continued to flourish even in periods of centralization (e.g. under the Bourbons in the eighteenth century) assume the existence of a consensus based on a division of interests within the Empire. (Traditionally Catalonia was given pre-eminence in the Mediterranean, and Castile – through Andalusia – was pre-eminent in the Atlantic and the New World.) In the eighteenth century other regions began to participate in imperial activities – the Basques in exploiting the new cacao wealth of Venezuela; the Asturians in the Mexican silver revival of the mid-eighteenth century – and with the free-commerce decrees of the 1780s Catalans became heavily involved throughout the New World. With the breakaway of Spain's American empire this imperial consensus broke down at the same moment as the Bourbon state collapsed under Napoleonic invasion. No overarching consensus replaced it. Catalans continued to benefit from the imperial connection but the reckoning, postponed for them for nearly a century, came with the 'Disaster' of 1898 and the loss of Spain's remaining colonies. It is with that loss of a consensus, which it could be argued was an aberration confined to the imperial period of Spanish history, that federalism became a key issue in the Spanish political debate: how to contain burgeoning nationalisms within the greater nationalism of the Spanish national state, so achieving Pi's vision of 'unity in variety'.

The parallel with the case of Britain is too close for comfort but for those with a penchant for the *longue durée*, Britain may be entering a similar phase of post-imperial disenchantment and loss of consensus as did Spain in the nineteenth century. Regional differences, papered over so long as the national gaze was fixed on the horizon of empire, now appear in exacerbated form. 'Internal colonialism' as Hechter has provocatively argued is not confined to developing societies.[2] Indeed, we can push the argument further and assert that it is an integral feature of underdeveloping societies. But that is another matter which cannot be pursued here.


## Notes

1.  It is a peculiarity of the Spanish language that the word for 'village' – *pueblo* – is also the word for 'people'.
2.  M. Hechter, *Internal colonialism: the Celtic fringe in British national development, 1536–1966*, London (1975)

# 2 Spain: the state of the autonomies

*Audrey Brassloff*

The pattern of power-sharing between the central government of Spain and its constituent regions that has emerged over the last decade does not fit neatly into the traditional classifications of the theory and practice of 'federalism' variously defined in a voluminous and disparate literature. It is *sui generis*. But then today's 'State of the Autonomies'[1] has not come about through the execution of a grand design; it is not the offspring of a homogeneous political philosophy, nor of a clearly thought-out theoretical position. Nor indeed does the Utopian nineteenth-century concept of federalism inherited from Pi y Margall (discussed in the previous chapter) appear to have had any direct impact. In reality various forces favouring varying degrees and kinds of decentralization ranged themselves against the 'unitary-staters': peripheral nationalists and regionalists out to maximize autonomy; parties of the left wedded to federalism and inter-regional solidarity; and centrist supporters of administrative devolution as a means of countering the bureaucratism and corruption of unchecked unitarism. Some favoured the generalization of autonomy all over Spain in order to dilute it, as they feared the high-profile sub-state nationalism of Catalonia and the Basque Country and, to a lesser extent, Galicia.

Where interests or opinions conflicted, the need for eclectic solutions and instant compromises could and did bring ambiguities and inconsistencies; progress was never rectilinear and at times proved to be positively tortuous. The State of the Autonomies was above all a pragmatic response in the late 1970s to the unique challenge of how – given the overriding political imperative of maximum national consensus – to replace the dictatorial state centralism of General Franco with a new antithetical system of popular participation in political decision-making at all levels, i.e. a system both democratic and territorially decentralized.

In the summer of 1987, debate over the desirability of moving the

24

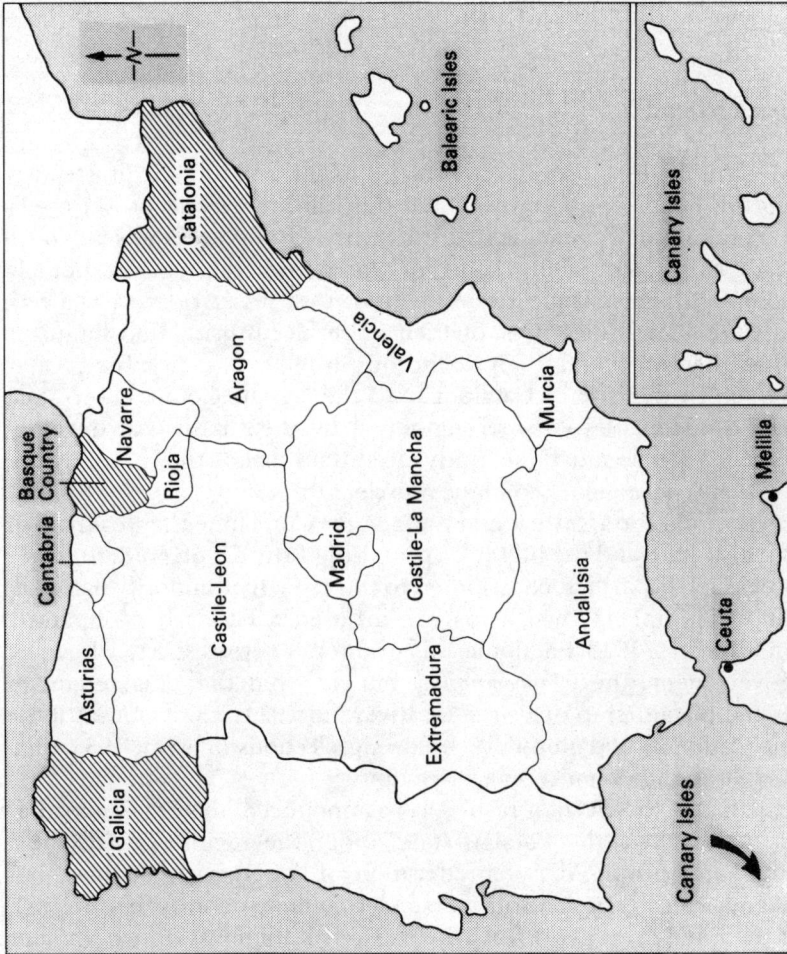

Spain, showing the Autonomous Communities

present system of centre-region power-sharing further in the direction of federalism was unexpectedly revived. The question had been brought up in the twilight of the Franco era and during the period leading up to the 1978 Constitution but, since then, although it had not been entirely forgotten, it had been pushed into the background. Before examining the new debate, it is useful to consider the whole background to the democratization and decentralization process wrought in Spain following the death of Franco in 1975.

## The background

An attempt to establish federalism in Spain had failed disastrously during the First Republic (1873) and thereafter the concept lost credibility. Political power remained at the centre throughout the years until 1931, in a scenario where some of the peripheral regions, notably Catalonia and the Basque Country (and, to a lesser degree, Galicia), which were acutely conscious of their cultural, historical and linguistic identities, became increasingly vociferous in their campaign for greater autonomy. In the case of Catalonia and the Basque Country, sub-state national consciousness was strengthened by their industrial development, which was so much more advanced than that of the rest of Spain, and by their consequent economic muscle.

Overcentralization, bureaucracy and at the same time the weakness of the Spanish state and the highly unpromising future it offered, together with regional disparities, contributed to the growth of minority nationalism at the periphery, which in turn aroused a backlash of 'Spanish' nationalism.[2] In 1913 Catalonia was granted a very restricted form of self-government (the *Mancomunitat*) but, as even that was rescinded under the dictatorship of Primo de Rivera in 1924, it was not until the advent of the Second Republic, following elections in April 1931, that decentralization became a realistic option.

Immediately the election results were announced, the Catalan leader, Macià, proclaimed 'the Catalan state under the regime of a Catalan republic' and proposed a confederation of the Iberian peoples, but representations from Madrid persuaded him to modify his claims.[3] What the Catalans pressed for, when a Constitution was drawn up later in 1931, was a federal republic for Spain and full political sovereignty for Catalonia. This was unacceptable to the Spanish Parliament: the organization of the country was obviously not based on independent units ready to meet on full federal terms, and anyway many of the regions did not feel the need for a federal organization. In addition, the 1873 experiment with federalism lingered as a distasteful memory.

At the same time, however, the unitary, centralized state which had rejected the main political forces of the opposition during the monarchy – a monarchy in turn rejected in 1931 – was equally unacceptable. So a compromise solution was reached between the existing unitary state and a federal state – 'the integral state' – a new concept, which did not divide the country into regions but made it 'regionalizable', creating a country in which there would be an over-arching '*gran España*' comprising regions that would each receive the level of autonomy appropriate to it in the light of the distinctiveness of its culture and general development and progress. Technically, the integral state of the Second Republic was but a variation of the unitary state, since sovereignty was not shared, and the regions' powers were not entrenched at the centre.[4]

It was a considerable achievement on the part of the Second Republic that the Catalan problem was resolved within this overall framework.

With the formula of the integral state, it was not proposed to effect a global re-organization of the Spanish state, but more modestly to satisfy the federalist aspirations of the Catalans, without on the other hand upsetting the unity which existed among the rest of the Spanish Republicans and Socialists, who were for the most part unitarists.[5]

This modest reorganization of the state was part and parcel of the Republic's aim to shake up society and set it on the road to democratic reform which Alfonso XIII's governments had not been prepared to envisage.

### Franco and the failure to homogenize (1939–75)

The Second Republic gave the right of autonomy to any region which desired it. Catalonia alone was able to exercise that option before the outbreak of the Civil War in 1936. The Basque Country exercised it very briefly before it fell to Franco's Nationalist forces in 1937 but Galicia, whose statute had also been approved by popular referendum, not at all. With Franco's victory came a generalized and ruthless attempt to eliminate any expression of regionalist identity that was not merely folkloric. Anything written or spoken that was not Spanish was banned and offenders were ordered to 'speak in Christian'. This type of repression was accompanied by indoctrination of the glories of Spanish national unity at all levels of education and by the pro-regime effusions of the state-run media. To the Francoist national unity was paramount and federalism or even devolution was seen as being synonymous with separatism and not to be tolerated.[6] Consequently, under Franco local government was just that: municipal and provincial, but non-existent at the regional level.[7] Even in post-Franco Spain, as a relic of his system, the constituency for the elections of both Congress and Senate remains the province.[8]

Francoist economic policy was equally centralist, with the provinces forming the largest political and administrative units on which, for the most part, state activity was based. During the period of the Development Plans (1964–75) emphasis was placed on sectoral rather than on regional development, and only in a few cases did these two priorities coincide. Existing regional imbalances continued and in some cases were exacerbated by the very fact of rapid and geographically differentiated growth: witness the contrast between the magic triangle Madrid–Bilbao–Barcelona and the continuing underdevelopment of Galicia, Andalusia and Extremadura, to take the starkest examples.[9]

The attempt at centralized homogenization provoked, not surprisingly, a counter movement. Catalanism flourished and the Basque Country experienced in the 1960s the start of a new terrorist branch of nationalism under ETA [10] whose violence continues more than twenty years later. As a backlash against Franco's authoritarian and centralizing political and economic policies – and under the 'demonstration effect' of the Catalans and Basques – autonomism, regionalism and separatism spread in varying degrees to other parts of Spain, such as the Canary Islands and Andalusia.[11]

### Democracy and the battles for autonomy (1975 onwards)

Franco's last message to the Spanish people referred twice in the same sentence to the unity of Spain although he did, exceptionally, make mention of 'regions' ('Keep the unity of the lands of Spain, exalting the multiplicity of its regions as the source of the strength of the unity of the Fatherland.') On 22 November 1975, two days after the Caudillo's death, his successor, King Juan Carlos, made a cautious reference to 'recognition, within the unity of the Kingdom and the state, of special regional characteristics as an expression of the diversity of peoples which constitute the sacred reality of Spain'. In the same speech, the king made an equally cautious, implicit reference to democracy in stating that 'a free modern society requires the participation of everyone in the decision-making process'.

Here were the twin challenges for Spain: the transition from an authoritarian regime to democracy, and the need to satisfy the demands made by 'special regional characteristics', in line with what, in the last years of Francoism, the opposition Democratic Coalition movement had committed itself to offering and recognizing in the future.[12] However, no-one could know in 1975 – or for the first years of the transition period – to what extent democracy in Spain would be authentic and to what extent a centralist state would respond to regional aspirations for decentralization and autonomy. At the least, these aspirations, and the commitment to meet them, meant abandoning a two-tier political and administrative system – municipal/provincial and central – for a three-tier system, introducing a regional layer to satisfy the demands of those territories with a strong sense of their own identity.

At the same time, the architects of the new Spain had to remember that the degree of state and sub-state feeling varied enormously from region to region; some did not necessarily desire to be 'differentiated parts' of the Spanish nation but merely to have a statute that would enable them to run their own regional affairs, and a decentralized government to bring power nearer to the people.[13] Asturias, Santander (now Cantabria), the Balearic Islands and Logroño (La Rioja) would fit into this category. Nor could the constitution-makers forget the weight of the long unitary tradition in Spain, the strength of Spanish national consciousness (as opposed to the minority nationalist consciousness in the periphery) and awareness of a common Spanish heritage. Juan Linz argues that most Spaniards outside the linguistic-cultural areas of the periphery simply feel Spanish and do not understand that one could feel something different from 'Spanish identity' at a level simultaneously emotional, symbolic and cultural. They may feel that they are from La Mancha or Extremadura, but that means loyalty to customs and a way of life which is not fraught with political implications. This is in marked contrast to the Catalans who feel that their nation is first and foremost Catalonia and only afterwards Spain, and even more to that not insignificant minority in the periphery, notably in the Basque Country, who feel themselves to be identified exclusively with a nation that is not Spain at all.[14]

These were some of the factors that had to be considered when the model of the newly-emerging Spainish State was being forged according to the 'bi-nomial democracy-autonomy'.[15] It was a highly complex situation in which the government under Adolfo Suárez [16] had constantly to be looking over its shoulder at the political right wing, especially the military, who as a body viewed with suspicion the introduction of democracy, the legalization of political parties and of authentic trade unions, and for whom the 'unity of Spain' was sacrosanct. Suárez was thus slow to grant political amnesty to Basque terrorists and this, despite the prospect of wide concessions of regional autonomy, exacerbated the attitude of the more extreme Basque nationalists who wanted separatism. As Preston observes;

This was not an aspiration shared by all Basques and was one that could only be achieved at the cost of provoking an intervention by the Spanish army. That would in turn mean a return to authoritarianism in the rest of Spain and civil war in the Basque Country.[17]

There was increasing pressure from Catalonia in pursuit of its nationalist rights. In the end, Suárez was persuaded of the desirability of recalling to Spain the man who symbolized Catalonia's aspirations and who was President of the Catalan *Generalitat* (Parliament and Executive) in exile, Josep Tarradellas. A deal for the restoration of the Catalan government was then worked out with him. This was part of a 1977 'pre-autonomies' system that would be generalized to the majority of the Spanish regions, in an interim move, before the framework of the Spanish state was defined in a new Constitution and sundry Statutes of Autonomy.

Legalized in time for elections in June 1977, almost all the political parties, except the right wing which remained wedded to rigid central-ism, included devolution in their political programmes and the PSOE (Spanish Socialist Party) and PCE (Spanish Communist Party) were committed to some form of federal state. The PSOE, at its 27th Congress in December 1976, declared itself in favour of 'the free right to self-determination by all the nationalities and regions which are to make up, on an equal footing, the federal state which we propose'.[18] A Minister for the Regions was appointed. He himself later pointed out that for a time he literally had no ministry in the material sense and that his greatest difficulty was shouldering responsibility for the regions in a country that as yet had no constitution and no regions – '*ministro para las regiones sin ministerio y sin regiones*'.[19] Two years later, by the time he left the post, there was a ministry and there were regions; in the intervening period, a Constitution had been drawn up and promulgated, and a new state framework had emerged.

**The making of the Constitution 1977–8**

For the makers of the 1978 Constitution, as for their predecessors in 1931, decentralization was the most difficult question to resolve. There was a tug-of-war over who had the right to be called a 'nation', an issue with far-reaching implications. A measure of its importance can be seen in the fact that it comes right at the beginning of the constitutional text. The preamble, having spoken first of 'the Spanish Nation', proclaims that Nation's will to 'protect all Spaniards and peoples of Spain in the exercise of human rights, of their cultures and traditions, and of their languages and institutions'. Article 2 proclaims 'the indissoluble unity of the Spanish Nation', and then states that the Constitution 'recognises and guarantees the right to autonomy of the nationalities and regions of which it is composed and solidarity amongst them all'. The three principles of unity, autonomy and solidarity are thus laid down: they encapsulate the guiding spirit of the Constitution but equally the problems that were to bedevil relations between central government and the regions in the search for equality (without uniformity) amongst them.

The Constitution is rich in ambiguities because of the very nature of the consensus politics which made it possible. In Article 2, the interpretation of 'Nation' is not in doubt, but the exact definition of 'nationalities' was never fully agreed, the term being used more to placate the Basque and Catalan nationalists who were out for maximal terms of recognition, than because of its precise content. 'Nationalities' appear nowhere else in the Constitution, but the term has reappeared in certain autonomy statutes, and is used generally to distinguish the 'historic regions' (see below) from the rest.[20] Elsewhere in the Constitution reference is made to 'regions', 'territories', 'peoples' and especially to 'Autonomous Communities', a term which had no precedent in Spanish constitutional law.

## The three routes to autonomy

The procedures leading to regional autonomy were laid down in Article 143 (the 'slow' route) and 151 (the 'fast' route). Catalonia, the Basque Country and Galicia enjoyed a special status as being 'historic regions' (a recognition of the statutes to which they had given approval by plebiscite in the 1930s) which entitled them to the speediest ride of all via a third route established by the Constitution's Transitional Provision No 2.

Under Article 151, a degree of autonomy equivalent to that of the historic regions could be achieved ultimately by a complicated system of local referendum returning a majority vote in favour from each one of a region's provinces. This mechanism 'was intended to avert future accusations that the Constitution had discriminated in favour of Basques and Catalans'.[21]

According to Article 143.1, 'bordering provinces with common historic, cultural and economic characteristics, island territories and provinces with historic regional status' could negotiate a Statute at local and central level which then had to be passed by the Spanish Parliament (Cortes). It was not originally intended that the Communities established via Article 143 should achieve the same level of devolved powers and responsibilities as those which proceeded via Article 151.

The intention was that all the non-historic regions, if they wished for a Statute (and it was thought at first that not all of them might so wish) would proceed along the slow – 143 – route and this indeed has happened, with the exception of (a) Andalusia and (b) Navarre:

(a) In the early 1980s, Prime Minister Suárez sought to dilute the powers granted to Catalonia and the Basque Country. His Minister for the Regions, Clavero Arévalo, acted to generalize devolved powers to the other regions ('café para todos').[22] Andalusia took the opportunity to step onto the complicated mechanism of autonomy via 151 and managed in the end to achieve it, despite a change of mind and brakes-on manoeuvring by the central government.

(b) Navarre, which did not wish to be considered part of the Basque Country, has a special regime governed by a Decree Law of 1969 and another Law of 1982 (Ley de Amejoramiento) which confirm its age-old charters guaranteeing local rights and privileges.

By February 1983 the political map of Spain, the so-called 'Spain of the Autonomies', was complete (see page 25). Seventeen Autonomous Communities of disparate sizes had come into existence, seven of them constituted by single provinces.[23] Statutory provisions, still pending, for the North African enclaves of Ceuta and Melilla will include the term 'self-government' but not 'autonomy', so as to avoid their being considered colonies located within another country.[24]

With some of the Autonomous Communities, historical–cultural–linguistic identity is more evident than with others. To take a few examples and leaving aside the 'historic regions' or 'nationalities': Andalusia and the Canaries have obvious distinctive characteristics; the Balearic Islands speak Catalan; Valencia speaks Valencian;[25] Asturias has its own, protected, dialect, Bable. Castile–La Mancha and Castile–León, on the other hand, seem more like administrative inventions to stop the proliferation of single-province Communities; and some others, like La Rioja and Cantabria, as was noted earlier, or Madrid and Murcia, have no federalist or autonomist past.

The constitution-makers of 1978 were entering uncharted seas. To a certain extent, their Constitution was based on the 1931 'integral' model and, as in 1931, the final destination of the ship of state was unknown, as they left so much for further legislation. In fact, over thirty State Laws (Leyes Orgánicas, Leyes Básicas) including separate Statutes of Autonomy for the seventeen different Communities, each with its own ceiling of powers to be negotiated within the framework of the Constitution, were to be enacted. The open-ended nature of the Constitution allowed a general consensus on the text to be achieved among the different parties, both national and nationalist, including, eventually, the Basque Nationalist Party (PNV) which successfully held out for recognition of the rights conferred by its ancient charter.[26] This open-endedness and the ambiguity mentioned previously also allowed various interpretations of what the new model of the Spanish state actually was, and these still fuel speculation today.

## The division of powers and responsibilities (competencias)

'*Competencias*'[27] in this context are the powers accorded to the Autonomous Communities to control specified areas of activity and authority which were previously the direct responsibility of the central state, and they imply the right and duty to provide appropriate services.

The powers referred to here are exercised by institutions which are based on the specific statutes of each Community and which, to a large extent, reflect institutions at national level. One major exception is that each Community has a regional legislative assembly consisting of a single chamber only, whereas the central Parliament is composed of both Congress and Senate. The constituency for regional elections is normally the province but can be the smaller territorial unit of the '*comarca*' as, for instance, is to be the case in Catalonia. Deputies are elected on the basis of proportional representation and in practice the leader of the majority party or coalition assumes the presidency of the Community. The President heads a regional executive of ministers (*consejeros*) in charge of departments which mostly, but not always, follow the national pattern. Political and administrative appointments in the regions tend to parallel rather than replace national appointments, which has led to the elephantization of Spanish bureaucracy. Each Community has a High Court of Justice which resolves disputes of a regional nature; in the final instance, however, the regional High Court is answerable to the national Supreme Court of Justice.[28]

Article 148 of the Constitution specifies the powers and responsibilities which the Autonomous Communities may assume, while Articles 149 and 150 specify those which are the preserve of the central state, and provide for the delegation or transference of powers to the Autonomous Communities. According to Article 148 the Communities may, *inter alia*, assume the power to provide services in education, health, culture, housing, local transport and agriculture. The central state holds exclusive jurisdiction over 31 matters, including defence, the administration of justice, international relations and general economic planning.

The most sensitive moment in the allocation of these powers was the negotiation of the first two Statutes, for Catalonia and the Basque Country, as the text of the Constitution allowed two different interpretations. One, which favoured the Catalan and Basque positions, effectively put no ceiling on their regional powers, limiting the powers of the central state to national defence, foreign affairs (with restrictions even on this point) and the national currency. This interpretation provoked a chorus of claims from the other aspirant Autonomous Communities, eager to obtain the same level of autonomy as the Catalans and Basques. Fearful of the virtual disappearance of the central state, Suárez's UCD

(Democratic Centre Coalition) government via another interpretation of the Constitution, negotiated amendments to the Catalan and Basque Statutes. These amendments upheld the government's position that powers ascribed to Autonomous Communities as 'exclusive' should be accepted as such without prejudice to the constitutional provisions which attributed the same exclusivity to the powers of the central state.[29]

The equivocation involved in this conflict of interests and perceptions has been the main source of friction between central and autonomous governments. The most striking case to date centred on the Organic Law for the Harmonization of the Autonomy Process (LOAPA), part of a series of agreements worked out in 1981 between the ruling UCD and the PSOE (without consultation with other national or regional parties) in an attempt to 'rationalize' the devolution process. This 'rationalization' move was introduced out of an awareness of misgivings among Army officers that the home-rule path being followed was leading Spain to de facto federalism and, more specifically, against the background of the attempted military coup of February 1981. The LOAPA sought to claw back some of the powers already agreed with the Autonomous Communities and to force regional parliaments to look to the central government for ratification of their laws. The Basques and Catalans therefore took it before the Constitutional Court, the supreme legal watchdog institution. This body (Article 161) 'has jurisdiction over the whole of Spanish territory and is competent to hear . . . appeals against the alleged unconstitutionality of laws and regulations having the force of law . . .' and also 'conflicts of jurisdiction between the State and the Autonomous Communities or between the Autonomous Communities themselves'.[30]

In August 1983 the Court pronounced 14 of the LOAPA's clauses to be unconstitutional. Nevertheless, the LOAPA has left its mark on most of the Communities that reached autonomy via the slow, 143, route; while it was still before the Court, some of its restrictive norms were accepted and incorporated into their Statutes and remain there today. The difference between the Communities that had achieved autonomy via Article 151 – the 'historic nationalities' plus Andalusia – and those which used the 143 route was thus increased. However, an exception, and a further complication in the already confusing pattern, was introduced in 1982 when, by virtue of specific laws – Leyes Orgánicas de Transferencias – two of the 143 Communities, Valencia and the Canary Islands, were granted a level of powers similar to that of the 151 Communities.

One might talk of a two-class autonomy system, both in the sense of the way autonomy was achieved and, largely but not exclusively linked with this, the level of competencias individual Communities were accorded. In respect of the latter, first-class Communities have a 'high level' of powers and responsibilities. In practice this means that their powers include control over the key services of education (Andalusia, the Basque Country, the Canaries, Catalonia, Galicia, Valencia) and of health (Andalusia, the Basque Country, Catalonia, Valencia, and eventually, the Canaries and Galicia).

Potentially there are no second-class Communities because in future all will be able to achieve the same areas and levels of responsibilities, even though some, like Asturias, have their powers ceiling written into their present Statutes. Article 148.2 allows all Statutes to be altered five years after initial approval. This was hardly to the liking of the Catalans and Basques, for whom:

the 1978 Constitution assumed the principle of autonomy because it was absolutely essential to resolve the claims to self-government made by Catalonia and the Basque country if indeed a democratic system was to be installed which aimed not just at the freedoms and rights of citizens but also of peoples . . . When the attack began via what has been called the generalization of the autonomies, the politicians tried to forget what was originally intended.[31]

### The financial profile

Power-sharing and devolved responsibility for services imply sharing of financial resources. The Constitution lays down the norms to be followed in matters of financial competence, and in accordance with Article 157.3 a law, LOFCA,[32] was passed to regulate the financing mechanism.

The central state is empowered under Article 131.1 to plan the country's overall economic activity and (Article 133.1) has the primary power to raise taxes. Articles 157 and 158 establish in general terms the sources of revenue of the Autonomous Communities. They are able to levy their own taxes (133.2), but only insofar as power is delegated by the central state. The LOFCA delegates almost no taxation power, only the collection and use of some 'ceded taxes'. The Basque Country and Navarre, by virtue of some historic rights, have each a specially favourable financial regime (Additional Provision No 1 of the Constitution) in that they have been given wider tax-raising powers (the 'special' or 'charter' regime) than the 15 other Communities (who have the 'common' regime).

For the 'common regime' Communities, the principal sources of revenue are the 'tax-sharing' grants from the central budget; these are basically related to the expenditure incurred by the Communities in respect of the services transferred from the central state according to the specific *competencias* established in their respective Statutes. There are

also specific central transfers, the most important of which finance
health services in those four Communities – Catalonia, the Basque
Country, Andalusia and Valencia – to which these responsibilities had
been devolved by the end of 1987; transfers of health responsibilities to
Galicia and the Canary Islands are pending.

The Communities are reluctant to be seen to add to the fiscal burdens
in their regions and so revenues from their own taxes are insignificant:
less than 2 per cent of total income derives from them and none at all in
13 of the Communities. Some state taxes are 'ceded'; they account for
approximately 10 per cent of overall Communities' income.

After long, hard, bi-lateral and multi-lateral negotiations, the financing mechanism to implement the constitutional norms – and so the
actual distribution of funds to individual Communities – was modified
(November 1986) from one described as 'transitional' to another which
was called 'definitive'. It remained based on the same three objectives:
to ensure autonomy; to maintain solidarity between regions; and to
guarantee financial equilibrium, i.e. control deficits.[33]

The proportion of central tax revenues allocated to the Communities
was established in a new complex set of formulae giving consideration,
inter alia, to such factors as size of population, territorial size, level of
services, relative poverty and specific regional conditions, e.g. the
Canaries and Balearics being islands. Advantages for the Communities
from the new system included the fact that, whereas in the 'transitional'
period funds were received from the central state to cover the effective
cost of the responsibilities as and when they were transferred (and so
revenues were not constant), under the new 'definitive' dispensation, a
percentage of state revenue was to be allocated for a five-year period
(1987–91) and there would thus be increased autonomy over spending
– and hence in the capacity for decision-making. It was also established
that Communities could not be made worse off under the new system.
On the other hand, they would not automatically participate in increases
in central revenues.

An important aspect of the problems of financing was left open:
payment for the costs of services relating to such historical realities as the
linguistic 'normalization' of some Communities and similar problems.
This meant, for instance, that the money needed to pay for the
extension of the vernacular in Catalonia and Galicia would have to be
saved from other expenditure areas. So long as that issue remained
unresolved, friction between the central authorities and the ethnic
nationalities was inevitable.

## Solidarity

There are clearly two elements in the financing of the Autonomous Communities that are conceptually separate but in practice linked. The primary aim is to give the regional administration sufficient resources to exercise the powers transferred to it and to provide public services such as health, education, social security, culture. But then there is also the aim of correcting regional disparities which in Spain are very pronounced and which are and will continue to be divisive. Hence the need for the solidarity enjoined in Article 2 of the Constitution.

This principle of solidarity is spelled out in Article 40.1 where public authorities are enjoined to promote a more equitable distribution of personal and regional income, and again in Article 138.1 where the state guarantees 'the establishment of a just and adequate economic balance between the different areas of Spanish territory . . .'

An Inter-territorial Compensation Fund (FCI) – established under Article 157.3 – has often been seen as the principal instrument of solidarity, insofar as it provides grants for capital investment, differentiated according to a formula which includes, *inter alia*, size of population, relative income levels, net emigration rates, relative unemployment rates and territorial size.[34] In fact, solidarity is most powerfully expressed in the tax-sharing grants for current expenditure. In this way, the economically weaker regions can enjoy, without having to increase fiscal pressure, a higher level of public services, financed in part by taxes collected in regions of greater fiscal strength. There is an explicit transfer of resources. The transfer between regions is, however, not direct. Technically, it is the central Treasury which effects this inter-regional compensation to ensure – or at least to further – horizontal equity by way of the fiscal system. Generally speaking, according to Josep Cullell, former head of the Economics Department of the *Generalitat*,[35] in countries having a federal system, or with regions enjoying a certain degree of autonomy, the starting-point is the principle of territoriality and only afterwards are mechanisms set up for compensation between the regions.[36]

Solidarity is not merely an ideal enshrined in the Constitution: it could well turn out to be the touchstone of the viability of the specific model of territorial organization and power-sharing represented in the present 'State of the Autonomies' or of some future amended system. 'In contemporary Spain, the trade-off between regional autonomy and inter-regional solidarity has come to be recognized as the key issue in the implementation of the decentralist 1978 Constitution.'[37]

The income contrasts are extremely painful: Extremadura, whose living standards are identified as being 'closer to the Third World than to Europe'[38] generates a regional product per capita of 50 per cent of that of Madrid, Andalusia 54 per cent and Castile–La Mancha 58 per cent. A quarter of the population of Spain lives in these three poorest Communities.[39]

It has been pointed out in this connection that the potential for territorial conflict that derives from the existence and perpetuation of inter-regional economic inequalities will constitute in Spain, as else- where, a longer-lasting phenomenon and one even more difficult to eliminate than the potential for territorial conflict which derives from differential factors of a historico-cultural-linguistic nature.[40] It is certainly an equal danger to the unity of the state.

## The Spanish model of power-sharing: definitions

There is no agreement among politicians and constitutional experts about the precise content or nature of the so-called 'State of the Autonomies'. It is 'describable but not definable'.[41] For many, 'it is evidently not a federal system . . . in which the sub-national units enjoy an equality of legislative independence. It corresponds well with the definition . . . of devolution.'[42] Others have referred to an 'imperfect or incomplete federation'; a 'semi-federal, semi-regional or semi- centralized state, at one and the same time'; 'shamefaced federalism'; a 'hybrid system of federalism and regionalism'; a 'quasi-federalizing concept'; a 'unitary state federalist in spirit . . . approximating more to the model offered by the Bonn constitution than that of Italy'; a 'covertly federal state'; a 'state based on the right to self-government' for which time alone will provide the final definition.[43]

A few of the arguments adduced to show that the Spanish model is not to be classified as federal are as follows (though not all experts concur):

1.  The Spanish Senate does not have the character of a 'House of Territorial Representation' (as it is referred to in Article 69.1) in the same way as the US Senate or the West German *Bundersrat*. The constituency for Senate elections is the province, and as each of them elects four Senators, representation is weighted according to provinces, not Autonomous Communities.

    The only concession to regional representation lies in the addi- tional Senators (less than 25 per cent of the total number) appointed by the parliaments of the Autonomous Communities. For this reason, if it is accepted that 'federalism tends to be marked by a concern with territorial representation and, most especially, the representation of regional units in the national legislature'[44] which is an aspect of the entrenching of the powers of federal constituent units at the centre, the Spanish model cannot be included.

2.. 'The Spanish system cannot be described as federal in the strict sense applied by jurisprudence for the simple reason that the so-called "nationalities and regions" do not have any originating power (that is sovereignty, however limited), nor therefore constituent competence, as have the member states of a federal state, to give themselves – or reform – their Statutes ... The Statutes of Autonomy are not norms that the Communities give to themselves, but are norms of the state which are approved by the Spanish Parliament, recognising to each region a certain sphere of autonomy (limited power).'[45]

3. Some purists go further: for them a federal state results from a pact between different sovereign bodies which decide to set up a new one, to which they yield up part of their powers. The Spanish state's point of departure is of a single sovereign body which recognizes the Autonomies and yields up part of its powers.[46]

4. The Spanish judicial system is dissimilar to that of a federal state which has a dual system of courts.[47]

However, although federalism was not the original point of departure for the Spanish model, it was not specifically ruled out. What the Constitution did forbid was 'the federation of Autonomous Communities' (Article 145.1). This was to prevent larger and more powerful territories banding together to the detriment of the power of the central state or indeed of the other territories, and to prevent a constant re-jigging of the regional map of the country.[48]

The constitutional fathers' unwritten watchword appears to have been *'on s'engage et puis on voit'*. They did not know how the battle would proceed, let alone how it would end.

**The federal debate renewed (1987 onwards)**

Federalism resurfaced as an issue in August 1987 on the initiative of the General Secretary of the Catalan Socialist Party (PSC), a federated member of PSOE[49]. It was taken up by the media, and critically examined by other political parties, both national and regional, and by constitutional experts. The PSC went on to vote unanimously at its fifth Congress, held in the following December, in favour of a federal development of the State of the Autonomies.[50]

What the PSC understood by the term 'federalism' was not clearly defined. Their perception was that the present role of the Autonomous Communities was too narrow, that they had little role to play in the running of Spain as a whole, that the central government was attempting to put the brakes on more power-sharing and that the central bureaucracy was still too powerful. They wanted appropriate mechanisms for the redistribution of powers between the Communities and the central and local administrations; this should and could be achieved via Articles 148 and 150 of the Constitution. The Senate would be converted into a real – in the sense of regional – 'House of Territorial Representation.'[51]

In reality, when the PSC spoke of 'federalism' or a 'federalized state', it was not so much to lay down a rigorous definition but essentially to give a name to the move towards the greater political and administrative autonomy which they demanded for the Autonomous Communities. These had to be authentic governments (not mere administrative units) which also had some say in the running of the country at the centre.

It must be borne in mind that the PSC proposals came at a very complex political time. After losses in the 1987 elections in most of the regions and in the municipalities, the Socialists had to make coalition pacts in some regions and town halls, and faced outright opposition in others. In moves to demand more powers and/or to embarrass the Socialist central administration, some regional governments were pressing for the revision of their Statutes, as they were entitled to do in accordance with the 'five-year rule' laid down in the Constitution. Moreover, with elections to the *Generalitat* due in the spring of 1988, the Catalan Socialists' proposal might be viewed by some as electoral opportunism, an attempt to promote their image as a political force truly committed to Catalan nationalism and thus to steal some of the clothes (though not the basic ideological wardrobe) of the ruling Liberal–Conservative *Convergéncia i Unió* nationalist coalition. Not surprisingly, CiU was dismissive of the PSC initiative.

Even within the PSOE, the PSC federalist proposals seemed at first unlikely to prosper, because of the official party stance at national level. The central government leaders talked in terms of consolidating rather than innovating, in such a way as to enable the Autonomous Communities to operate more efficiently but within the terms of their present Statutes. The Minister responsible (currently the Minister of Public Administrations) indicated that the process for the 'slow-route' Autonomous Communities would have to be conducted via Article 150.2 of the Constitution which allows the central government to transfer or delegate certain powers.[52] That way the government kept the initiative and set the pace for the process, and ministers referred to the need not to 'break the great national consensus' that had made the present Constitution possible.

In the event, however, in January 1988, the 31st PSOE Congress did take on board the Catalan federalist proposals while maintaining its negative attitudes towards altering the Statutes of the 'slow route' Communities. Resolutions passed included recognition of the need to articulate ways in which the Autonomous Communities could share in shaping 'the will of the state'. The Congress undertook to promote not only the autonomy of the Communities but also that of local government, including a commitment to pitch the allocation of public funds to the municipalities at the average European level. In practice this meant an alliance of 'autonomists' and 'municipalists' for the further decentralization of the central state. On the other hand, it also meant that the powers of the Parliaments of the Autonomous Communities *vis-à-vis* local government might be curtailed, or at least more clearly defined, for the text approved by the Congress stated the need for a clear demarcation of the competencies of each of the three tiers of the administration of the State: the local, the regional, and the central. Socialists at both national and local level feared a repetition of what happened in Catalonia when, in the mid-1980s, the Liberal–Conservative majority in the *Generalitat* used its exclusive powers in local government to dissolve the Greater Barcelona Council (*corporacion metropolitana de Barcelona*). This had in practice been the municipal government of Barcelona and twenty-six other adjacent municipalities, almost all of them with a Socialist majority.

Pascual Maragall, the socialist mayor of Barcelona, one of the promoters of the new federalist debate, stated that it was the first time that recognition had been given to the fact that 'public resources belong to all the public sector, not just to the central administration or to the one that collects and distributes them'. He also claimed that the undertaking by the Socialists always to allocate maximum resources (within the bounds of efficiency and redistribution) to the administrative level closest to the people was a political priority that would differentiate the Socialists from the nationalists, who were only interested in promoting the autonomy of the Autonomous Communities to the detriment of the municipalities.[53]


**Towards a federal future?**

The federal issue has thus been brought back from the sidelines, its outcome as yet unresolved. With the State of the Autonomies still evolving, and the debate about the ideal balance of power between the centre and the constituent regions of Spain rarely off the political stage, various alternative future scenarios, sometimes distinct, sometimes overlapping, can be discerned.

1. Evolutionist minimalist regional autonomy;
2. Radically revisionist neo-centralism;
3. Radically European regionalist;
4. Nationalist particularist;

5.  Mixed federo-regional;
6.  Federalist maximalist.

### 1. Evolutionist minimalist regional autonomy

This envisages a uniform regional structure. It would imply all present Autonomous Communities proceeding to exhaust to the full the potential for transfer of powers by the central government which is explicit and implicit in the Constitution and the Autonomy Statutes. This potential has not to date been realized, in particular by the non-nationalist regions. It would result in a broader and more equal – though still limited – degree of self-government, considerable administrative decentralization but with the clear supremacy of the centre unchallenged. This might not be fundamentally different from the present situation, though even such an 'evolutionist minimalist' model would run counter to the present endeavours of the central government effectively to slow up progress of the autonomy process.

### 2. Radically revisionist neo-centralism

Jordi Solé Tura, one of the draftsmen of the 1978 Constitution, points to the possible emergence of a new technocratic centralism brought in by politicians who consider the Communities a concession to the past and an obstacle to rationalization of the state and of the Spanish economy in the future. This neo-centralism would benefit from Spain's integration into the European Community and from the growing presence of the multinational corporations. The Autonomous Communities would then consolidate as mere decentralized administrative units.[54]

Such a 'radically revisionist' scenario seems unrealistic, given the strength of minority nationalism whose political demands Spain's new democracy was pledged to meet, and greater or perceived government intervention in the dynamics of the Basque and (especially) Catalan economy would inevitably exacerbate old resentments. Nor would (effective) abolition of regional self-government be acceptable to most of the other Communities now in being.

### 3. Radically European regionalist

Integration into Europe suggests also a completely antithetical option for Spain: the erosion of the central national state by ever-increasing supra-national (European) decision-making, associated with a widening scope for the sub-national and regional communities, leading to a 'radically European regionalist' scenario. Moreover, in a European dimension, opposition has already been expressed to the central government arrogating to itself functions that properly belong within the competence of Autonomous Communities in the application of EC norms. This has already happened with EC agriculture regulations, where the Spanish central government has taken upon itself powers to administer aid to the agricultural and livestock sectors.[55] In this connection, it is interesting to note that all the Spanish Autonomous Communities bar two – Navarre and Castile–La Mancha – are members of the Assembly of European Regions, which is one of the institutional expressions of the Utopian(?) dream, indulged in many EC countries, of a Europe of the Regions.[56]

## 4. Nationalist particularist

Another outcome could be seen as 'nationalist particularist' which recognizes self-government for the historic nationality regions while the others become institutions of purely administrative decentralization of the central main-nation-state, with little or no decision-making power.

This might actually please Catalan, Basque and Gallego nationalists, and indeed the Catalan President is quoted as saying that if anything is to be 'federated' in Spain it is:

the historic nationalities, that is, Galicia, the Basque Country, Catalonia and the major part of the peninsula, that which, starting historically with Asturias, León and Castile, occupies the rest of the peninsula, except for Portugal.[57]

However, it is unlikely that the other Communities, having tasted autonomy, will be willing to relinquish their newly-acquired constitutional rights. Nor should the dangers to national harmony (*convivencia*) and indeed to the central state itself, inherent in such a proposal, be underestimated. During the Second Republic the philosopher Ortega y Gasset warned against the creation of two different Spains, one comprising two or three aggressive regions, and another more docile to the central power, for 'we shall find ourselves with a centrifugal Spain facing a centripetal Spain: worst still, with two or three regions which are semi-states facing Spain, our Spain.'[58]

*5. Mixed federo-regional*

A variant would be a continuation of

a mixed model which some have called 'federo-regional' and which would imply an unequal degree of self-government among the different nationalities and regions, on the basis of the differential elements of a historical, cultural and sociological character and also on the basis of the different conditions and capacities of both.[59]

Such a model would imply distinguishing between maximum and optimum levels of power.

This road – sometimes giving a bumpy ride – seems to be the one that has been taken by Spain up to now whatever the complexion of the central government in power, at least since the debacle of Suárez's attempt to serve an equal slice of the autonomy cake to all regions in 1980. Any central government, willingly or not, has to recognize the 'differentiating factor' between the historical nationalities – Catalonia and the Basque Country and to a lesser extent Galicia – and the remainder. This was made especially manifest in the victory of minority nationalism in the Constitutional Court's findings over the LOAPA and in the resurgence of the nationalist vote in Catalonia and the Basque Country in recent autonomy and local elections. (The anti-system radical nationalism of ETA in the Basque Country presents a problem apart.) To recognize such a special status is deeply unpopular elsewhere in Spain, but it cannot be ignored.

*6. Federalist maximalist*

The State of the Autonomies may develop all its potential and end up operating as a federal state – in the sense of a much more pronounced shift of power to the regions – irrespective of whether it officially receives that label or not. Many commentators agree that this could be a realistic possibility (even if only in the very long run) now that the PSOE – though not necessarily the PSOE government – has taken up the federal cause again.

In spite of the frequent claims to the contrary, this could not be done within the present Constitution. At the very least, 'federalization' would involve a revision of Title VIII in order to allow the Senate to function as a House of full regional representation, and to give increased taxation powers to the Autonomous Communities. So, arguably it would require fundamental constitutional change. Seen against the norms of the present and of the recent past, this could be seen as 'maximalist'.

As a start, all regions would attain the same 'high level' of self-government available already to the 'first-class', 'high-level' Communities (a catching up process allowed for in the 1978 Constitution) even though resentment among high-profile minority nationalists (Basques and Catalans) at this 'same level for all' treatment would surely be rekindled. But over and above that, considerably increased powers for the Autonomous Communities would be implied, involving some say in the central functioning of the State.

A reduction in the present number of regions, with some re-grouping, would also appear necessary, given their unequal economic strength and the fact that some have seemed barely viable from the start.[60] The drawing-up of new Statutes might re-awaken old fears and rivalries in a context that would demand a high degree of co-operation and co-ordination.

## Conclusion

The 1978 Constitution addressed the two central issues of the Spanish state: political democracy and regional self-government. During the First and Second Republics similarly, partial moves towards territorial devolution had gone hand in hand with moves towards greater general political democracy. With the Restoration of 1874 and with Franco's victory in the Civil War, these joint endeavours were submerged.

The present perception of flourishing regional diversity and autonomy – expressed in the concept of 'the Spain of the Autonomies' – as strenthening the unity of the Spanish state runs counter to the centuries-old struggle to overcome particularist forces and interests in the vigorous pursuit of countrywide unification and centralization which led to a widespread sense of identification with the overall Spanish state.

In assessing the relevance of Spain's new regionalist structure to the resolution of conflicts between the nation-state and sub-state nationism, it must be remembered that only three of the seventeen Autonomous Communities, comprising less than 30 per cent of the country's population, are based on their own separate sub-state nationality. The other fourteen are all of the same (Spanish) nation, most of them speak the same (Spanish) language with differences of dialect only, though many of them have a 'distinct historic and/or regional identity' attested in their Statutes. This contrasts with the federalist or regionalist structures for the healing of ethnic confrontation in other countries of Europe where, (as in Yugoslavia, Czechoslovakia, and potentially in Belgium), the 'federalist' state is made up of constituent regions each of which roughly corresponds to a differentiated nationality.

If the Spanish autonomy structure is to a large extent geared to ethnic issues, it is arguably even more strongly geared to, and relevant for, the evening-out of the persistent polarization of regions, an issue potentially equally dangerous'to the unity of the state: the regional disparities in economic structure, income, wealth and general social welfare.

In disadvantaged Communities there are inevitably high, but possibly illusory, hopes that the political bargaining power of self-government will lead to a more favourable regional share-out of total national resources and that increased regional decision-making, guided primarily by consideration of local interests, will allow for more efficient use of all resources.

In some advantaged Communities, perceptions predominate that their already proven and superior regional efficiency in resource use will be further enhanced by the reduction of the influence of the Centre and that maximum self-government will equate with minimum outflow of resources from the region into the rest of the country.

The difficulties in establishing criteria for a countrywide redistribution of resources between the favoured and the disadvantaged regions that are both equitable and politically realistic may very well underlie the debate that has resurfaced over the most desirable pattern of centre–periphery structures.

The situation at present is in a state of flux. Some of the rules are permissive; options opened up by parts of the Constitution and of the Statutes of the individual Autonomous communities may yet or may never be taken up. The system of automny finance that superseded the 'transitional' in 1986 may be called 'definitive' but is clearly not unalterable.[61] Organic Laws to execute constitutional provisions have been sometimes challenged before the Constitutional Court, whose interpretation does not always stay narrowly within the text, partly because of a lack of clarity in the Constitution which is related to the consensus–compromise imperative of the late 1970s.

The constitutional debate about the form of the Spanish state is not over. It has been frequently rekindled – most recently in the second half of 1987. The portents are ambiguous. The present political climate in Spain overall and the central government's instincts favour very cautious advance, after a period of improvizations, which were almost inevitable given the nature of Spain's transition to democracy. The administration on the one hand wants to be seen to be involved in constructive negotiations with Basque and Catalan nationalism, and on the other hand wants to set the (slow) pace for the development of the autonomy powers of the other regions. It does not wish to tinker with either the Constitution or with the Statutes of Autonomy.

However, in the long term, a move in the direction of federalism, however defined, cannot be ruled out. The present Prime Minister, Felipe González, who in opposition and later in government has been closely involved in the democratizing and decentralizing process, called the Catalan Socialists' recent initiative 'an effort at thinking-through the issues which sees the State of the Autonomies in the context of international views on federal states and co-operative federalism'.[62] Indeed, on an earlier occasion, Felipe González stated that he had 'the perspective of the year 2000 for the culmination of this process which would leave us at the doors of a federal structure of the state'.[63]

So a final analysis, evaluation and classification of the precise 'theoretical nature' of the Spanish state-region power-sharing model will have to wait for its formal completion. Nevertheless, one can discern the rough outlines of various roads along which the State of the Autonomies may proceed, and the patterns that may emerge.


## Acknowledgement

I am grateful to Dr. Joaquim Solé Vilanova of Barcelona University for his comments and suggestions. Any shortcomings in this chapter are my responsibility entirely.


## Notes

1. The 1978 Constitution, (in Article 3 and others) refers to 'Autonomous Communities', whose rights are recognized within the unity of the Spanish nation. It was on this basis that the expressions 'The State of the Autonomies' and 'The Spain of the Autonomies' were subsequently minted and have been widely used in the literature.
2. See I. Olábarri Gortázar, 'El conflicto entre nacionalismos', in F. Fernández Rodríguez (co-ord), *La España de las Autonomías*, Instituto de Estudios de Administración Local, Madrid (1985), 74.
3. Details of the central government–Catalan negotiations in A. Hernández Lafuente, *Autonomía e integración en la Segunda República*, Madrid (1980), 51–6.
4. See I. Olábarri Gortázar, 'La cuestión regional en España, in *La España de las Autonomías*, Espasa-Calpe, Madrid (1981), Vol. 1, 181, footnote 138.
5. Ibid, 180, footnote 136.
6. See S. Giner, 'Ethnic nationalism, centre and periphery', in Abel and Torrents (eds), *Spain – Conditional Democracy* (1984), 86.
7. See M. Hebbert, 'Regional Policy in Spain', *Geoforum 13* (1982), 114.
8. The provincial organization of the country, based on the French model, was generalized in 1833 by Javier de Burgos: forty-nine (later fifty) provinces, forty-seven on the mainland and three for the islands (Balearics and Canaries).
9. See J. R. Cuadrado Roura, *La política regional en los Planes de Desarrollo*, Espasa-Calpe, Madrid (1981) Vol 1, 550–4.

10. Acronym signifying Basque Homeland and Freedom.
11. J. P. Fusi extends this even to Castile. 'Spain: The Fragile Democracy', *West European Politics 5,* No 2 (1982), 227.
12. The Democratic Coalition comprised the left and regional parties, and some which would later form part of the UCD, the governing coalition of the first stage of the period of transition from dictatorship to democracy.
13. See G. Ariño Ortiz, 'El Estado de las Autonomías, una interpretación jurídica', in F. Fernández Rodríguez (co-ord), *La España de las Autonomías*, op. cit. (note 2), 283.
14. J. Linz, 'Un sociólogo ante el problema: una España multinacional y la posibilidad de una democracia consociacional', in G. Trujillo (ed), *Federalismo y nacionalismo*, Madrid (1979) 135.
15. The term is used to contrast with 'the bi-nomial dictatorship-centralism forces' by Antoni Monreal, 'The New Spanish State Structure', in M. Burgess (ed), *Federalism and Federation in Western Europe* (1986), 61.
16. Carlos Arias Navarro, the last Prime Minister under Franco and the first of the monarchy, was forced to resign a few months after King Juan Carlos' accession, as Arias was unable to handle either the Franco die-hards or the political opposition. The King then appointed Adolfo Suárez.
17. P. Preston, *The Triumph of Democracy in Spain* (1986), 124.
18. Quoted by M. Turrión, 'Sempre en Galiza', *El País*, 24 March 1978.
19. M. Clavero Arévalo, *España desde el centralismo a las Autonomías*, Barcelona (1983), 25.
20. The term 'nationalities' reappears in the Statutes drawn up for Catalonia, the Basque Country, Galicia and – more curiously – Andalusia. Most regions are referred to in their Statutes as 'historic entities'.
21. L. F. Alonso Teixidor and M. Hebbert, 'Regional Planning in Spain and the Transition to Democracy', in R. Hudson, J. R. Lewis (eds), *Regional Planning in Europe* (1982), 20.
22. With the generalization of devolved powers to the different regions, it was said that Clavero Arévalo had served up 'coffee for everyone' instead of 'champagne for the historic nationalities'. Later, when the system of financing was determined, the Catalans were to complain that the Basques and Navarrans (because of their favourable tax-raising regime) had been given brandy to accompany their coffee.
23. The seventeen Autonomous Communities are Andalusia, Aragon, Asturias, Balearic Islands, Basque Country, Canary Islands, Cantabria, Castile–La Mancha, Castile–León, Catalonia, Extremadura, Galicia, Madrid, Murcia, Navarre, La Rioja, Valencia. (The seven single-province Communities are Asturias, Balearic Islands, Cantabria, Madrid, Murcia, Navarre and La Rioja).
24. See *El País*, 24 February 1987.
25. Valencian is considered by many to be a variety of Catalan.
26. This recognition comes in Additional Provision 1 and Repeal Provision 2 of the 1978 Constitution.
27. In the absence of a precise equivalent in English, 'competencia' has been variously translated as 'power', 'competence', 'function' and 'responsibility'.
28. For a fuller account of the institutions of autonomy, see P. J. Donaghy and

M. T. Newton, *Spain – a Guide to Political and Economic Institutions*, CUP, 1987, 107–12.

29. See E. García de Enterría, 'El futuro de las autonomías territoriales', in E. García de Enterría (ed) *España: Un presente para el futuro* Vol 2, Instituto de Estudios Económicós, Madrid (1984), 103–7.

30. There have been a large number of cases brought for the Court's decision on matters affecting regional government powers. They include: Andalusia's Agrarian Reform Law (mainly concerned with the expropriation of certain large estates) which the Court declared not prejudicial to private property and private enterprise, and several affecting the use of languages other than Castilian (cases lodged by all the 'historic nationalities') where the criterion followed by the Court has been based on Article 3 of the Constitution which establishes that the languages of the Autonomous Communities have rights and are to be protected, but that these rights do not constitute obligations.

31. M. Fernández, *La Vanguardia*, 4 April 1985.

32. Organic Law for Financing the Autonomous Communities.

33. J. Ruiz Huertas, 'Financiación autonómica, perfiles de un compromiso', *El País*, 20 June 1987. For details of financing in the 'transitional' period, see J. M. Basañez, 'La financiación de las Comunidades Autónomas', in Banco de Bilbao, *Situación 1986/4*, 62–70, and A. Brassloff, 'La España de las Autonomías', in *Vida Hispánica*, Winter 1985, 9.

34. It was envisaged that the FCI would be enhanced by transfers from the European Regional Development Fund. Assistance was also anticipated from other European Community institutions.

35. *La Vanguardia*, 25 July 1986.

36. A further element of solidarity, though not specifically geared to Communities, continues to exist insofar as differential transfers under various titles from (taxes) and to (social security payments, etc) individuals reduce regional disparities in income per head: in this way, differences in the regional disposable income per head are smaller than those in regional income per head. Data from Banco de Bilbao, *Renta Nacional de España 1985*, Vizcaya, (1988) show that regional income per head in the poorest quarter of Spain's population is 54 per cent that of the richest quarter; equivalent disposable income per head is 66 per cent.

37. M. Hebbert, 'The New Decentralism', in Healey, McDougall and Thomas (eds), *Planning Theory Prospects for the 1980s* (1982), 114.

38. *The Economist*, in its special Survey of Spain, 11 March 1986, 29.

39. Calculation based on data from *Renta Nacional de España*, op. cit. in note 36.

40. J. López-Aranguren, *La conciencia regional en el proceso autonómico español*, Madrid (1983), 194.

41. J. Tornos *et al.*, *Informe sobre las Autonomías*, Barcelona (1987), 31.

42. L. F. Alonso Teixidor and M. Hebbert, op. cit. (note 21), 22.

43. All quoted by G. Ariño Ortiz, 'El Estado de las Autonomías – realidad política, interpretación jurídica', in *La España de las Autonomías*, Espasa-Calpe, Madrid (1981), Vol 2, 24. The subtitle of his chapter makes a telling reference to 'a Juridical-State Enigma'.

44. P. King, *Federalism and Federation*, (1982), 19.

45. G. Ariño Ortiz, in F. Fernández Rodríguez (co-ord.), op. cit. (note 2), 280.
46. L. Sánchez Agesta, *Revista Informativa de la Oficina de Información Diplomática*, 170, Madrid, (October 1987), 5.
47. G. Ariño Ortiz, op. cit. (note 2), 281.
48. However, in Transitory Provision No. 4, the Constitution specifically allowed for the possible future incorporation of Navarre into the Autonomous Community of the Basque Country.
49. The issue had never completely disappeared and references to a federal model for Spain had been made in earlier years by the same PSC General Secretary as well as the President of the Andalusian Parliament, and others.
50. *El País*, 14 December 1987.
51. Ibid.
52. *El País*, 13 December 1987.
53. *El País*, 24 January 1988.
54. J. Solé Tura, *Nacionalidades y nacionalismos en España*, Madrid (1985), 160.
55. J. Tornos *et al.*, op. cit. (note 41), 102.
56. M. Kolinsky discusses 'The nation-state in Western Europe: erosion from above and below' in L. Tivey (ed), *The Nation-State*, (1981), 82–103.
57. Quoted by J. Solé Tura, 'Un debate que ha empezado mal', *El País*, 30 September 1987.
58. Quoted in E. García de Enterría, op. cit. (note 29), 113.
59. G. Ariño Ortiz, op. cit., 284.
60. For instance, a study published by the Revista Española de Investigaciones Sociológicas considered that the survival of Castile–León and Castile–La Mancha as Autonomous Communities was 'very problematical'. *El País*, 12 December 1983.
61. For example, as early as January 1988, Catalonia, Castile–León, Aragón, the Balearic Islands and Andalusia demanded from the central administration economic compensation for certain favourable financial arrangements which the Basque government had obtained in the previous December. *El País*, 27 January 1988.
62. Interview with the editor of El País, *El País Semanal*, 8 November 1987.
63. 1980 statement quoted in *El País*, 19 October 1987.

# 3 Constitutional reform in Belgium: from unitarism towards federalism

*Robert Senelle*

Since 1970 the structure of the Belgian state has undergone fundamental changes. These changes have been made primarily in order to
give political recognition and status to the different linguistic and
cultural communities that exist within the boundaries of Belgium. The
process of restructuring has not come to an end so it is not yet possible to
see it in full perspective. The purpose of this chapter is to describe as
exactly as possible the most important reforms that have so far been
effected, to discuss their impact and possible future evolution, and in
particular to ask how far they involve the transformation of a unitary
state into a federal one. The emphasis will be on constitutional issues and
the text of the Belgian constitution as it stands at the end of 1987 is
appended (p 77) to enable the reader to follow developments more
easily. The opening section will outline the historical background of the
present period of change.

## Belgium: an old nation with current problems

The roots of the present-day kingdom of Belgium are to be found in the
principalities of the Southern Low Countries. During the fifteenth and
sixteenth centuries, the Dukes of Burgundy gradually succeeded in
grouping these principalities, together with the territories in the
Northern Low Countries, into a large personal union sharing the same
socio-economic culture and sovereign.

Thus contrary to the opinion often voiced abroad, Belgium is not an
artificial body which came into existence because of a concern for
political and military equilibrium on the part of the Great Powers in
1830. The constituent parts of the old Burgundian state spoke French
and Dutch. The present nine provinces are the successors of the old
principalities, which preceded the creation of the Belgian states. For

51

more than a thousand years and until recently the annual session of the council of each of the principalities – later the nine provinces – was declared open by the governor first in the name of the King of Spain, afterwards in the name of the Emperor (House of Habsburg), and finally, since 1830, in the name of the King of Belgium.

The current borders between the Belgian provinces were established at the end of the eighteenth century, but they have inherited traditions that go back well beyond this. There is probably not a single inhabitant of the province of West Flanders or East Flanders who does not have a feeling of pride for the prestigious County of Flanders, the cradle of world-famous Flemish painting; inhabitants of the Belgian provinces of Brabant and Antwerp and of North Brabant in the Netherlands recall the Duchy of Brabant; inhabitants of the province of Liège take pride in the episcopal principality of Liège. These few examples may suffice. It should not be forgotten that the coat of arms and blazon of the ancient Duchy of Brabant were adopted by the new Kingdom of Belgium in 1830. These symbols of a distant past go back, from an institutional point of view, to the early Middle Ages.

The tragic religious wars of the second half of the sixteenth century were to result in the partition of the seventeen provinces of the Burgundian state. With the fall of Antwerp, seized by the Spanish army in 1585, the Southern Low Countries, which at present constitute the territory of the Kingdom of Belgium, came first under the rule of the Spaniards and then of the Habsburgs, while the Northern province evolved into the separate Republic of the United Netherlands.

The reunification in 1815 of the seventeen provinces by William I, King of the Netherlands, ended after the uprising by the Belgians against William I's autocratic policies in 1830. In spite of these political events, it is worth noting that the language boundary separating the Dutch-speaking part in the north from the French-speaking part in the south was to remain unaltered throughout the centuries, with only a few minor exceptions (See map on p 53).

Until the steamroller of the French armies forced Jacobin centralism on them in 1792, the Belgian principalities were linked together by an almost federal structure. The policy of Frenchification so disastrous to Belgium was launched when the law of 9 Vendémiaire Year IV (1 October 1795) took effect. By this measure the annexation of the Belgian provinces to France by the French National Convention in March 1793 was ratified. The French occupying forces created an absolute predominance of the French language so as to ensure that the annexation to France was taken for granted, and at the same time aimed at systematically extirpating Dutch. French became the language used for administrative matters, in the army, education, justice, culture and for public life; and steps were taken to ban the Dutch language.

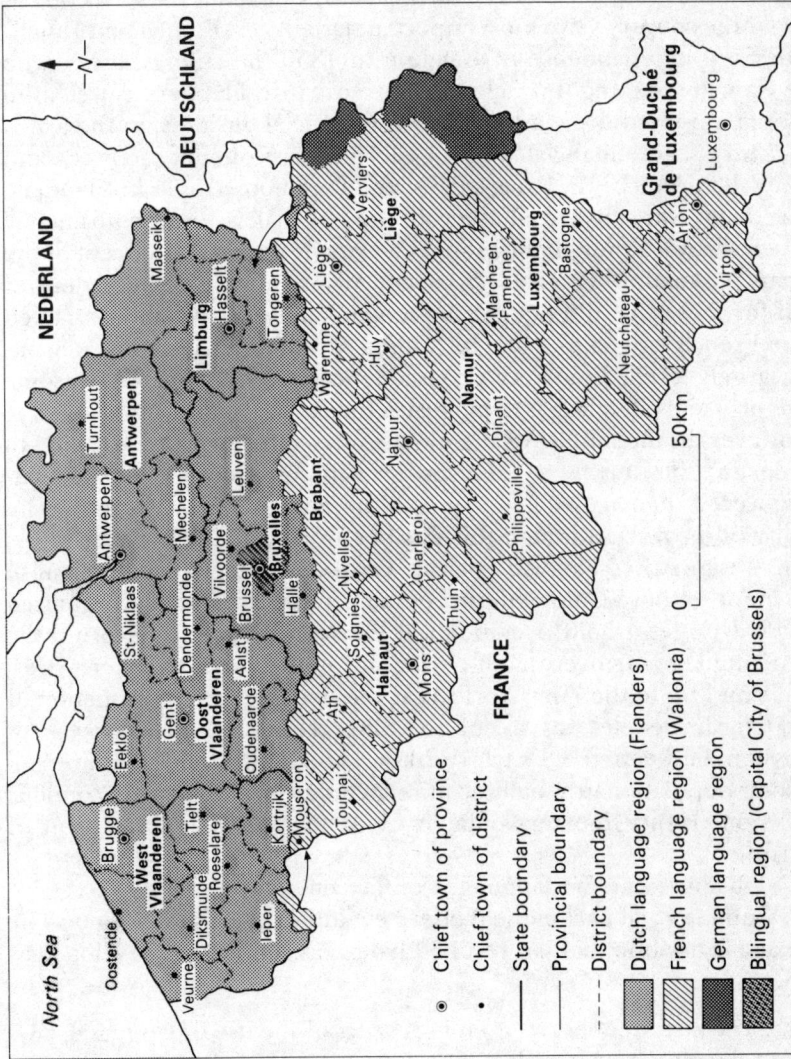

Belgium, showing provinces, districts and language regions

From Napoleon's time onwards, up to 1970, the structure of the Belgian state remained strictly centralist. Belgium however, contains (according to current estimates) five and a half million Flemings who belong to the Dutch cultural area, three and a quarter million Walloons who form a part of French culture and about 70,000 German-speaking Belgians. The inhabitants of Brussels – nearly one million – speak one or other of the country's two most important languages, French and Dutch.

After the independence of Belgium in 1830 the ruling classes, who were French-speaking throughout the country, in Flanders as well as in Wallonia, imposed French in all forms of official business, in the army, the church, the financial world, education, economic activity, and cultural life. Dutch, the language of the common people in Flanders, decayed and was considered as a collection of dialects utterly unsuitable for such affairs, although it was spoken by no less than 60 per cent of the Belgian population. Political power and prestige were definitely out of reach for those that did not speak French. The social advantage gained by the French language at the beginning of the nineteenth century has been largely levelled out yet its consequences are still apparent in some of the problems Belgium is coping with today.

However, in the middle of the nineteenth century a halt was called to the decline of Dutch as an ever growing number of intellectuals rediscovered their native language and became aware of its right to an identity of its own. Although this was not a reversal, it was nevertheless the first sign of a Flemish revival. Gradually the so-called Flemish movement gathered momentum, became more adequately organized and tried to get a hold over political life with a view to restoring the Dutch language in government circles and state affairs. In other words, initially and up to the First World War the struggle for emancipation of the Flemish people was a cultural one. However, the subjects of discussion between the Dutch-speaking population and the French-speaking population gradually acquired a financial and a socio-economic dimension. Hence the unavoidable trend towards a federal form of government.

It is obvious that the language conflict has played, in its successive phases, an essential part in the modern evolution of Belgian society. The language legislation that has resulted from this conflict has developed as follows:

1. 1831: constitutional freedom in respect of the use of language; laws and decrees are promulgated in French; there exist 'Flemish' translations, but only the French text has legal validity.

2. 1873: a law imposes the use of Dutch on the courts (in criminal cases) in the Flemish part of the country, unless requested otherwise by the accused.

3.  1878: a law imposes the use of Dutch on the government authorities in the Flemish part of the country, unless requested otherwise by the interested party.

4.  1883: in the Flemish part of the country part of the teaching in secondary education is henceforth in Dutch.

5.  1890: magistrates must prove that they have command of Dutch in order to be eligible for appointment in the Flemish part of the country; at Ghent National University lecturing in some of the subjects (including criminal law and criminal procedure for future Flemish magistrates) is henceforth in Dutch.

6.  1898: laws and decrees are sanctioned, ratified and promulgated in Dutch as well as in French; both texts have legal validity.

7.  1912: at the Catholic University of Louvain, too, lecturing in some of the subjects is henceforth in Dutch.

8.  1913: military officers must henceforth also have command of Dutch.

9.  1921: law concerning the use of languages in administrative matters:

    – the central national administration becomes bilingual, as do its officials;
    – local administrations become monolingual (the language of the region becomes the medium of communication);
    – the Brussels communal administrations have the choice between the country's two languages;
    – protection of the French-speaking minorities in the Flemish part of the country;
    – language censuses every ten years whereby a commune can change its language statute.

10. 1928: training of soldiers must be in their mother tongue, while military officers must be bilingual.

11. 1930: official use of the Dutch language at Ghent National University. The free universities of Brussels and Louvain are gradually transformed into two separate linguistic entities.

12. 1932: abolition of individual bilingualism of officials of the central national administration; matters must be dealt with in the language of the dossiers without resorting to translators. Officials are distributed over two language rolls (Dutch and French), with a fair balance in respect of appointments; in primary and secondary education in the Flemish part of the country bilingualism is abolished; Dutch becomes the medium of communication. In Brussels,

the theoretical principle 'mother tongue' medium of communication is applicable.

13. 1935: law concerning the use of the country's languages in judicial matters: 'language of the region – language of proceedings' principle is applicable and the accused may apply for the proceedings to be conducted in the other language; in Brussels the language of the accused is the language of proceedings.

14. 2 August 1963 and 23 December 1970: laws concerning the use of the languages in administrative matters: leaving aside the bilingual region of Greater Brussels, this legislation establishes homogenous linguistic regions in which the public services, generally speaking, use only the language of the region, both internally and in their dealings with other services and with private individuals.

The ground for these last two steps towards linguistic standardization had been prepared by the law of 8 November 1962, which contained the demarcation of the linguistic boundary between the French and Dutch-speaking regions on the basis of the work done by the Harmel Centre (see below) and altered the boundaries of the provinces, districts and communes so that each section of the country would be administered by an authority using the same language. Likewise, with a view to ensuring the stability of the linguistic boundary, the 1962 law abolished the changes in the linguistic regime which the results of the last ten-yearly census could have imposed on a commune where either 50 per cent or 30 per cent of the inhabitants declared that they most frequently spoke the national language which was not that of the linguistic group to which the commune was attached.

The demarcation of the linguistic regions by the law of 2 August 1963 therefore presented no further problems, except insofar as the limits of the bilingual district of Greater Brussels were concerned and the linguistic status of several communes along the linguistic boundary. The 1963 legislators had not been able to reach complete policy agreement and so six outlying communes of Greater Brussels were grouped together in a separate administrative district coming under the Deputy Governor of the province of Brabant, and were given their own statute. Under the law of 23 December 1970, these communes, while retaining their own statute, were attached to the administrative district of Halle-Vilvoorde, which is in the Dutch-speaking region.

This completed the demarcation of homogenous linguistic regions in Belgium. These regions were to form the territorial basis of the 'cultural communities' referred to in Article 3b of the Constitution, which was approved by the Constituent Assembly in 1970, and which will be discussed in a moment.

To entrench the territorial integrity of the cultural communities, Parliament decided that the boundaries of the four linguistic regions, as they were at the time when Article 3b was approved, could thereafter only be altered or corrected by a law passed by a specially qualified majority, so that in future, the legislators will not be able to hive off any part, be it large or small, of a linguistic region without the consent of a majority of the parliamentary representatives of the linguistic region in question. The boundaries of the four language areas will be described when we discuss the 1970 constitutional revision.

## From language legislation to constitutional reform

The beginning of post-war constitutional reform can be traced back to the so-called Harmel Centre, set up by the law of 3 May 1945, under the name 'Research Centre for the national solution of the social and legal problems in the Flemish and Walloon Regions'. The final report of the Harmel Centre, which was published on 24 April 1958 in the form of a parliamentary paper, contained important conclusions on the regional-ization of the country's institutions: equal representation of Flemings and Walloons in the administration; definitive demarcation of the language boundary, and the setting-up of a Walloon Cultural Council and a Flemish Cultural Council for the purpose of conducting a cultural policy of their own; and the division of the province of Brabant according to the language boundary.

One of the first important consequences of the work of the Harmel Centre were the new laws of 1962 and 1963 concerning the use of languages in administrative matters and introducing for the first time since 1831 the absolute monolingualism of the language areas. As has already been indicated, these laws contained amongst other things: abolition of the language census whereby communes could change their language statute; definitive demarcation of the language boundary; the congruence of the boundaries of the provinces with the language boundaries; the requirement that the communal administrations of Greater Brussels become bilingual and that there should be an equal number of Dutch-speaking and French-speaking officials in the national administration. These language laws, which were nearly always passed with a majority approaching or exceeding two-thirds and which were based on the territoriality principle, are in fact of a federal nature.

Under the Lefèvre Government (1961–5) the movement to harmon-ize political relations between the two communities was finally launched. After a working party had handed over on 24 October 1963 a report to the Government headed by Lefèvre, a declaration concerning the revision of the Constitution with a view to reforming the institutions was made, for the first time, in the House of Representatives on 3 March 1965. However, the fall of the Lefèvre Government did not allow this revision to be brought to a successful conclusion. Subsequently various commissions have advised the government on the reform of the institutions.

The Eyskens Government (1968–71) included for the first time a Minister of Dutch Culture and a Minister of French Culture, two Ministers of National Education and two Ministers with the status of Secretaries of State for Regional Economy. For Dutch culture, French culture and common cultural affairs separate budgetary laws were passed. It was under this Government that a Constituent Assembly was convened and constitutional revision took concrete shape.

## The 1970 constitutional revision

The reform of the Belgian state has taken place in three successive stages. The 1970 Constituent Assembly duly endorsed in its broad outlines the programme submitted by the Eyskens Government, even though it was left to the legislature to lay down the competence and composition of the regional bodies that were to be established. In doing so, the 1970 Constituent Assembly sought to preserve the unity of general state policy and at the same time to reconcile this unity of policy with the constitutional recognition of cultural communities, language areas and regions.

First, let us consider the cultural communities. To establish cultural autonomy, Article 32b was incorporated into the Constitution. This laid down that in cases specified by the Constitution, the elected members of each House of Parliament (the House of Representatives and the Senate) were to be divided into a Dutch and a French language group. This article remains valid today. The members of the two parliamentary language groups thus formed, constituted the 'cultural councils' which were to be the organs of the Dutch and French cultural communities respectively. Article 3c provided further that the Dutch, French and German cultural communities could exercise such powers as were conferred on them by the Constitution or by laws passed under the Constitution. The cultural council of the Dutch cultural community and the cultural council of the French cultural community were specifically granted the necessary authority to lay down legally valid provisions (decrees) for the members of their own community in the matter of cultural affairs, cultural co-operation, educational matters (with the exception of certain subjects defined by the Constitution) and the regulation of the use of languages in the field defined by the Constitution.

Now let us look at the language areas. These were mentioned earlier, when the history of Belgian language legislation was described. According to Article 3b of the Constitution, incorporated in 1970, Belgium now finds itself divided into four linguistic areas: the Dutch language area, the French language area, the German language area and the bilingual area of the capital city, Brussels. The first area consists of the provinces of Antwerp, Limburg, East and West Flanders, and in Brabant, the district of Louvain, together with the new district of Halle-Vilvoorde which has been amputated from the nineteen boroughs of the Brussels urban area which constitute the bilingual area.

The French area consists of the provinces of Hainaut, Luxembourg, Namur and Liège, with the exception of the boroughs belonging to the German language area and lastly, in Brabant, the district of Nivelles. The German language area is made up of twenty-five boroughs in the East of the province of Liège.

In the region of Comines and Mouscron, previously part of West Flanders, the Dutch-speaking minority is legally protected. The French-speaking minority enjoys the same protection in Ronse, Voeren, the German-speaking area and six boroughs on the outskirts of Brussels. The same applies to the German-speaking minorities in the Malmedy region and a certain number of eastern boroughs of the province of Liège. Six boroughs on the outskirts of Brussels listed below have their own status and are directly answerable to the Vice-Governor of Brabant.

The old Brussels district is split into three administrative districts:

(a) The bilingual district of Brussels-Capital, made up of the nineteen boroughs of the Brussels urban area where the principle of bilingualism laid down in the law of 1932 is currently interpreted as being:
   – at the level of administration, bilingualism applying externally and internally, with equality of cultural representation in the higher ranking posts;
   – in education, the setting up of a programme to create Dutch language pre-primary State schools;

(b) The monolingual Flemish district of Halle-Vilvoorde;

(c) The district of the six peripheral Flemish boroughs, namely Drogenbos, Kraainem, Linkebeek, Sint-Genesius-Rode, Wemmel, and Wezembeek-Oppem where the plan is for a special linguistic regime in administration, the law, and education to benefit the many French speaking families which have settled there.

Every commune of the realm forms a part of one of these language areas. No modification or correction may be made to the boundaries of the four areas other than by a law passed by special majority. The

Constitution laid down as a rule that the decrees of the cultural council for the Dutch cultural community in the Dutch language area and the decrees of the cultural council for the French cultural community in the French language area had the force of law and specified in which cases it was possible to deviate from this rule.

Finally, the regions: according to Article 107d of the Constitution, incorporated in 1970, Belgium comprises three regions, the Flemish region, the Walloon region and the Brussels region. This article is still in force. It provides that legislation may establish regional bodies, composed of elected representatives, and grant them authority to deal with such matters as the law may specify, with the exception of those mentioned in Article 23 (use of languages) and 59b (cultural affairs). Such facultative laws must be passed by a qualified majority within both parliamentary language groups. From this it is apparent that the Constituent Assembly gave a clearly defined content to the autonomy of the cultural communities, while relying on (ordinary) legislation as far as the regions are concerned.

Although Article 32 of the Constitution, which stipulates that the members of both Houses of Parliament 'represent the nation', remained untouched by the 1970 revision, it is clear that it no longer applied without reservation after that date. As we have seen, the revision subdivided the Houses into two language groups – the Dutch and the French – who, acting in their capacity as cultural councils, could make legally binding decisions on certain matters for their own particular language areas. Through the existence of this authority, the members of the cultural councils were holders of the rights of sovereignty, as they enacted the law in the field of the subject-matter reserved for them.

Furthermore, a qualified majority of both parliamentary language groups was required when voting on draft laws and bills submitted in pursuance of Article I (exemption of a territorial area with its own status from the division into provinces); 3b (modification of the boundaries of the language areas); 59b, Sections I and 2 (laying down the manner in which the cultural councils exercise their authority, the cultural matters which fall within the scope of the cultural councils, as well as the forms of co-operation), and article 107d (laying down the composition and the authority of the regional bodies).

It is obvious that after 1970 Belgium was no longer a classic unitary state. The following features characterized it:

1.   The national legislature retained full authority. The authority of the cultural councils and the regional bodies was an assigned authority.

2.   According to the explicit provisions of Article 32b the division into language groups was effected (solely) 'in the cases specified by the Constitution'.

3.   According to the second paragraph of Article 3c each cultural community possessed (only) those powers which were conferred upon it by the Constitution or by laws passed by virtue of the Constitution.

4.   Subject to application of the unaltered Article 32.

It is clear that Belgium had not yet become a classic federal or regional state. A federal form of government implies the existence of two legal systems, a federal and a regional legal system, which clearly differ from one another. Apart from the cultural councils, the cultural communities of 1970 did not have the necessary structures and competences; they lacked judicial and executive bodies of their own. The rules passed by the cultural councils were confirmed, proclaimed and implemented by the King.

Only a few years after the constitution had been changed in 1970, however, it was called into question again. Between 1970 and 1980 there had indeed been a remarkable gathering of momentum on the political plane. An overall and definitive settlement of the regional problem was demanded by all political parties. The pace of state reform was quickening.

## The 1980 constitutional revision

During the negotiations for the formation of the second Tindemans Government (June 1977–October 1978) a new political agreement, the so-called Community Pact, on a fundamental reform of the Belgian state was confirmed by most of the parties. This Pact was subsequently further supplemented by the so-called Stuyvenberg Agreement and gave rise to the tabling, on 11 June 1978, of a draft law containing various institutional reforms. However, due to the dissolution of Parliament, this draft law lapsed.

Under the political agreement which, after the parliamentary elections of 17 December 1978, led to the formation of the first Martens Government (April 1979–May 1980) it was agreed that the reform of the state should be carried out in three phases: a first phase, during which special executives for the communities and regions were to be established; a second so-called provisional and irreversible phase, whereby a number of legislative competences in various fields were to be assigned to the communities and the regions; and lastly a third phase, during which a definitive state reform was to be worked out by the Parliament and the government.

The first phase, which remained limited to policy at the executive level, was carried into effect by a number of royal decrees on the basis of the law setting up provisional community and regional institutions. To implement the second phase, two draft laws were submitted on 1 October 1979. Parliamentary resistance to these draft laws resulted in the resignation of the government on 3 April 1980.

During the negotiations which led to the formation of the third Martens Government in May 1980, agreement was reached on the principles and main lines of definitive state reform, except for the Brussels problem. With a view to the implementation of the agreement, the government immediately tabled proposals for the revision of a number of constitutional provisions, together with two draft laws for the reform of the institutions: a first draft grouping together the provisions which had to be sanctioned by a special majority and a second draft containing those provisions which could be sanctioned on the basis of ordinary majority. Articles 3c, 26b, 28, 59b, 107c, 108, 110, 111, 113 and 135 of the Constitution were amended or inserted and the special law and ordinary law on institutional reforms were proclaimed on 8 and 9 August 1980, respectively.

The first of these laws dealt with the organization and competences of the new bodies that were to be set up, and the second with the problem of the financial resources to which the communities and regions are entitled.

The 1980 Constituent Assembly limited the revision of the Constitution to three articles which were strictly necessary for the approval of the draft special law and the draft ordinary law. The amendment of Article 59b was the cornerstone of the new state structure. By it the 'cultural communities' became simply 'communities'. The competences of the communities are extended from cultural matters in the narrow sense to what are called 'personalized' matters, including such things as medical care, social services, and education. (A full list is provided on p 69–70). The right of initiative is conferred upon the community councils and their executives. Article 59b also makes it henceforth possible for the regional powers mentioned in Article 107d of the Constitution to be exercized by the community councils. The special law of 8 August on institutional reforms puts this into effect immediately as regards Flanders, while it creates the possibility for it to be done in the future for Wallonia. (In the meantime the regional council there remains distinct from the community council.)

The power of the new regional authorities is decisively affected by Article 28b, inserted into the Constitution in 1980. This article affords the possibility of conferring the force of law upon the 'rules' that are made by the regional authorities in pursuance of the tasks conferred upon them by the national parliament. The special law of 8 August 1980 provides that for the Flemish and Walloon regions rules called decrees can be issued with the force of law.

Article 107c of 1980 relates to the prevention and settlement of conflicts of competence between laws, decrees and regional 'rules', and also between different decrees and between different regional 'rules'. For this purpose a Court of Arbitration is to be set up, and the legislator is instructed to determine the composition, competence and operation of this court. On 18 June 1983, the law concerning the institution, competence and operation of the Court of Arbitration was enacted. Article 108 was supplemented in 1980 by a provision which makes it possible to delegate the organization and exercise of administrative supervision of provincial and communal institutions to the communities or to the regions.

The aim of the revision of Articles 110, 111 and 113 in 1980 was to provide the communities and the regions with a fiscal system of their own. In pursuance of this, the ordinary law of 9 August 1980 provides for the following financial resources for the Flemish community, the French community and the Walloon region:

1. non-fiscal resources of their own;
2. credits chargeable to the National Budget (= endowment);
3. rebates on the yield of certain taxes and levies imposed by the law;
4. a fiscal system of their own;
5. loans.

Owing to its limited size, no decree-making authority was conferred, in the 1970 constitutional revision, on the German cultural community. In the 1980 constitutional revision its designation was admittedly changed to 'German-speaking community' (Article 31c), but its position still remained unchanged. Only in 1983 was Article 59c of the Constitution inserted to grant it autonomy equivalent to that of the other two communities, including decree-making authority. The new Constitution provision requires, for its implementation, an ordinary law, which was proclaimed on 31 December 1983, as the law on institutional reform for the German-speaking community.

As mentioned earlier, only the Brussels region remained outside the implementation of Article 107d of the Constitution because of the lack of the majorities required for this purpose. The Brussels region, then, is not as yet a legal entity separate from the state and continues to be governed by the co-ordinated law of 20 July 1979 setting up provisional community and regional institutions and the decrees implementing them.

### 1987: the start of a new phase of constitutional revision

A 'declaration of amendment', which marks the first stage in any act of constitutional reform in Belgium, was unanimously approved by the

King and both Houses of Parliament in 1987. With its passage, and the election of a new Parliament at the end of that year, a third phase of revision has begun to succeed the two that have already been described. While the new declaration does not deal exclusively with the issue of state reform, many of the amendments it recommends are highly relevant to it. These amendments will be summarized below, though at the time of writing (1989) they have not yet been adopted.

First, it is recommended that the division of Belgium into regions (as provided under Article 107d) be given recognition in the first heading or chapter of the Constitution, alongside the division into language areas and communities. It is also proposed that the unclear division of powers between the national and central authority, on the one hand, and the regional or community authorities on the other, about which there has been much criticism since 1980, should be remedied by new articles defining the exclusive powers of the national government and the residuary and concurrent powers. The Constituent Assembly is also given the possibility of inserting rules for the regional and community governments equivalent to the provisions for the national government into Chapter III of the Constitution.

Highly significant, when considering how far Belgium is moving in a federal direction, are the recommended amendments affecting the Senate. These are aimed at ensuring that, while the House of Representatives will continue to represent the nation, the Senate will represent the communities and/or regions. It should be added that such a reform has been envisaged for some time as part of the overall process of state restructuring.

According to the declaration, it is proposed to give the three communities full powers in educational matters, with the exception of matters relating to the 'Schools Pact' (an agreement between the Belgian political parties to maintain a financial balance between the state educational network and the Catholic network). The Constituent Assembly may also approve new provisions relating to the community and regional councils, particularly with regard to the direct election of their members – another highly significant recommendation when viewed in the context of federalism. The declaration also makes it possible that the Court of Arbitration may be transformed into a Constitutional Court with the task of ensuring the observance of the Constitution as a whole. Lastly, the financial powers of regions and communities, and their powers with regard to the administrative organization of local authorities, may undergo modification.

### The structure of Belgium's community and regional institutions

So far the discussion has concentrated on the changes that have taken place in Belgium's Constitution since 1970. The detailed provisions relating to the organization and competences of the new community and regional authorities sanctioned by the Constitution were largely set out in the special law of 8 August 1980, and for the German-speaking community, the law of 31 December 1983. Their stipulations will be summarized in this and the following two sections.

First, let us consider the organization of the community and regional councils. Community matters in the Flemish community, the French community and the German-speaking community are taken care of by the Flemish council, the council of the French community and the council of the German-speaking community respectively. All regional matters in the Flemish and Walloon region are dealt with by the Flemish council and the Walloon regional council respectively.

It should be pointed out that Flemish council simultaneously exercises the powers with regard to community matters in the Flemish community and regional matters in the Flemish region. Such a transfer of power occurs in Flanders only, whereas the Walloon regional council and the council of the French community have retained their respective attributions. However, they can at any moment decide to assign the competence of the Walloon regional council to the council of the French community, though the decision must be taken on the basis of a two-thirds majority of the votes cast in each of these bodies.

As the German-language region forms part of the Walloon region, the Walloon regional council is competent for all regional matters in this region. The Constituent Assembly of 1980, has, however, created the possibility of a future transference of certain regional attributions to the council of the German-speaking community.

*Composition of the councils*

Composition of the Flemish council, the council of the French community and the Walloon regional council:

*Final phase*

1. The Flemish council consists of directly elected members of the Dutch-language group in the Senate.

2. The council of the French community consists of directly elected members of the French-language group in the Senate.

3.  The Walloon regional council consists of members of the French-language group in the Senate who were directly elected in the provinces of Hainaut, Liège, Luxembourg and Namur, and in the circumscription of Nivelles.

*Transitional phase*

Until the necessary changes in the Senate have been effected the councils are composed in the following way:

1.  The Flemish council consists of members of the Dutch-language group in the House of Representatives, together with members of the Dutch-language group in the Senate who are directly elected by the electorate.

2.  The council of the French community consists of members of the French-language group in the House of Representatives, together with members of the French-language group in the Senate who are directly elected by the electorate.

3.  The Walloon regional council consists of members of the French-language groups in the House of Representatives and the Senate who are directly elected in the provinces of Hainaut, Liège, Luxembourg and Namur, and in the circumscription of Nivelles.

Whenever the council of the French community exercises the competence vested in the Walloon regional council, this council is composed in an analogous way to the Flemish council.

*Composition of the council of the German-speaking community*

The council of the German-speaking community consists of twenty-five members, elected for four years by the electorate of the German-speaking region. The first elections were held on 26 October 1986.

*The executives*

The executives of the community and regional insitutions consist of the 'Flemish executive', which is the executive arm of the Flemish community; the 'executive of the French community'; the 'Walloon regional executive' and the 'executive of the German-speaking community'.

*Composition of the Flemish and French/Walloon executives*

Each executive is elected by the council from among its members. The Flemish executive comprises nine members including its president. One member at least belongs to the bilingual region of Brussels–Capital. The executive of the French community comprises three members including its president. One member at least belongs to the bilingual region of Brussels–Capital. The Walloon regional executive comprises six members including its president. When the executive of the French community is vested with the competence of the executive of the Walloon region, this executive consists of nine members, including the president.

### Composition of the executive of the German-speaking community

The executive of the German-speaking community consists of three members including the president, who are elected by the council of the German-speaking community. In contrast to the others, the German executive may consist of persons who are not members of the council, provided they have been domiciled in the German-speaking region for at least one year, and are entitled to vote.

### The competences of Belgium's community institutions

The competences of the Flemish and French communities are as follows:

### Cultural matters

1. The defence and promotion of the language;

2. The promotion of training and research workers;

3. The fine arts;

4. The cultural heritage, museums and other cultural and scientific institutions;

5. Libraries, record libraries and kindred services;

6. Radio and television broadcasting, with the exception of broadcasts by the National Government and of commercial advertising;

7. Youth policy;

8. Permanent education and cultural promotion;

9. Physical education, sport and open-air activities;

10. Leisure and tourism;

11. Pre-schooling in nursery and day care units;

12. Further education and para-academic training;

13. Artistic training;

14. Intellectual, moral and social formation;

15. Social advancement;

16. Professional reconversion and retraining, with the exception of rules governing intervention in the expenses incurred by the selection, professional training and rehabilitation of personnel recruited by an employer with a view to founding a business enterprise or to the enlarging or retooling of an existing enterprise;

17. Applied scientific research with respect to the matters listed above;

### Educational matters

Education exclusive of everything appertaining to the 'Schools Pact', compulsory school attendance, educational structures, diplomas, subsidies, salaries and school population norms. Education hence means above all university education and art teaching, with the exclusion of schools of music.

A fairly long series of exceptions with regard to community competence in the educational field simply proves that three substantial areas are still reserved to the National Parliament: questions relating to the 'Schools Pact', further agreements at national level, and major options in the matter of schooling. Each community may nevertheless introduce new orientations, ways and methods of teaching.

### Other educational competences

1. With respect to state schooling and free schools which are subsidized or approved by the public authorities:

    – the definition and supervision of compulsory school attendance;

    – the various subjects and streams, together with their syllabus and timetables, but solely to the extent that this area is not included among the conditions governing the recognition of diplomas, a matter reserved to the National Parliament;

    – the organization of the school inspection services;

    – the diplomas required of teaching personnel;

    – promotional schemes;

    – holiday and vacation regulations;

- in general, everything pertaining to the improvement and encouragement of school attendance.

2.  With respect to state schooling:

- organic rules and regulations governing day and boarding schools.

*The use of languages*

1.  for administrative matters;

2.  for education in schools set up, subsidized or approved by the public authorities;

3.  for social relations between employers and their personnel, together with acts and documents compiled by business enterprises in terms of existing laws and regulations.

*Personalized matters*

The personalized matters referred to in Article 59b, para. 2, b of the Constitution, are as follows:

1.  In the sphere of health policy;

(a) The policy covering treatment and care dispensed within and outside hospitals and clinics, except for:

(i)  organic legislation;

(ii)  financing such facilities when this is organized by the organic legislation;

(iii) sickness and disability insurance (social security);

(iv) basic rules with respect to planning;

(v)  basic rules for the financing of infrastructural work, including heavy medical equipment.

(vi) national standards governing official approval, but only to the extent that they may have repercussions on the areas of competence referred to in (ii), (iii), (iv) and (v) above;

(vii)definition of the conditions for, and designation of, a university (teaching) hospital, in accordance with the legislation governing the hospitals.

(b) Education in health care and hygiene, together with work and services centred on preventive medicine, except for prophylactic measures on the national plane.

2. In the sphere of aid to individuals:

(a) Family policy, including all forms of aid and assistance to families and children.

(b) Social assistance policy except for:

   (i) organic rules and regulations governing the CPAS (*Centres Public d'Aide Sociale*);

   (ii) definition of the minimum amount and the conditions governing the granting and financing of the legally guaranteed minimum income, in accordance with legislation instituting the right to a minimum level of subsistence.

(c) The policy surrounding the reception and integration of immigrants.

(d) The policy with respect to handicapped people, including their training, rehabilitation and vocational guidance, except for:

   (i) The rules and financing of allowances to handicapped people, including their personal files;

   (ii) Rules governing financial grants for the employment of handicapped workers, awarded to employers who take them on.

(e) Old-age policy, except for the definition of the minimum amount, and the conditions surrounding the granting and financing of the income legally guaranteed to senior citizens.

(f) The care and protection of minors, except for matters pertaining to civil, criminal and judicial law.

(g) Social aid to prisoners and ex-prisoners, except for the execution of penal rulings.

3. In the sphere of applied scientific research:

Applied scientific research in all areas coming within the exclusive competence of the Councils.

*International co-operation*

Formal assent to any treaty or agreement relating to co-operation in the sphere of personalized, cultural and educational matters is given either by the council of the French community, or by the Flemish council, or by the two councils acting together should both of them be involved. Such treaties are tabled in the competent council by the executive concerned.

Such are the competences of the Flemish and Dutch communities. Since the end of 1983 the German-speaking community has been vested with the same competence as the other two. In addition the council and executives of the German-speaking community may exercise all further competences vested in them by law by means of decrees and rules. Finally the German-speaking community may exercise completely or partially, within the German-speaking region, the competence vested in the Walloon region.

*The competences of Belgium's regional institutions*

The competence of the new regional bodies in Belgium extend to the following:

1. Territorial development;
2. The environment;
3. Rural redevelopment and nature conservation;
4. Housing;
5. Water policy;
6. Economic policy;
7. Energy policy;
8. Subordinate authorities;
9. Employment policy;
10. Applied research;
11. International co-operation;
12. Territorial application of decisions made by regional authorities.

**Where are we now?**

The 1980 state reform was regarded by some as establishing the definitive structure of the Belgian state. This reform was, however, simply the extension of the cultural and regional autonomy begun in 1970. It was no more than an important transitional phase, a second step towards the ultimate goal, that is to say, a Belgian federal monarchy.

That this development is progressing fairly slowly need not surprise us. In states with a federal tradition, the revision of the structure of the state is not a speedy process either. The overall revision of the Federal Constitution of Switzerland took more than ten years. The system for the financing of the Länder in the Federal Republic of Germany materialized after five years of parliamentary activity and even so represented but a fraction of the problem raised by the need for reform. Belgium, however, does not have a federal tradition. Where most federal states have come into existence from a joining together of previously independent and autonomous territories, just the opposite is happening in Belgium. Here, starting from a Napoleonically centralized state, self-government is now being conferred on parts of that state.

It goes without saying that the transformation of the unitary Belgian state into a federal form might have been effected simply through the remodelling of the present nine provinces into Swiss-style cantons. The great advantage of this constitutional structure lies in the fact that it would have prevented the emergence of a federalism consisting of only two or three component parts. Oddly enough, a solution of this kind never had any real chance. The political division of the country along the language boundary which separates the Dutch-speaking from the French-speaking population came to appear unavoidable to the majority of politicians. As a result, state reform was effected on a cultural and not on a provincial basis. But for the last ten years the provinces in Belgium have once more been under discussion in the political forum. The 1970–1 state reform bypassed them although the final settlement of the institutional question in a new federal Belgium logically entailed their abolition as political entities. Ten years later a reassessment of the provinces as intermediary administrative bodies seems probable. It should nevertheless be noted that the communities and regions have so far not yet spoken out on the definitive position of the provinces in the new form of government. Only time will tell whether a cantonal solution for the institutional problem of the Belgian state is still a possibility.

Criticism may be levelled at the existing way of selecting the members of the community and regional councils. The directly elected members of the central Belgian Parliament make up the Flemish, Walloon and French 'Parliaments' (councils) respectively, albeit according to the language group to which they belong and their place of residence. These members of Parliament thus have on the Flemish side (where the community council and the regional council coincide) a twofold and on the Walloon-French-speaking side (where the regional council and the community council are distinct bodies) even a threefold capacity as sovereign legislators and supervisors of the executive power. This brings about a delicate situation.

The citizen casts his vote at election time on the basis of his preference for a specific political alignment at the Belgian level (and decides on possible coalitions for the central government). Indirectly and, in most cases, unconsciously, he thereby also determines the political relationships and possibilities in his region and community. Once a government coalition has been formed at the centre, the members of Parliament are placed in a hybrid situation in which they must decide on coalitions and political choices at regional or community level. Their attitudes at that level inevitably have repercussions in the central Parliament and on the stability of the central government and vice versa. Bearing in mind the obvious tensions on points of competence and interests between the central government and the newly created communities and regions, any unequivocal assumption of political responsibility at any level becomes hard to realize. Thus it may happen that, for example, members of the Flemish 'Parliament' approve a specific point of view with regard to their community and that the same members take up a different position in the central Parliament because they do not want to embarrass the central government there. Moreover, this state of affairs acts as a brake on the inner dynamism of the community and regional 'Parliaments' respectively. One can well imagine that a directly elected Flemish legislative body would experience different political conditions from the present-day Flemish council and would take up a more independent position vis-à-vis the national authority.

It is not only the composition of the existing structures that can be criticized. The 1980 legislation did not entirely succeed in establishing a clear demarcation of competence between the central government and the communities and regions. At first sight the distribution of compe-tences is simple: the communities and regions possess exclusive powers granted to them, while the central government retains the residual competence. In practice, however, this distribution of competence may provoke conflicts. When devising a distribution of competence within a federally organized state, it is a fundamental condition that one should have clear insight into the criteria or key according to which one want to redistribute the tasks devolving upon the various authorities and that these powers should be defined in straightforward, unequivocal terms. It is difficult to claim that the existing Belgian law fully comes up to this. The distribution of competences carried out in 1980 is the result of many a compromise. A lot of competences – especially at regional level – were distributed in an arbitrary manner between the central govern-ment and the regions.

The financial arrangement too, is open to criticism. The reality is that the financial resources of the new bodies consist for the most part of an 'endowment' and only in a very incidental way of so-called shared taxation revenue, while a fiscal system of their own was denied to the communities and regions until the end of 1984 and can only have an impact in the future.

The result is that the financial resources of communities and regions are very inflexible and that a direct connection between the policy conducted by communities and regions and their financial circumstances is lacking. Budgetary and fiscal mechanisms should be improved so that the communities and regions can become genuine policy framers.

In addition to the small volume of financial resources, another more fundamental disadvantage of the existing financing system comes to the fore – the manner in which the financial resources are made available to the various areas making up the whole. The financing system of most federal states is based on the principle that each of the areas is itself responsible via-à-vis its population for the financing of its expenditure policy, on the basis of its own fiscal system. The central subsidizing system, founded on the idea of mutual solidarity, is incidental and designed solely to correct any excessive imbalances between the regions.

In Belgium this arrangement has been reversed. The provision of financial resources under the Belgian state reform is not in keeping with the principles of financial responsibility. At the moment a discrepancy between expenditure and the proper financial means is manifest. This is an absolute negation of the basic rules of sound financial policy.

It is, then, obvious that the provision of financial resources to the regions as organized at present is not capable of supporting and guaranteeing the autonomy of the regional authorities. Proper regionalization requires that the national government should, parallel with the competence to spend, delegate to the regions equivalent authority to raise revenue.

**Whither Belgium?**

It is generally accepted that the basic principles of federalism can be summed up as follows: the co-existence of two legal systems with their own legislative and executive power; respect for the principle '*Bundesrecht bricht Landesrecht*' (federal law sets aside state law); the existence of a supreme constitutional court; participation of the individual states in the federal legislative process; and federal solidarity, amongst other things, in the financial field.

There can be no wellbeing for the Flemish and Walloons outside a genuinely federal Belgium with a strong central authority. It is necessary therefore to fall back on the classic criteria which are applicable to any federally organized state. These criteria have up to now made possible the peaceful co-existence of the different constituent parts of foreign federal states. Swiss and German federalism serves as a model in this connection. Belgium must become a genuine federal monarchy.

It has been shown that three communities in Belgium are already recognized as genuine people's communities. They must have their own legislative assembly which they themselves have elected, so that the relationship between the individual state and the federation can become fully operative, and the internal tutelage of regional political initiatives within the unitary party-political structure can diminish in importance. Furthermore, the financial and economic relations between the communities must be based on the full responsibility of each of them, supplemented by interregional and national solidarity to be calculated in an objective manner.

Every federal state has a constitutional court which sees to it that the laws, regional decrees and acts of political bodies are in line with the constitution. The Belgian Court of Arbitration has, quite correctly, the sole authority to deal with conflicts of competence between, on the one hand, the national and the regional authorities and, on the other hand, the regional authorities themselves.

It will be particularly important to change the current Belgian practice of distributing competences according to the technique of exclusive powers. Experience abroad and the development there towards what is conventionally called 'co-operative federalism' shows that a technique of concurrent powers is the optimal formula with respect to the distribution of competence between the national and the regional authorities. Therefore the present system of a rigid distribution of competence must be abandoned in favour of a more flexible one. It is also of paramount importance that the present Senate should be reformed and allocated a new role as a federal council where the constituent parts of the Belgian state are represented as such and regional disputes can be settled. Here the system of the Federal Republic of Germany, and in particular the organization of the Bundesrat, could serve as a model. It is finally a striking fact that even if the rule of the preponderance of national law over regional law has not been expressly written into all federal constitutions, all federal countries nevertheless apply this rule, in order to promote indispensable legal security over the whole territory of the federation. This too requires further consideration in Belgium.

In sum the reform of the Belgian state, begun in 1970 and carried further in 1980, needs to be brought to a successful federal conclusion. The role of the monarchy is absolutely fundamental for the harmonious achievement by this process. The King must continue to exist as a moderating figure above the political struggle. It is not a good thing that in a country without a federal tradition the electorate should have to be periodically consulted on the choice of Head of State. Even if the person chosen were trilingual, the result would always be open to challenge in the eyes of those individual states making up the whole from which the elected Head of State does not come. Without the monarchy Belgium is not viable today.

A federal monarchy? Why not? The popular King Baudouin, who has been caused many worries by the Belgians, but who, with dogged perseverance and an unflagging sense of duty, embodies the cohesion between the communities amid the constitutional storms, is the last bond between the component parts of the Belgian state. Owing to an unexpected repetition of history, this sovereign must do the work of his

Burgundian predecessors over again albeit in the opposite sense, i.e. by ensuring the transition from a unitary state structure, which has proved intolerable, via a regional, towards a federal model. A genuine federal structure with the preservation of the country's political unity, is the only possible lasting solution for the further co-existence of Flemings, Walloons and German-speaking Belgians in one and the same state.

Despite the occasional high tide of verbal violence, the Belgians live peacefully side by side and take a philosophical view of the slowly, but steadily progressing state reform. The large majority of the Belgians wish to continue to live together in one and the same federal state. Yet they are aware that the process of transforming the unitary form of government previously existing in Belgium into a classic federal structure of state, is only possible after a lapse of time in order to allow the country to adapt slowly to the new state structure. It is obvious that a new spirit of 'Bundestreue' must find reception with the Dutch-speaking, the French-speaking and the German-speaking population. Once this goal is achieved, the process of transforming the Belgian state may be called a success.

## Conclusion

One of the most remarkable political phenomena in Europe in the second half of the twentieth century is, without doubt, the rise in the consciousness of the various constituent parts of culturally non-homogenous countries about their cultural and linguistic individuality. This is especially true of Spain and Belgium. At the general level, the unitary, centralized state finds itself obliged to adapt its constitution to these new trends. Belgian post-war history is a typical example of the slow but inevitable transformation of a unitary state into a federated structure, the core of the process being the institutionalization of the culturally diverse parts. This chapter has tried to indicate the scale of the federalism that has so far been achieved, and has argued that only a fully federal Belgium will permit Walloons, Flemish and German-speaking Belgians to live in peace and allow them jointly to work for the good of the Belgian body politic.

# APPENDIX

## THE BELGIAN CONSTITUTION

### HEADING I

### CONCERNING THE TERRITORY AND ITS DIVISIONS

**Art. 1**. Belgium is divided into provinces.

These provinces are: Antwerp, Brabant, West Flanders, East Flanders, Hainaut, Liège, Limburg, Luxembourg, Namur.

It is up to the law, if necessary to divide the territory into a larger number of provinces (rev. 7.9.1983).

An act of Parliament may exempt certain territories, whose boundaries it shall determine, from being divided into provinces, place them directly under the executive authority and subject them to an individual status.

Such an act must be passed by a majority vote in each linguistic group of each of the Houses, on condition that the majority of the members of each group is present and that the total number of votes in favour in each of the two linguistic groups attain two-thirds of the votes cast (rev. 24.12.1970).

**Art. 2**. The subdivisions of the provinces can only be established by law.

**Art. 3**. The boundaries of the State, the provinces and the boroughs may only be changed or rectified by virtue of a law.

**Art. 3b**. Belgium comprises four linguistic regions: the French language region, the Dutch language region, the bilingual region of Brussels-Capital, and the German language region.

Every commune in the Kingdom belongs to one of these linguistic regions.

The boundaries of the four regions may only be altered or amended by an act of Parliament passed on a majority vote in each linguistic group of each of the Houses, on condition that the majority of the members of each group are present and that the total votes in favour within the two linguistic groups attain two-thirds of votes cast (rev. 24.12.1970).

### HEADING Ib

### CONCERNING THE COMMUNITIES

**Art. 3c**. Belgium comprises three communities: the French Community, the Flemish Community, and the German-speaking Community.

Each community enjoys the powers vested in it by the Constitution or by such legislation as shall be enacted in terms thereof (rev. 24.12.1970).

### HEADING II

### CONCERNING THE BELGIANS AND THEIR RIGHTS

**Art. 4**. Belgian nationality is acquired, retained and withdrawn in accordinace with the rules laid down by civil law.

The present Constitution and the other laws governing political rights determine which conditions, apart from nationality, are necessary for the exercise of those rights.

**Art. 5**. Naturalization is granted by the Legislative power.

Only full naturalization places the foreigner on an equal footing with the Belgian citizen where the exercise of political rights is concerned.

**Art. 6**. There is no distinction between orders in the State.

All Belgians are equal in the eyes of the law; they alone are acceptable for civil and military posts, with some exceptions which may be established by law in special cases.

**Art. 6b**. Enjoyment of the rights and liberties to which Belgians are entitled must be ensured without discrimination. To this end, laws and decrees shall guarantee amongst other things the rights and liberties of ideological and philosophical minorities (rev. 24.12.1970).

**Art. 7**. Individual liberty is guaranteed.

No person may be prosecuted except in cases laid down by the law and in the form it prescribes.

Apart from the case of *flagrante delicto*, no person may be arrested save on a motivated order by a judge, which must be signified at the time of the arrest or within twenty-four hours at the latest.

**Art. 8**. No person may be withdrawn from the judge assigned to him by the law, save with his consent.

**Art. 9**. No penalty may be decreed nor applied save in accordance with the law.

**Art. 10**. The home is inviolable; no entrance into a private house may be made save in those cases laid down by the law and in the manner it prescribes.

**Art. 11**. No person may be deprived of his property save in the public interest, in cases laid down by the law and in the manner it prescribes, and on condition that just compensation is made previously.

**Art. 12**. The penalty consisting of confiscation of property may not be decreed.

**Art. 13**. The civilian death penalty is abolished and may not be reinstated.

**Art. 14**. Freedom of worship and its public exercise, together with freedom to manifest personal opinions in every way, are guaranteed save for the punishment of offences perpetrated in exercising those liberties.

**Art. 15**. No person may be constrained to assist in any way in the acts and ceremonies of any form of worship, nor to observe its days of rest.

**Art. 16**. The State has no right to intervene either in the appointment or the induction of ministers of any form of worship, nor to forbid them to correspond with their superiors and to publish their acts save, in the latter case, for the ordinary responsibility bound up with the press and publishing.

The civil wedding must always precede the nuptial benediction, save in exceptional cases to be established, where necessary, by law.

**Art. 17**. Education is free; any preventive measure is forbidden; the punishment of misdemeanours is regulated only by law.

Public education provided at the expense of the State, is also regulated by law.

**Art. 18**. The press is free; no form of censorship may ever by instituted: no cautionary deposit may be demanded from writers, publishers or printers.

When the author is known and is resident in Belgium, the publisher, printer or distributor may not be prosecuted.

**Art. 19**. Belgians have the right to hold peaceful, unarmed meetings; they must comply with the laws which may regulate the exercise of this right without, however, subjecting it to prior authorization.

This clause does not apply to open-air meetings which remain entirely subject to the police laws.

**Art. 20**. Belgians have the right to associate; this right may not be subjected to any preventive measure.

**Art. 21**. Every person has the right to address petitions signed by one or several people to the public authorities.

The constituted authorities alone have the right to send in collective petitions.

**Art. 22**. The secrecy of letters is inviolable. The law shall determine which agents are responsible for the violation of secrecy in the case of letters sent by post.

**Art. 23**. The use of the languages spoken in Belgium is optional; it may only be regulated by law and only in the case of acts by the public authorities and of legal matters.

**Art. 24**. No prior authorization is necessary to bring an action against civil servants with regard to their administrative acts, except as elsewhere specified for Ministers.

## HEADING III

### CONCERNING THE AUTHORITIES

**Art. 25**. All powers stem from the nation.

They are exercized in the manner laid down by the Constitution.

**Art. 25b**. The exercise of given powers may be conferred by a pact or law on institutions coming under international civil law (rev. 20.7.1970).

**Art. 26**. Legislative authority is exercised collectively by the King, the House of Representatives and the Senate.

**Art. 26b**. The laws enacted in implementation of Article 107d shall determine the force in law of the rules which the bodies thereby created shall apply in those matters they shall specify.

Such laws may confer on those bodies the authority to issue decrees having the force of law within the jurisdiction and in the manner they shall determine (rev. 17.7.1980).

**Art. 27**. The right of initiative is vested in each of the three branches of the Legislative authority (rev. 15.10.1921).

**Art. 28**. The authoritative interpretation of laws is the sole prerogative of Acts of Parliament.

The authoritative interpretation of decrees is the sole prerogative of the decree itself (rev. 17.7.1980).

**Art. 29**. The Executive authority is vested in the King as laid down by the Constitution.

**Art. 30**. The Judiciary authority is exercised by the courts and tribunals.

Their decisions and judgements are delivered in the name of the King.

**Art. 31**. Interests which are exclusively municipal or provincial are regulated by the municipal or provincial councils in accordance with the principles laid down by the Constitution.

## CHAPTER I

*Concerning the Houses of Parliament*

**Art. 32**. The members of both Houses represent the nation, and not merely the province or subdivision of a province which elected them.

**Art. 32*b***. For those cases prescribed in the Constitution, the elected members of each House are divided into a French language group and a Dutch language group in such manner as is laid down by law (rev. 24.12.1970).

**Art. 33**. The sessions of both Houses are public.

Nevertheless, each House may go into secret committee at the request of its president or of ten members.

It then decides, on the basis of an absolute majority, whether the sitting is to be resumed in public on the same subject.

**Art. 34**. Each House verifies the powers of its members and pronounces judgement on any contestations that may arise in this regard.

**Art. 35**. No person may be a member of both Houses simultaneously.

**Art. 36**. The member of either House who is appointed by the government to any salaried post other than that of Minister, and who accepts, ceases to sit immediately and does not resume his functions save as the result of a new election (rev. 7.9.1983).

**Art. 37**. At each session, each House nominates its president, its vice-presidents and makes up its steering committee.

**Art. 38**. Every resolution is passed on the basis of an absolute majority of votes cast, except as shall be prescribed by the House and Senate rules with respect to elections and candidatures.

Should there be an equal number of votes on both sides, the proposal under discussion is thrown out.

Neither of the two Houses may adopt any resolution without the majority of its members being present.

**Art. 38*b***. Except in the case of budgets and laws requiring a special majority, a reasoned motion signed by at least three-quarters of the members of one of the linguistic groups and introduced after the report has been tabled and before the final voting in public session, may declare that the provisions of a draft or proposed bill which it specifies are of such a nature as to have a serious effect on relations between the communities.

In such cases, parliamentary procedure is suspended and the motion is referred back to the Cabinet which, within a period of thirty days, gives its reasoned findings on the motion and invites the House to reach a decision either on those findings or on the draft or proposed bill in such form as it may have been amended.

This procedure may only be applied once by the members of a linguistic group in respect of one and the same draft or proposed bill (rev. 24.12.1970).

**Art. 39**. Voting is done either by word of mouth or by sitting and standing; all laws generally are voted on by the calling of names and word of mouth. The election and presentation of candidates are voted on by secret ballot (rev. 31.7.1984).

**Art. 40**. Each House has the right of investigation.

**Art. 41**. No bill may be passed by either House until after it has been voted on article by article.

**Art. 42**. The Houses have the right to amend and to divide up the articles and amendments proposed.

**Art. 43**. It is prohibited to present petitions in person to the Houses.

Each House has the right to refer the petitions addressed to it back to the Ministers. The latter are bound to provide explanations regarding their contents whenever the House shall request it.

**Art. 44**. No member of either of the two Houses may be prosecuted or sued as a result of the opinions and votes he has expressed in the exercise of his functions.

**Art. 45**. No member of either of the two Houses may, during the session, be prosecuted or arrested as a punishment save with the permission of the House to which he belongs, except in the case of *flagrante delicto*.

No bodily constraint may be used towards a member of either of the two Houses during the session, save with the same permission as above.

The detention or prosecution of a member of either of the two Houses is suspended during the session and throughout its duration if the House shall so require.

**Art. 46**. Each House, through its own rules, shall determine the way in which it shall exercise its powers.

## SECTION I

### Concerning the House of Representatives

**Art. 47**. Members of the House of Representatives are directly elected by all citizens aged 21 years and over, resident for at least six months in the same borough, and who do not come under any of the causes of disenfranchisement laid down by the law.

Each elector is entitled to only one vote (rev. 7.2.1921 and 28.7.1981).

**Art. 48**. The constitution of the electoral bodies is regulated for each province by the law.

Elections are held on the basis of the proportional representation system as specified by the law.

Voting is compulsory and secret. It takes place in the borough save in exceptional cases to be specified by law (rev. 15.11.1920).

**Art. 49**. Section 1. The House of Representatives comprises 212 members.

Section 2. Each electoral district has as many seats as results from dividing its total population by the national divisor, which is obtained when the total population of the Kingdom is divided by 212.

Remaining seats are allocated to those districts with the largest surplus populations not yet represented.

Section 3. The distribution of members of the House of Representatives as between the districts (constituencies) is effected in proportion to the population by the King.

For this purpose, a population census whose results he publishes within six months is carried out every ten years.

Within three months following such publication, he determines the number of seats allocated to each constituency.

The new distribution applies with effect from the next general election.

Section 4. Electoral districts are determined by legislation: this also lays down the necessary qualification to be on the electoral list and how the electoral procedure shall be conducted (rev. 28.7.1971).

**Art. 50**. To be eligible, it is necessary:

1. to be a Belgian by birth or to have been granted full naturalization;

2. to enjoy civil and political rights;

3. to be aged twenty-five years or over;

4. to be legally resident in Belgium.

No other condition of eligibility may be required (rev. 15.11.1920).

**Art. 51**. The members of the House of Representatives are elected for a term of four years.

The House is renewed every four years (rev. 15.10.1921).

**Art. 52**. Each member of the House of Representatives is entitled to an annual indemnity of 12,000 francs.

He is furthermore entitled to travel free on all lines of communication that are operated or contracted out by the State.

The law specifies those methods of transportation which members may use free of charge apart from those mentioned above.

An annual indemnity, chargeable to the endowment destined to cover the expenses of the House of Representatives, may be attributed to the president of that assembly.

The House determines the amounts that may be levied on the indemnity under the heading of contributions to the retirement or pension funds it has deemed useful to set up (rev. 15.11.1920).

## SECTION II

*Concerning the Senate*

**Art. 53**. The Senate is composed:

1. of members elected on the basis of the population in each province, in accordance with Article 47. The provisions of Article 48 are applicable to the election of those senators;

2. of members elected by the provincial councils in the proportion of one senator to every 200,000 inhabitants. Every surplus of at least 125,000 inhabitants confers the right to elect an additional Senator. However, every provincial council shall nominate at least three senators;

3. of members elected by the Senate on the basis of half the number of senators elected by the provincial councils. If the number is an odd one, it is increased by one digit.

These members are designated by the Senators who were elected according to the provisions of 1 and 2 of the present article.

The election of Senators who are elected according to the provisions of 2 and 3 of the present article, is carried out according to the proportional representation system as laid down by the law (rev. 15.10.1921).

**Art. 54**. The number of Senators directly elected by the electorate is equal to half the number of members of the House of Representatives (rev. 7.9.1983).

**Art. 55**. The senators are elected for a term of four years. The Senate is entirely renewed every four years (rev. 15.10.1921).

**Art. 56**. To be elected senator, it is necessary:

1. to be Belgian by birth or to have been granted full naturalization;

2. to enjoy civil and political rights;

3. to be legally resident in Belgium;

4. to be at least forty years of age (rev. 15.10.1921).

**Art. 56*b***. (rev. 3.6.1985).

**Art. 56*c***. Senators elected by the provincial councils may not belong to the assembly which elects them nor have been a member thereof during the two years preceding the date of their election (rev. 15.10.1921 and 11.6.1970).

**Art. 56*d***. In the event of a dissolution of the Senate, the King may dissolve the provincial councils.

The act of dissolution contains a summons to the provincial electors within forty days and to the provincial councils within two months (rev. 15.10.1921).

**Art. 57**. Senators receive no salary.

They are, however, entitled to the reimbursement of their expenses. This indemnity is fixed at four thousand francs a year.

They are furthermore entitled to travel free of charge on all lines of communication operated or contracted out by the State.

The law lays down those means of transportation which they may use free of charge apart from the lines mentioned above (rev. 15.10.1921).

**Art. 58**. The sons of the King or, failing these, Belgian princes of that branch of the royal family which is in the line of succession, are senators by right at the age of eighteen years. They are only entitled to speak and vote at the age of twenty-five years (rev. 7.9.1983).

**Art. 59**. Any assembly of the Senate which is held outside the time of the session of the House of Representatives shall automatically be null and void.

## SECTION III

### *Concerning the Community Councils*

**Art. 59b.** § 1. There is a Council and an Executive of the French Community and a Council and an Executive of the Flemish Community, the composition and functioning of which are regulated by law. The Councils are composed of elected representatives.

With a view to the implementation of Article 107d, the Council of the French Community and the Council of the Flemish Community, together with their Executives, may exercise the forms of competence vested respectively in the Walloon Region and in the Flemish Region, in obedience to the conditions and methods laid down by the law.

The laws referred to in the preceding paragraphs must be enacted in terms of the majority vote specified in Article 1, last paragraph.

§ 2. The Community Councils, each in its own sphere, shall regulate by decree:

1. cultural matters;

2. education, excluding all matters appertaining to the Schools Covenant, compulsory education, teaching structures, diplomas, subsidies, salaries, and the standards governing the student population;

3. co-operation between the Communities and international cultural co-operation.

A law enacted in terms of the majority vote specified in § 1, paragraph 3, shall define the cultural matters referred to in (1) and the forms of co-operation referred to in (3) of this paragraph.

§ 2b. The Community Councils, each for its own account, shall regulate by decree the personalized matters, as also co-operation between the Communities and international co-operation in such matters.

A law enacted in terms of the majority vote specified in Article 1, last paragraph, shall define these personalized matters and the forms such co-operation shall take.

§ 3. Furthermore, the Community Councils, each for its own account, shall regulate by decree, to the exclusion of the Legislative, the use of languages in the following areas:

1. administrative matters;

2. the education provided in schools which are set up, subsidized or recognized by the public authorities;

3. industrial relations between employers and their personnel, together with such business instruments and documents as are required by the law and the regulations.

§ 4. The decrees issued in terms of § 2 have the force of law respectively in the French-language region and in the Dutch-language region, and also with regard to institutions established in the bilingual region of Brussels-Capital which, by virtue of their activities, must be considered as belonging exclusively to one or other of the Communities.

Such decrees as are promulgated in pursuance of § 3 shall have the force of law respectively in the French-language region and in the Dutch-language region, except as regards:

– boroughs or groups of boroughs which are adjacent to another language region, and in which the law prescribes or permits the use of a language other than that of the region in which they are located;

– departments whose activities extend beyond the language region in which they are established.

– national and international institutions designated by law, whose activities are common to more than one community.

§ 4b. The decrees issued in terms of § 2b have the force of law respectively in the French language region and in the Dutch language region and also, except if a law passed on the basis of the majority vote specified in Article 1, last paragraph, shall provide otherwise, with regard to those institutions, established in the bilingual region of Brussels-Capital which, by virtue of their organisation, must be considered as belonging exclusively to one or other of the Communities.

§ 5. The right of initiative is vested in the Executive and in the members of the Council.

§ 6. The law determines the overall credit which is made available to each Community Council, which controls the allocation thereof by decree.

This credit is calculated in the light of objective criteria laid down by the law.

Equal endowments are established in matters which, of their very nature, do not lend themselves to objective criteria.

In obedience to the same rules, the law shall determine the proportion of this credit which must be set aside for the development of each Community within the territory of Brussels-Capital.

§ 7. The law defines those measures aimed at preventing any discrimination for ideological and philosophical reasons.

§ 8. The law sets up the procedure aimed at averting and settling any conflicts between laws and decrees, and between one decree and another (rev. 24.12.1970 and 17.7.1980).

**Art. 59c.** § 1. There is a Council and there is an Executive of the German-speaking Community, the composition and functioning of which are regulated by law.

The Council is composed of elected representatives.

Article 45 applies analogously to the members of the Council.

§ 2. The Council shall regulate by decree:

1. cultural matters;

2. personalized matters;

3. education, as far as for what is regulated under Article 59b, § 2, 2.

4. co-operation between the communities and international cultural co-operation as well as international co-operation in the matters referred to in 2.

These decrees have force of law in the German-speaking Region.

The law lays down the cultural and personalized matters referred to in 1 and 2, as well as the ways of co-operation referred to in 4.

§ 3. On the motion of their respective Executives the Council of the German-speaking Community and the Walloon Regional Council may, by mutual consent and by separate decree, decide that the Council and the Executive of the German-speaking Community shall, within the German-speaking region, exercise completely or partially the competence vested in the Walloon Region.

This competence shall, as the case may be, be exercised by means of decrees, orders or regulations.

§ 4. The Council and the Executive of the German-speaking Community exercise, by means of orders and regulations, any other competence vested in them by law.

Article 107 applies to these orders and regulations.

§ 5. The right of initiative is vested in the Executive and in the members of the Council.

§ 6. The law determines the overall credit which is made available to the Council, which controls the allocation thereof by decree.

§ 7. The law defines those measures aimed at preventing any discrimination for ideological and philosophical reasons.

*Transitional Provision*

Up to the date of commencement of the laws referred to in § 1, first clause, § 2, third clause, § 6 and § 7, the law of 10 July 1973 concerning the Council of the German Cultural Community remains implemented (rev. 1.6.1983).

## CHAPTER II

*Concerning the King and his Ministers*

### SECTION I

*Concerning the King*

**Art. 60**. The constitutional powers of the King are hereditary in the direct line of natural, legitimate heirs of H.M. Leopold Georges Chrétien Frédéric of Saxe-Coburg, from male heir to male heir, in order of primogeniture, to the perpetual exclusion of women and their descendants.

Shall be deprived of this right of succession any prince who marries without the consent of the King or of those people who, failing him, exercise his powers in the cases laid down by the Constitution.

However, he may be relieved from this disqualification by the King or by those who, failing him, exercise his powers in the cases laid down by the Constitution, on condition that both Houses agree thereto (rev. 7.9.1893).

**Art. 61**. Should there be no male descendants of H.M. Leopold Georges Chrétien Frédéric of Saxe-Coburg, the King may nominate his heir with the consent of both Houses, which is expressed in the manner prescribed by the following article.

If no nomination has been made according to the method outlined above, the throne shall be vacant (rev. 7.9.1893).

**Art. 62**. The King may not simultaneously be the Head of another State save with the consent of both Houses.

Neither of the Houses may debate on this subject unless at least two-thirds of its total number of members are present, and the resolution is only passed if it secures at least two-thirds of the total number of votes cast.

**Art. 63**. The King's person is inviolable; his Ministers are accountable.

**Art. 64**. No act of the King's is effective unless it is countersigned by a Minister who, in doing so, renders himself accountable therefore.

**Art. 65**. The King appoints and dismisses his Ministers.

**Art. 66**. He confers ranks in the Armed Forces. He appoints persons to posts in the general administrative departments and those connected with external relations, except in such cases as are laid down by law.

He does not make appointments to other offices except under the express ruling of a law.

**Art. 67**. He issues the regulations and decrees necessary for the implementation of laws, without ever being able to suspend the laws themselves nor exempt people from implementing them.

**Art. 68**. The King commands the armed forces on land and sea, declares war, makes treaties of peace, alliance and commerce. He advises the House of the contents thereof as soon as the interest and security of the State shall permit, enclosing all relevant documents.

Commercial treaties and those which might affect the State or individually become binding on certain Belgians, only become effective after they have received the consent of both Houses.

No cession, exchange or addition of territory may take place save under a law. In no case may the secret clauses of a treaty render the public clauses null and void.

**Art. 69**. The King sanctions and promulgates the laws.

**Art. 70**. The Houses automatically assemble every year on the second Tuesday of October, unless they have been convened previously by the King (rev. 30.6.1969).

The Houses must sit during at least forty days every year.

The King pronounces the closure of the session.

The King has the right to convene the Houses in an extraordinary session.

**Art. 71**. The King has the right to dissolve the Houses, either together or separately. The act of dissolution contains a summons to the electorate within forty days, and to the Houses within two months.

**Art. 72**. The King may prorogue the Houses. However, this adjournment may not exceed one month in duration, nor be repeated during the same session, without the consent of the Houses.

**Art. 73**. He has the right to reprieve or reduce the sentences delivered by judges, except in regard to what has been laid down for the Ministers.

**Art. 74**. He has the right to coin currency in implementation of the law.

**Art. 75**. He has the right to confer titles of nobility, without ever being able to grant privileges on that account.

**Art. 76**. He awards military decorations in obedience to the prescriptions of the law in this respect.

**Art. 77**. The law fixes the amount of the civil list for the duration of each reign.

**Art. 78**. The King has no other powers save those formally vested in him by the Constitution and the special laws passed in accordance with the Constitution itself.

**Art. 79**. On the death of the King, the Houses shall meet unconvened by the tenth day at latest following the date of decease. If the Houses have been dissolved previously and a summons has been included in the act of dissolution for a time which is later than the tenth day, the outgoing Houses will resume their functions up to the assembly of those which are to replace them.

If only one House has been dissolved, the same rule shall be followed in respect of that House.

Dating from the death of the King and until the oath of office is taken either by his successor to the throne or by the Regent, the constitutional powers of the King are exercised, in the name of the Belgian people, by the Ministers meeting in Council and on their own responsibility.

**Art. 80**. The King comes of age on his eighteenth birthday.

He does not ascend the throne until he has formally taken the following oath before both Houses meeting together:

'I swear to observe the Consitution and the laws of the Belgian people, to maintain national independence and the integrity of the territory.'

**Art. 81**. If, on the death of the King, his successor is a minor, the two Houses shall meet in a single assembly in order to arrange for the regency and the guardianship of the new King.

**Art. 82**. If the King is unavoidably prevented from reigning, the Ministers, after establishing that impossibility, shall immediately convene both Houses. Arrangements are made for the regency and guardianship of the King by both Houses meeting together.

**Art. 83**. The regency can only be conferred on one person.

The Regent does not take office until he has taken the oath laid down in Article 80.

**Art. 84**. No alteration to the Constitution may be made during a regency regarding the constitutional powers of the King and the Articles 60 and 64 and 80 and 85 of the Constitution (rev. 31.7.1984).

**Art. 85**. When the throne is vacant, the Houses shall meet in a joint session to make temporary arrangements for the regency until the Houses meet again after they have been entirely renewed; this meeting shall take place at latest within two months. The new Houses, meeting together, shall make definite arrangements in regard to the vacancy.

## SECTION II

*Concerning the Ministers*

**Art. 86**. No person may become a Minister unless he is Belgian by birth or has been granted full naturalization.

**Art. 86b**. With the possible exception of the Prime Minister, the Cabinet comprises an equal number of French speaking and Dutch speaking ministers (rev. 24.12.1970).

**Art. 87**. No member of the royal family may become a minister.

**Art. 88**. Ministers are only entitled to speak and vote in one or other of the Houses when they are a member of it.

They are authorized to enter either House and must be heard whenever they so request.

The Houses may request the presence of the ministers.

**Art. 89**. In no case may any verbal or written order from the King exempt a minister from his responsibility.

**Art. 90**. The House of Representatives has the right to impeach Ministers and to bring them before the Court of Cassation, which alone has the right to judge them in the presence of both Houses, except as shall be laid down by the law with regard to the exercise of civil proceedings by the injured party and to the crimes and misdemeanours that the ministers may have committed outside the exercise of their official functions.

A law shall specify the cases of responsibility, the penalties to be imposed on ministers, and the procedure to be adopted in their regard, either on the basis of an accusation accepted by the House of Representatives or on the legal action brought by the injured parties.

**Art. 91**. The King may not reprieve a minister sentenced by a Court of Cassation save at the request of one of the two Houses.

**SECTION III**

*Concerning the Secretaries of State*

**Art. 91***b*. The King appoints and dismisses the Secretaries of State.

These are members of the Government. They do not form part of the Cabinet. They are attached to a Minister.

The King determines their powers and the limits within which they may be given authority to sign.

The constitutional provisions relating to ministers apply to them with the exception of Articles 79, paragraph 3, 82 and 86*b* (rev. 24.12.1970).

**CHAPTER III**

*Concerning the judiciary power*

**Art. 92**. Contestations arising out of civil rights come under the exclusive jurisdiction of the law courts.

**Art. 93**. Contestations arising out of political rights come under the jurisdiction of the law courts except in such cases as are laid down by the law.

**Art. 94**. No tribunal or court of arbitration may be set up save under a law. No extraordinary commissions or courts may be set up under any denomination whatsoever.

**Art. 95**. There is one Court of Cassation for the whole of Belgium.

This court does not deal with the content of the affairs submitted to it, save in regard to the judgment of ministers.

**Art. 96**. Hearings in the courts and tribunals are public unless such publicity is prejudicial to good order or morals; in this case, the court shall so declare in an official ruling.

In matters connected with political or press misdemeanours, a session *in camera* can only be ordered on a unanimous basis.

**Art. 97**. Every judgment shall be motivated. It is pronounced in open court.

**Art. 98**. A jury is empanelled for all criminal affairs and for political and press misdemeanours.

**Art. 99**. Justices of the peace and judges of the various courts are directly appointed by the King.

Counsellors of the Courts of Appeal, the presidents and vice-presidents of the Courts of First Instance within their jurisdiction, are appointed by the King on the basis of two double lists, one submitted by the courts concerned and the other by the provincial councils.

Counsellors of the Court of Cassation are appointed by the King on the basis of two double lists, one submitted by the Senate and the other by the Court of Cassation.

In both cases, candidates named on one list may also be named on the other list.

The names of all candidates are made public at least fifteen days before the appointment is made.

The courts shall choose their own presidents and vice-presidents from among themselves.

**Art. 100**. Judges are appointed for life. They are retired at an age determined by law, and receive the pension laid down by the law.

No judge may be deprived of his office or suspended except by a specific judgment.

The transfer of a judge can only be made on the basis of a new appointment and with his consent (rev. 23.1.1981).

**Art. 101**. The King appoints and dismisses the officials of the Public Prosecutor's department in the courts and tribunals.

**Art. 102**. The salaries of members of the Judiciary are fixed by law.

**Art. 103**. No judge may accept a salaried post from the government unless he exercises it without charge, and except for the cases of incompatibility laid down by the law.

**Art. 104**. There are five Courts of Appeal in Belgium:

1. that of Brussels, whose jurisdiction includes the province of Brabant;

2. that of Ghent, whose jurisdiction includes the provinces of West Flanders and East Flanders;

3. that of Antwerp, whose jurisdiction includes the provinces of Antwerp and Limburg;

4. that of Liège, whose jurisdiction extends to the provinces of Liège, Namur and Luxembourg;

5. that of Mons, whose jurisdiction extends to the province of Hainaut.

*Provisional arrangement*

A law determines the date of entry into force of Article 104 and shall regulate its implementation. The draft bill must be tabled before the Legislature within two years following promulgation of the present article.

The existing text shall apply until such time as the said law comes into force (rev. 11.6.1970).

**Art. 105**. Special laws regulate the organization of military tribunals, their powers, the rights and obligations of the members of such tribunals, and the duration of their term of office.

These shall be commercial courts set up in places to be specified by the law which also regulates their organization, their powers, the method of appointing their members and the duration of the latters' term of office.

The law also lays down the organization of the labour courts, their powers, the procedure for appointing their members and the duration of the latters' term of office (rev. 21.4.1970).

**Art. 106**. The Court of Cassation delivers its verdict on conflicts of authority in the manner laid down by the law.

**Art. 107**. The courts and tribunals shall not apply any general, provincial or local decrees and regulations save insofar as they are in accordance with the law.

## CHAPTER III-B

### The Prevention and Settlement of Conflicts

**Art. 107c**. § 1. The law organizes the procedure aimed at averting conflicts between laws, decrees, and the regulations referred to in Article 26b, and as between one decree and another and also as between the regulations referred to in Article 26b.

§ 2. There shall be, for the whole of Belgium, a Court of Arbitration whose composition, competence and functioning shall be defined by law.

This Court shall rule on the conflicts referred to in § 1.

*Transitional clause:* Article 107*c* comes into force within a period of six months dating from its promulgation. As a transitional measure, the law shall work out a procedure designed to prevent and settle conflicts between laws and decrees, and as between one decree and another (rev. 29.7.1980).

## CHAPTER III-C

### *Concerning the regional institutions*

**Art. 107*d*.** Belgium comprises three regions: the Walloon Region, the Flemish region and the Brussels Region.

The law confers on the regional bodies which it sets up, and which are composed of elected representatives, the power to rule on such matters as it shall determine, to the exclusion of those referred to in Articles 23 and 59*b*, within such jurisdiction and in accordance with such procedure as it shall determine.

Such a law must be passed with a majority vote within each linguistic group of both Houses, provided the majority of the members of each group are present and on condition that the total votes in favour in the two linguistic groups attain two-thirds of the votes cast (rev. 24.12.1970).

## CHAPTER IV

### *Concerning provincial and borough institutions*

**Art. 108.** Provincial and municipal institutions are regulated by the law.

The law sanctions the application of the following principles:

1. the direct election of members of provincial and borough councils.

2. the attribution to provincial and borough councils of all matters of provincial and borough interest, without prejudice to the approval of their acts in such cases and in accordance with such procedure as the law may determine.

3. the decentralization of authority in favour of provincial and borough institutions.

4. public sittings by provincial and borough councils within the limits prescribed by law.

5. publication of budgets and accounts.

6. the intervention of the oversight authority or of the legislative authority to prevent infringement of the law or injury to the general interest (rev. 20.7.1970).

In implementation of a law passed on the basis of the majority vote specified in Article 1, last paragraph, the organization and exercise of administrative oversight may be regulated by the Community or Regional Councils (rev. 17.7.1980).

Several provinces or several boroughs may co-operate or join together, under such conditions and according to such procedure as shall be determined by the law, for the purposes of settling and jointly pursuing objectives of provincial or of borough interest. This notwithstanding, it is forbidden for several provincial councils or several borough councils to hold meetings for deliberating together (rev. 20.7.1970).

**Art. 108*b*.** Section 1. The law shall create urban areas and federations of communes. It shall determine their organization and their powers, applying the principles laid down in Article 108.

For each urban area and for each federation there shall be a council and an executive body.

The Chairman of the executive body shall be elected by the council from amongst its members; his election shall be ratified by the King; the law shall determine his status.

Articles 107 and 129 shall apply to decrees and regulations issued by the urban areas and federations of communes.

The boundaries of urban areas and federations of communes may not be altered or amended other than by legislation.

§ 2. The law shall set up the body within which each urban area and the nearest federations of communes shall act in concert, under such conditions and according to such procedure as it shall specify, to examine common problems of a technical nature coming within their respective field of jurisdiction.

§ 3. Several federations of communes may come to an understanding amongst themselves or enter into association, under such conditions and according to such procedure as the law shall determine, for the purpose of settling and jointly pursuing objectives coming within their jurisdiction. It is not permissible for their councils to hold joint meetings for deliberating together (rev. 24.12.1970).

**Art. 108c.** Section 1. Article 108b applies to the urban area to which the capital of the Kingdom belongs, subject to the undermentioned provisions.

§ 2. For those cases laid down in the Constitution and by legislation, the members of the urban area council are divided into a French language group and a Dutch language group in the manner prescribed by law.

The executive body is composed of an uneven number of members. With the exception of the Chairman, there are the same number of members in the French language group as in the Dutch language group.

§ 3. Except in the case of budgets, a reasoned motion signed by at least three-quarters of the members of a linguistic group in the urban area council and tabled before the final voting in public sessions may declare that such provisions as it specifies in a draft or proposed regulation or decree by the urban area council are likely to do grave harm to relations between the communities. In this case, the procedure in the urban area council is suspended and the motion is referred back to the executive body which, within thirty days, pronounces its reasoned judgment on the matter and amends the draft or proposed instrument where necessary.

The oversight power in respect of the regulation or decree adopted after this procedure is exercized by the King on a motion by the Cabinet.

This procedure may only be applied once by the members of a linguistic group in respect of one and the same draft or proposal.

§ 4. In the urban area there is a French committee for culture and a Dutch committee for culture, which are composed of an equal number of members elected respectively by the French language group and by the Dutch language group in the urban area council.

Each has the same powers in respect of its cultural community as the other organizing authorities:

1. in pre-schooling, post-educational and cultural matters;

2. in education.

§ 5. The French committee and the Dutch committee for culture together constitute joint committees. Decisions of the joint committees are only adopted if they obtain, in each committee, the majority of votes cast.

The joint committees are competent in the matters laid down in Section 4 which are of common interest and for promoting the national and international mission of the urban area.

§ 6. The committees referred to in Sections 4 and 5 also fulfil the functions vested in them by the legislature, the cultural councils or the Government.

The law regulates the organisation and operating procedures of these committees (rev. 24.12.1970).

**Art. 109**. The establishing of birth, marriage and death certificates and the keeping of the registers come exclusively within the competence of the borough authorities.

## HEADING IV

### CONCERNING FINANCES

**Art. 110**. § 1. No tax for the benefit of the State may be levied save in terms of a law.

§ 2. No tax for the benefit of the Community or the Region may be levied save in terms of a decree or a regulation referred to in Article 26*b*

With regard to the taxes referred to in the preceding paragraph, the law shall define those exceptions which have been proved to be necessary.

§ 3. No charge or levy may be imposed by a province except by a decision of its council.

With regard to the taxes referred to in the preceding paragraph, the law shall define those exceptions which have been proved to be necessary.

The law may abolish, in whole or in part, the taxes referred to in paragraph 1 above.

§ 4. No charge or levy may be imposed by the urban area, federation of boroughs, or individual boroughs except on a decision by their council.

With regard to the taxes referred to in the preceding paragraph, the law shall define those exceptions which have been proved to be necessary (rev. 20.7.1970 and 29.7.1980).

**Art. 111**. Taxes for the benefit of the State, the Community and the Region are voted annually.

The regulations establishing them are effective during one' year only unless they are renewed (rev. 29.7.1980).

**Art. 112**. No privilege may be established where taxes are concerned.

No exemption nor moderation of taxes may be established save through a law.

**Art. 113**. Apart from the provinces, the polders and fenland, and cases formally excepted by law, decree or the regulations referred to in Article 26*b*, no payment may be required of citizens except by way of taxes for the benefit of the State, the Community, the Region, the urban area, the federation of boroughs, or the borough (rev. 29.7.1980).

**Art. 114**. No pension and no gratuity chargeable to the public treasury may be granted save in accordance with a law.

**Art. 115**. Each year the Houses pass the law on State accounting and vote on the budgets.

All the receipts and expenditures of the State must be included in the budgets and in the accounting.

**Art. 116**. The members of the Audit Office are appointed by the House of Representatives and for a term of office laid down by the law.

This Office is in charge of the examination and winding up of the accounts of the general administration and of all vouchers on the public treasury. It ensures that no article of expenditure in the budget is exceeded, and that no transfer takes place. It winds up the accounts of the various State administrative offices and is in charge of collecting, for this purpose, any information and accountable receipts that may be necessary. The general accounts of the State are submitted to the Houses along with the comments of the Audit Office.

This Office is organized by a law.

**Art. 117**. The salaries and pensions of ministers of religion are chargeable to the State; the sums necessary for this purpose are included in the annual budget.

## HEADING V

### CONCERNING THE ARMED FORCES

**Art. 118**. The method of recruiting for the Armed Forces is laid down by law. It also regulates the promotion, rights and obligations of the military.

**Art. 119**. The armed forces contingent is voted annually. The law which establishes it is only effective for one year unless it is renewed.

**Art. 120**. The organization and attributions of the gendarmerie are the subject of a law.

**Art. 121**. No foreign troops may be admitted to the service of the State, nor may they occupy or pass through the territory, save under the terms of a law.

**Art. 122**. (rev. 31.7.1984).

**Art. 123**. (rev. 24.8.1921).

**Art. 124**. The military may not be deprived of their rank, honours and decorations, or pensions save in the manner laid down by the law.

## HEADING VI

### GENERAL CLAUSES

**Art. 125**. The Belgian nation has adopted the colours red, yellow and black, and for its coat of arms, the Belgian Lion with the device: 'Unity is strength'.

**Art. 126**. The city of Brussels is the capital of Belgium and the seat of the government.

**Art. 127**. No oath may be imposed save in accordance with the law, which lays down the wording thereof.

**Art. 128**. Any foreigner who is on Belgian territory enjoys the same protection granted to persons and property, save in exceptional cases to be established by law.

**Art. 129**. No law, decree or administrative regulation of a general, provincial or municipal character is compulsory until it has been published in the manner laid down by the law.

**Art. 130**. The Constitution may not be suspended, either in whole or in part.

## HEADING VII

### CONCERNING REVISIONS OF THE CONSTITUTION

**Art. 131**. The Legislative Power has the right to state that it is necessary to revise such constitutional provision as it shall designate.

Following this statement, both Houses are automatically dissolved.

Two new Houses will be convened in accordance with Article 71.

These Houses, in agreement with the King, shall pronounce judgment on the points submitted for revision.

In this case, the Houses may not debate unless at least two-thirds of the members of each of them are present and no alteration shall be adopted unless it secures at least two-thirds of the total votes cast.

**Art. 131b.** No revision of the Constitution may be entered upon, not pursued in time of war or when the Houses are prevented from meeting freely on the national territory (rev. 15.1.1968).

## HEADING VIII

### TRANSITIONAL ARRANGEMENTS

**Art. 132.** Until such time as the Université Catholique de Louvain (1) including its ancillary branches of intermediate and technical education, is transferred outside the Dutch language region, the Cultural Council for the French cultural Community (2) shall, notwithstanding Article 59b, Section 4, paragraph 1, have jurisdiction over this institution.

The linguistic system at present in force, both as regards education and administrative matters, will continue to apply until such appointed time (rev. 24.12.1970).

**Art. 133.** (rev. 31.7.1984).

**Art. 134.** Until a law has been passed in this regard, the House of Representatives shall exercise discretionary powers in impeaching a minister, and the Court of Cassation shall exercise similar powers in judging him, the misdemeanour being specified and the penalty being determined.

Nevertheless, the penalty may not exceed that of penal internment, without prejudice to cases expressly provided for under the penal laws.

**Art. 135.** Until a law enacted in implementation of Article 59b, § 1, paragraph 1, has arranged for the composition of the Councils and the Executives of the French Community and the Flemish Community, the Council of the French Community comprises members of the French linguistic group in both Houses and the Council of the Flemish Community comprises members of the Dutch linguistic group in both Houses; the right of initiative is vested in the King and in the members of the Community Councils, and Articles 67, 69 and 129 are applicable to the decrees (rev. 17.7.1980).

**Art. 136.** (rev. 21.4.1970).

**Art. 137.** The fundamental law of August 24, 1815 is abolished, as also the provincial and local statutes. However, the provincial and local authorities shall retain their powers until such time as other arrangements have been made by law.

**Art. 138.** Dating from the day on which the Constitution comes into force, all laws, decrees, ordinances, regulations and other acts which are contrary to it shall be abolished.

**Art. 139.** (rev. 14.6.1971).

**Art. 140.** The text of the Constitution is drawn up in French and in Dutch (rev. 10.4.1967).

---

(1) French language wing of the Catholic University of Louvain.
(2) This now refers to the Council of the French Community.

# 4 Autonomy and the unitary state: the case of Corsica

*Peter Savigear*

The government of France rests on a strong tradition of centralism. Over the centuries the unitary state has been victorious, shaped by the centralizing efforts of the old monarchy, the Revolution of 1789, the Jacobinism of 1792–4, Bonapartism, constitutional monarchy and successive republican regimes. Although a tradition of federal ideas certainly exists in France (one need think only of Proudhon), in practical politics federalism is known there chiefly by its defeats, in 1793, and again in 1871 (the Communards). Some quasi-federal plans have been made, but on the whole these have been reserved for overseas territories. At home devolution has not, traditionally, been accorded any encouragement.

Nevertheless even within France, centralization has not swept away all variety among peoples and traditions. France has the basic building-blocks for some kind of 'multiple autonomy', if not of outright federalism, in the form of the old pre-revolutionary provinces. Some of these possess a history of independence and a remarkable cultural individuality. The size of the country alone suggests a federal solution; few unitary states are as large as France. And the central state has given at least some recognition to this diversity within the national frontiers. As long ago as 1951 regional languages were recognized and their use in schools authorized by the *Loi Deixone*. This law preserved something of local identities, although it applied only to Breton, Catalan, Occitan and Basque in its first formulation and it accorded no political recognition. It was but a nod in the direction of regional diversity.

In the last thirty years, however, there have been signs that a deeper change in traditional attitudes may be taking place. There has been a significant increase within France of demands for regional autonomy, and a growing willingness among some politicians at the centre to consider granting greater powers to the regions. The pages that follow aim to examine the way in which, in relation to one particularly sensitive

96

area of France, the island of Corsica, the unitary state has attempted to come to terms with the upsurge in regional demands and claims.


## Corsica in the French state

The wild, mountainous and rather remote island of Corsica was conquered by French troops in 1769 after the Republic of Genoa, nominally sovereign of Corsica, had failed to crush a rebellion that had begun in 1729. On several previous occasions French help had been requested and provided, but finally the Treaty of Versailles, signed in January 1768, passed responsibility for administration of the island from Genoa to the King of France.[1] However, it was not until May of the following year that the French were able to defeat the Corsican national leader Pascal Paoli who had seized a few years of independence for his people between 1755 and 1769.[2]

Special administrative and constitutional arrangements were applied immediately after the conquest. A reorganization of justice and municipal administration, including representative institutions, occurred, disturbing the local practices of self-government by which the Corsicans had traditionally ruled their lives. Corsica became a *pays d'état*, a model for the kind of regime which the ministers Turgot and Necker hoped to introduce in the older provinces of France. However scarcely had the island been absorbed into the French monarchy when the Revolution occurred, and the constitutional status was transformed. In 1789 Corsica became part of the unitary French state[3] and Genoa's residual claim to sovereignty was rejected. The island was provisionally made a single department in 1790, but divided into two by the Convention in 1793, named after the rivers Golo and Liamone. Natural ruggedness and difficulties in communication reversed the decision in 1811 and Corsica remained a single department until 1975 when it was again divided to form the two departments of *Haute-Corse* and *Corse-du-Sud*, this change taking effect in 1976.

Pascal Paoli returned to France after his exile in Britain (where he fled after the defeat of 1769) and arrived in Corsica in July 1790. He was nominated President of the administrative council and commander of the National Guard. However relations soon soured. The people were divided between those favouring French rule, 'one and indivisible', and those, following Paoli who feared the consequences of integration and an ever more pressing centralization. Paoli finally broke with the Convention in 1794 and turned to the British, seeking a special status for Corsica under the sovereignty of King George III. The life-span of the *Royaume Anglo-corse* as it was called, was cut short; war-time strategic factors led to British withdrawal and in 1796 French rule was re-imposed. Corsica became *la plus proche des terres lointaines* of the French state.

Loyalty to France was scarcely in doubt after this date. The Corsican Napoleon Bonaparte saw to that; he was also the creator of efficient centralizing institutions and practices, bringing to fruition the unitary state of his predecessors. Corsicans were bound closer to the state of France. They studied on the mainland, and they served the state, in its armies, in the administration of metropole and empire. Another Bonaparte ruled as Napoleon III. In the wars of the nineteenth and twentieth centuries the Corsicans fought for France. After 1922 Mussolini's irredentist claims were rejected, and Corsica was the first part of metropolitan France to be liberated, in October 1943. Between 1796 and the end of the Second World War there were few coherent demands for independence, or for a federal relationship between Corsica and the French state.

However the unitary state had acknowledged that certain special conditions applied to Corsica. A particular fiscal regime was inaugurated in 1801 by the Miot decrees, reducing certain stamp duties and taxes, supplemented by a special customs arrangement in 1811. A degree of fiscal peculiarity continued and until recently affected commodities like tobacco, alcohol and fuels. The unitary state thus did not mean total uniformity.

Demands for autonomy and a greater recognition of Corsican individuality were not completely repressed. The earliest demands (as in the case of the Flemish movement in Belgium) concentrated on cultural matters such as the preservation of the language and literature, and the need to encourage interest in Corsican traditions and customs. Journals and other publications appeared during the nineteenth century devoted to all aspects of historical, scientific and cultural life, but only a few voices called for constitutional changes. These voices became stronger in the twentieth century, especially after 1920 with the journal *A Muvra* and the formation of the *Partitu corsu d'azione*, a small but active political association. Even these demands were muted; Italian Irredentism had produced a strong reaction and Corsicans proclaimed their loyalty to France. The demand for autonomy became more serious after 1945.

By the late-1950s the pressure for autonomy was organized and more accurately focused. These demands were fostered by two beliefs which were themselves encouraged by events and crises in French political life at that time. The first of these beliefs was that Corsica had been treated like a 'colony' although it had been constitutionally a part of metropolitan France. This 'colonial' exploitation had been accomplished by French business from the continent, by an unsympathetic administration, indifferent to Corsica and Corsicans, and above all by more than 17,000 *pieds noirs* from Algeria who arrived after 1962 when Algeria became an independent state. Official attitudes and new development organizations contributed to this view of an exploited Corsica, stifled and in the hands of alien developers.

Among the targets of the growing autonomist movement of the 1960s was SOMIVAC (*la société pour la mise en valeur de la Corse*) responsible for land allocation and development plans for agriculture and irrigation. Such institutions were regarded as excessively supportive of *pieds noirs*. Cartels and fraud in the wine trade led to violence in 1975 and the autonomists' denunciation of malpractice ended in a clash with security forces at Aléria in August 1975 in which two members of the CRS (*Compagnie républicaine de sécurité*) died. These were among many events which sustained support for the autonomists in the years before 1981.[4]

The second belief that drove the autonomists was their hostility towards those Corsican established interests known always as the 'clans', the '*clanisti*' in the Corsican language, that had dominated the island's politics through the centuries. Layer upon layer of client relationships exercised a controlling influence in the island not so much for the sake of financial gain as for the sake of political power. Corsica shared this characteristic with other areas, notably those Mediterranean countries where family and client ties were stronger than those of class, and where their interests were understood.[5] In such societies, political principles become subordinated to clan interests. In Corsica these client networks had learned to use the institutions of the French state, most obviously the locally elected offices at the level of the commune and the department. In particular, clans managed to control elections through their extended influence and through corruption – at least so the autonomists maintained. Critical voices raised against the clans were ignored, and failed to change the system from within. Reforming candidates failed to win seats and could not compete and during the 1970s the critics turned increasingly to direct action and to a barrage of public attacks through the press and demonstrations.

The response of the unitary state to the developing movement for autonomy was cautious. Direct action and violence did not produce political changes. However economic and financial measures brought some benefit to the island. New institutions and subsidies were established to assist the key sectors of the economy, tourism, agriculture, improvements to the infrastructure. By the mid-1980s the state was spending over 500 million francs in Corsica. A large increase in investment through an interministerial commission occurred between 1974 and 1980. Additional subsidies were regularly provided for further improvement. There were other concessions to nationalist opinion – the local language was recognized as coming within the *Loi Deixone*, and, for the first time since 1770, a university was established at Paoli's former capital, Corte.[6] The island also benefited from European Community funds.[7]

However these injections of capital and investment programmes were still administered through the institutions of the unitary state, and these in turn were dominated at local level by the influence of the clans. They controlled the distribution of funds and favours. Structural reform was slow to come to Corsica.

## The Special Statute for Corsica: 1982

Finally in 1982 the Socialist government under President François Mitterrand and Prime Minister Mauroy introduced a programme of decentralization which included a Special Statute for Corsica. The legislation came in two parts, a general text applicable to the majority of the French regions, 'à l'ensemble de la France', and an exceptional law applying only to Corsica and introducing autonomous government to that region alone. The minister responsible for the whole programme was M Gaston Defferre. The Special Statute, as the legislation for Corsica was known, was not extracted from the government by force. It was a matter of principle, an extension of socialist commitment to autogestion or self-rule, and based on a socialist draft law for Corsica prepared in 1976.

The legislation was 'special' because this was not intended to be a model for other regions, nor has it been. Decentralization elsewhere, as proposed by the Defferre ministry, was not to be the same as autonomy for Corsica. The principle of the unity of the state was not to be affected by particular arrangements made for an island with peculiar needs.

The 1982 Statute was a derogation from the Constitution of 1958, and was unsuccessfully challenged in the Constitutional Council on the grounds of being contrary to the Constitution. By this law Corsica became not simply a region with its own regional assembly like the other regions, but an autonomous region with a Corsican Assembly and its own executive or government.

The executive was indirectly elected from the members of the Assembly and by them. These deputies, sixty-one in all, were directly elected by proportional representation. The institutions and the new tier of administration which the Corsican government required, came into existence in 1982.

The special arrangements for Corsica have not been affected by the change of government in Paris which occurred in March 1986. Indeed it would be politically insensitive now to suggest abolition whatever the fate of the other decentralized regions of France. The law of 2 March 1982 explicitly recognized the specificity of Corsica 'résultant, notamment, de sa géographie et de son histoire'.[8]

The Assembly and the executive, under the authority of its president, have been given considerable powers over the two departments of Corsica, *Haute-Corse* and *Corse-du-Sud*. The factors that affect the daily lives of the 247,000 inhabitants of the island are now largely in the hands of their own representatives. Beneath the regional administration are those of the two departments and the communes. Exercising some reserved powers, notably policing and security, is the former centralized prefectoral administration – the prefects having reverted to their earlier title, *commissaires de la République*.

Corsica is thus a special region. Autonomy extends particularly to budgetary matters, and, unlike other regions, the executive is under no obligation to present its budget to Paris and responsible only to the Corsican Assembly and its committees in the first instance. The former system of prefectoral tutelage and scrutiny is no longer applicable. The sole matters still scrutinized by the officers of the Ministry of the Interior are those to which decentralization does not apply, those matters that are merely subject to a deconcentration of power. Such powers include the police and public order responsibilities of the mayors of the communes. Judicial review of the operation of autonomy lies with the existing legal system, acting on the advice of the *commissaires* who are empowered to refer breaches of the law.

The heart of autonomy lies in the competences transferred to the regional government. The identity and integrity of the region are in the hands of the Corsican Assembly and these are to be protected by regional responsibility for important economic and social matters. There are extensive competences in planning and development of the urban and rural environment. The Assembly has authority to designate areas for industrial and tourist development. The matters covered by the French term *l'aménagement du territoire* are transferred to the region. These powers in the general area of economic development also cover the responsibilities of the agencies established in 1957 and under central government authority, SOMIVAC in particular. They include agricultural projects and research, irrigation schemes – these are of great importance for rural communities – and the regional park which covers 78 communes of the interior. Special funding for development projects is available to the region; a *caisse de développement* is established. In accordance with the 1982 law, the two departments of the region are able to assist businesses finding themselves in financial difficulty, by direct and indirect aid as article 48 of the law permits. Thus the major part of the economy of Corsica is in the hands of the Assembly.

Responsibility for other aspects of the region's infrastructure is also moved to the region. This includes energy policy and transport. The financial and development responsibility for the road system lies with the Corsican Assembly, and this body shares control of the railway with the national organization, the SNCF. All control and future policy for airports and airlines now rests with the region. Transport in the widest sense has therefore been transferred, although the region does not have competence in transport between Corsica and the mainland – a matter of irritation for the islanders, since this is vital in commercial costing.

Employment policy has also been transferred to the region, a result of its wide competence in economic matters. Training and apprentice schemes form part of this responsibility, both vital to a region with high unemployment – currently around 11 per cent.[9]

In addition to these issues broadly covered by the term *formation professionelle*, the region has competence in education, from primary schools to the university, and related cultural and scientific and sporting activities. In a state sharply attuned to contemporary developments, the region has competence in audiovisual matters through le *Conseil corse de l'audiovisuel*. The transfer of administrative competences has therefore been extensive, so great indeed that it seems difficult for the 61 representatives in the Corsican Assembly and the bureaucracy to demonstrate skills and rapid grasp of these many issues. The region needs time to explore the avenues that have been opened by the legislation of 1982.

One of the difficulties has been finance. The region has been transferred funds to match the transfer of competences so that a proper responsibility can be exercised. Additionally the region can raise taxes, receive revenue from particular sources, like vehicle registration, and it can raise loans on national and international markets. Each of the two departments raises substantial amounts from taxation and licences as well as from local rents. However more than 50 per cent of the budget comes from central government subventions; in this way the grip of Paris remains firm.

At all levels of the administration, the region, the two departments and the communes, there is a similar problem, namely severe debt and such poverty that the exceptional costs of administration must be met by central government and transfers to the island. The many communes, 360 in all, rely heavily upon such transfers. The smaller communes, those with less than 700 inhabitants (this means 312 communes in Corsica) find 65 per cent of their income in this way. This money covers the various competences exercized at this level and subsidized projects and production. The remaining resources come from investments and local taxes – on professions, land, housing, and related matters. The two departments also have high costs and low income. Less than half the income comes from indirect taxation, and the bulk from the state. In this respect *Corse-du-Sud* is less dependent upon the state than *Haute-Corse*. The region receives some direct compensatory aid, but two-thirds of locally raised funding comes from special taxation, on vehicles and tobacco. Loans amounted to 9.6 per cent of the income (total 321,500,000 francs) in 1987.

These mixed sources of income, received by the three main levels of administration, provide the picture of Corsican financial difficulties. Total amounts are relatively low – a regional budget of 350 million francs in 1986 – but cost per head of population is high – 1,371 francs, contrasting with a national average in 1986 of 475 francs. Central government and state support per person in the two Corsican departments is equally significant in comparison to the national average, at 2,000 francs this figure is almost double the average. It has not been easy to move towards financial autonomy. The official commentary sums up the position all too crisply: 'L'importance des frais de personnel, le faible poids des recettes fiscales, compensé par celui plus élevé des transferts, sont les principales caractéristiques du budget des communes insulaires.'[10]

But financial arrangements have encountered other difficulties. Compensatory funding from Paris to cover the transfer of responsibilities has been slower than anticipated. The region has great difficulty in seeking loans on any market; it is the poorest in France and cannot afford long-term interest repayments. Moreover the total resources of the region are too limited to risk major loans. The return on regional investments is still sluggish and restricted. In short, Corsica cannot yet generate enough wealth for extensive economic development.

Although the regional budget is autonomous, there is a careful scrutiny of finances, particularly those at the level of the communes. A regional Chamber of Accounts has been created with this responsibility and here too Paris exerts an important authority. The regional *Cour des Comptes* is itself responsible to the Paris-based *Cour des Comptes*, and its members are appointed by the government in Paris and not by the Corsican Assembly. Ultimate financial control therefore rests with the central government. This should not, however, detract from the great regional authority.

Fears that autonomy for Corsica might bring demands from other regions for greater transfer of competences have been unfounded. No collapse of the unitary state has occurred. But this is perhaps because the central government has retained the initiative. The Special Statute for Corsica was not negotiated between the government in Paris and the region of Corsica. It was not a treaty between equals, but *octroyé*, granted by the state. What the French state has given away, it can also take back. There is no assurance that a future government may not revise the new relationship, however politically awkward this might be. The accommodation is fragile and the case of Corsica is not simple.

**Autonomy in practice**

Autonomy has not worked smoothly. Financial support has been tardy. The principle of autonomy has also been threatened. Details of the operation of policy have revealed ambiguity, sometimes resolved in favour of Paris, as in the case of communications between Corsica and the continent, where responsibility remains with the national government. In addition, the new institutions have not always operated autonomously; in some cases responsibility has been shared with older, centrally funded organizations.

Competence in tourist development for the island is divided between the region and the *Agence régionale du tourisme et des loisirs*, created by the government of the unitary state before autonomy was granted. Much the same applies to commercial and industrial development which has been divided between the regional government and the *Société de développement régional*. Even rural planning for Corsica is shared between regional and departmental organizations on the one hand and the very much older institutions of the communes on the other. On some issues the regional voice has been totally ignored. This was the case with a proposed power cable link between Corsica and Italy, rejected by the regional executive and Assembly.

There are other considerations which have influenced the working of Corsican autonomy. One of the hopes and aims of regional devolution and the election of an assembly according to a system of proportional representation had been to restrict the impact of the traditional clans. This was the explicit aim and hope of the autonomists.[11] But the new institutions have not broken the mould. With the election of the first Corsican Assembly in 1982, it was clear that the old interests, even the same individuals, would control the region and the new institutions.

This grip was perpetuated in the subsequent elections in 1984 and 1986. Leading roles in the committees have also gone to well-known and acknowledged clan figures or their henchmen, with only a few exceptions. Too few votes went to new political parties and too few new politicians emerged through the institutions. The established parties, the RPR (*Rassemblement pour la République*) and MRG (*Mouvement des radicaux de gauche*) in particular, with familiar leaders, held the majorities in the Corsican Assembly as they did in the general councils of the two departments. The Assembly has therefore been restricted by the control exercized by these traditional groups, intent on retaining their influence rather than introducing a contest of political principles.

The distribution of seats and party strength followed the familiar pattern, sharing authority. In *Corse-du-Sud* Jean-Paul de Rocca-Serra, the 'Silver Fox' as he is known, and the RPR list dominate whereas in *Haute-Corse* their support was strong enough to give the list the position of largest party in the Assembly. The second largest list in the regional elections has consistently been the leftist MRG and *Union socialiste et radicale*, as it was termed in 1986.

Political power has been shared between the left and the right, with the latter basing its strength in the southern department. Both groups have steadily increased their appeal and number of votes. In 1986 they had thirty-seven of the sixty-one seats between them, nineteen for RPR and eighteen for the left. The departmental general councils also divide in this way, the right dominating in the South and the MRG and its dominant personality M Francois Giacobbi (also a Senator for Corsica) in *Haute-Corse*. Moreover some of the remaining smaller political lists are aligned with the established clan groups. In these circumstances the opposition to the traditional interests, the autonomists, nationalists and even the communists have little chance to use the new institutions of autonomous Corsica to break the existing form. This regional 'power sharing' has meant that the Corsican Assembly has never had a clear, overall, majority since 1982, and no distinct balance between government and opposition. Regional government has always been a coalition, a product of compromise and bargain.

Even the ending of a '*cumul des mandats*', the holding of several democratic mandates simultaneously, did not change the position of the clans when such mandates were limited to two in 1986. The supporters of the principal clans were enough to fill the many offices available at communal, departmental and regional levels. When one or two mandates were given up, it was easy to find clan supporters to stand for election. This change and the introduction of proportional representation did not bring a great change in the fortunes of the clans.

If the new institutions reinforce the existing interest groups, these in turn have not been keen to push autonomy to its limits. The accepted leaders of the two dominant political clienteles, Senator Giacobbi and the deputy Dr Jean-Paul de Rocca-Serra, mayor of Porto-Vecchio for many years, both voted against the legislation in 1982, the former in the Senate and the latter in the Chamber of Deputies in Paris. These two men have held senior office in the Corsican executive since 1982, and Dr Rocca-Serra has been President since 1984. The RPR political list on the island, that of Dr Rocca-Serra, has stressed the element of deconcentration of power as much as that of decentralization. The title of the list conveys as much, *Rassemblement de la Corse dans l'unité nationale*. In the nineteenth century the clans had managed to exercize their influence through the then new institutions of the French administration at communal and departmental levels. They kept their hands on the funds, and many a prefect lamented his lack of control over the local clans. A similar experience greeted the autonomous regional government in 1982. The autonomists mourn the abiding influence of the clans in 1988 just as they did before 1982.[12]

Moreover the autonomists and nationalists proved unable to attract a large proportion of the vote. Clan loyalties were strong. The autonomist/nationalist share of the vote has declined from 14 per cent in the first elections for the Corsican Assembly in 1982 to stabilize around 10 per cent. Furthermore the 'movement' has divided, between the autonomist UPC (*Union du Peuple corse*) established more strongly in *Haute-Corse*, and the nationalists, once formed as the MCA (*Muvementu corsu per l'autodetermazione*) and reconstituted as *A Cuncolta* after the MCA was banned by the state, essentially for being placed close to the violent *Front pour la libération nationale corse* (FLNC). This nationalist list is stronger in the department of *Corse-du-Sud*. Autonomist political influence has therefore not been able to weaken that of the established clans and their popular leaders. Indeed in 1984 two of the UPC deputies attempted to form a political alliance with other groups in the Assembly in order to exert some continuing pressure on policy. The expedient failed and new elections were required in August 1984 to break the deadlock, and this resulted in a further decline in support for the autonomists. Ironically, this movement also seems to need its clan to ensure consistent support. At no time have there been more than seven autonomist or nationalist deputies in the Corsican Assembly.

The most powerful party lists are those that have dominated Corsican politics throughout the Fifth Republic, the centre-right forms of Gaullism, currently the RPR, and the MRG. The socialists have never managed to build a powerful clientele and their share of recent votes has been poorer than those of other lists, even the autonomists on some occasions. In 1981, M Mitterrand who was promising autonomy for Corsica, only obtained 20 per cent of the vote in the first ballot for the presidential elections. New parties, like the *Front National*, have been successful as a result of a popular and locally influential leader. In the case of the *Front National* this has been M Pascal Arrighi, an experienced politician, well known in Corsica since 1958.

The apparently unbreakable hold of the clans has been exasperating to their opponents and an indication that Corsican politics are *sui generis*, a world which follows a logic of its own. Thus the Corsican Assembly is restricted in its operations by the continuing dominance of client interests at communal level. If the clans dominate the Assembly, they smother the communes. Although Ajaccio and Bastia contain almost half the total population of the island, many of these people have come into the towns in recent years from the villages of the interior. It is there, in the rural communes, that the clans find their basic loyalties, and the mayors of those small communes wield great influence, absorbing funds and creating client relationships. The importance of local clienteles comes from the large numbers of such communes on the island. Only nineteen Corsican communes have more than 2,000 inhabitants, and 115 have less than 100. Moreover, in the years after 1975 it has been communes with populations of 500 to 2,000 that have grown in numbers and have experienced some economic expansion with development projects drawing significant funding.[13] In these communes the autonomists and nationalists have failed to shift the established interests. Autonomy only works with the co-operation of these local leaders, and that itself shows that not enough has changed at local level for the Special Statute to bring the transformation that many had expected.

One factor above all others helps to explain the persistence of client politics. The electorate is small and divided into many tiny communities where all faces are known, and strangers with no local voting rights stand out clearly. Corsica is the smallest of the French regions, with barely 200,000 voters. These are subject all the more easily to the influence of clans. Politics are based on personal acquaintance, bargaining and the distribution of favours and office. Autonomy offered ever greater opportunities for the play of interest, as did the system of grants and benefits which flowed from the French state after 1945. Proportional representation, which was expected to provide a fairer and truer reflection of preferences, still allowed the clans to divide and splinter rivals. There is also little evidence to suggest that electoral malpractice, not an exclusively Corsican phenomenon, has diminished. In 1986 a commission of inquiry exposed serious misconduct of the elections at Bastia. New elections were held after those of the Spring were declared invalid. Autonomists and nationalists argue that there can be no reduction of clan influence without proper democratic procedures throughout the region's institutions.

There have been attempts to democratize institutions and break the hold of client systems outside the Assembly. All representative bodies are targets, but some have drawn particular attention from the autonomists. Successes have been achieved, most notably in union and work organizations, e.g. the so-called 'élections prud'homales', by the autonomist *Sindicatu di u travagliadori corsi* (STC), and in the local parent representative bodies by the *Associu di i parenti corsi* (APC). However these matters are relatively peripheral although they possess a local significance in parts of Corsica where autonomists and nationalists are strong. More significant are those matters between the region and the unitary state which have not been affected by the Special Statute and which form the real limits of autonomy.

Of the responsibilities that remain with the government of France, defence, foreign policy and control of the judiciary and the currency are not at issue between the region and the centre, not even in the autonomist camp. Only a tiny number of separatists challenge the central government's right to wield them. But there are certain other powers retained by the centre that have caused criticism and resentment in the island, and certain other factors that have emerged as constraints upon the authority of the regional government.

As will already have become apparent, the communes retain a central role, in every sense of the term. Regional government operates through the departmental administration, but it is the mayors and their municipal officers who apply the policies. The mayors thus keep their responsible role despite the change from a central to an autonomous regional government. They are elected by people immersed in the culture of the island and only partly controlled by the region. The mayors of Corsica wear two hats, a 'decentralized' hat as the officers of the regional administration, implementing regional policy in those areas where competence has been transferred, and a 'deconcentrated' hat for matters subject to the authority of the prefect, now *commissaire de la République*, and the *sous-préfets*, still operating in the *arrondissements* of the two departments. As the representatives of central government the mayors are responsible for police and public order – important matters in contemporary Corsica.

The communal administration serves the central government and thus limits the authority of the Corsican Assembly. The communes still handle the grants and the development plans for their inhabitants. Their influence extends to local improvements, to roads and detailed matters as well as to the implementation of grander schemes. The Assembly proposed a regional coastal development (*Plan nautique régional*) in 1982. This envisaged a network of pleasure ports, attracting the yachting community of the Mediterranean. However, this could only be achieved with the co-operation of the communes concerned. In this example planning and development may clash with public order and security, and the mayors are at the centre of these responsibilities. On other matters the overlap is quite obscure. Education and training are clearly regional responsibilities, but the communes retain their competence in primary education, school building and administration. The crucial question is therefore: who scrutinizes the mayors and their communal administration and arbitrates between their various powers? The answer goes to the root of the relationship that now exists between the region and the unitary state in France.

The former tutelage of the prefect has been abolished except in those matters where authority has been deconcentrated rather than de-centralized. Financial control lies with the central state. In the key matter of arbitration, the region is seriously constrained in its authority because the Special Statute was *octroyé* and not negotiated, and because, in the French system, there is no court specifically designed to arbitrate between an autonomous region and the central government.

The sole resort in any dispute between these two authorities is the Constitutional Council. However the members of this body, according to the 1958 Constitution, are representatives of the central state, appointed by the President of France and by the presidents of the National Assembly, the Chamber of Deputies and the Senate, and former heads of state. Even the Senate, a body representing the departments of France, is not an unequivocal champion of the regions in the manner of the West German Bundesrat, the voice of the *Länder*. The odds are therefore against the French regions. In the case of Corsica it is not even certain that the senators actually favour autonomy; M Giacobbi voted against the 1982 legislation. This raises the question whether the unitary state has really shifted ground in relation to the region of Corsica beyond the granting of a few responsibilities to the regional executive there.

Another factor which constrains the regional executive to look to Paris relates to the economic competences which have not been transferred. Control of communications between Corsica and France is a vital matter for the economy. Apart from state aid, pensions and other welfare payments, the largest single source of income is apparently tourism, amounting to some 20 per cent of total annual earnings in the 1980s, or 200 million francs. The cost of transport is obviously crucial, yet the Regional Assembly has no competence here. The centre has therefore withheld a key competence, one in which there has been a history of bitterness and monopoly that may only change with the economic results of the creation of the single European market and free competition in 1992.

Another matter which has been withheld from the region is policing. This has a special significance in Corsica as a result of nationalist and other violence during the last twenty years. Regional control of policing can be seen as a test of self-government, the recognition of the integrity of a people capable of maintaining order, appointing and disciplining their own police. Where this has been withheld, there has been a demand for change. This has occurred in Spain and Italy where centralized policing has aroused local feeling. Responsibilities need to be carefully defined, not an easy matter as the West Germans have discovered in distinguishing the roles of *Landpolizei* and *Grenzschütz-polizei*. However in France the centre has retained control of policing. Although the mayors are responsible for municipal policing and the delightfully named rural *gardes champêtres*, they are answerable to the prefects in these matters. Beyond these forces public security is the responsibility of the state through the central system and, in Corsica, a specially appointed commissioner for police. Where circumstances demand reinforcements, the central government can alone provide them, security companies (CRS), and, as elsewhere in France, additional *gendarmerie*.

Throughout the state, rural policing is a general responsibility of the *gendarmerie* who are under the authority of the Ministry of Defence in the last resort. Therefore in principle the unitary state can apply its authority whenever and however it pleases even in this autonomous region of Corsica. On a daily basis there is consultation, but the region has no formal competence, despite the continuing high level of violence both politically motivated and criminal which has fed off the bombings and increasing assassinations associated with separatist groups. Policing and public order are central to economic development of the region, yet the Assembly and Corsican executive have no direct authority in these matters.

There is a further matter which lies within the competence of the Corsican Assembly but which has been difficult to exercise. The French regions, including Corsica, were granted competence by the 1982 legislation to negotiate on trade and environmental issues with other regions, and with foreign governments and their regions. (This competence has incidentally been an important part of the life of the autonomous Spanish region of Catalonia in the years since 1975. Treaties are negotiated directly and not through Madrid.)

Relations with the European Community are part of the same area of regional competence. Such negotiations were invited by the legislation of 1982, not without control; the authorization of the central government in Paris is required. However the principle is acknowledged – transfrontier co-operation is encouraged, 'contacts réguliers avec des collectivites décentralisées étrangères ayant une frontière commune avec la région'.[14] It is a little unclear what this means in the case of Corsica; the sea complicates the issue. But whatever the nature of the competence, Corsica is restricted by its small market, limited productivity and budget. Risks cannot be taken with foreign trade. Contacts through the regional delegation for foreign trade have been relatively few, only six 'missions' being organized between 1984 and 1987. It is ironical that a French region with no historical or cultural identity, like *Rhône-Alpes*, has been far more successful and enterprising in this respect than Corsica with its acute sense of nationalism and debilitating poverty. Corsica cannot match *Rhône-Alpes* despite its Special Statute and greater autonomy. In these matters large regional budgets, economic prosperity and the two and a half million people of the *Rhône-Alpes* make the difference. This region has agreements directly negotiated with Catalonia and Baden-Württemberg, as well as others agreed within France. The contrast has not escaped the Corsican autonomists and nationalists, nor those in Brittany, both of whom have pointed to the encouragement given to 'le séparatisme rhônalpin'.[15]

Clear-cut autonomy has thus not been established in Corsica by the legislation of 1982. Local demands have been only partially satisfied and a mixture of disappointment and anger remains. The unitary state and the clan system of political influence have apparently emerged victorious. A little has been conceded here and there. Perhaps true autonomy cannot come from the 1958 Constitution of France because no real negotiations can take place between region and state; all is *octroyé*. The French state may be constitutionally unable to move towards a federal system without major constitutional change, which will allow such negotiations and which would construct a real and effective means of arbitration between two levels of power. The Corsican nationalists and separatists are pointing to the need for a more fundamental revision of the relationship. They do not believe that the central state can abandon its authority; this can only be wrested from it, if necessary by violence.

Meanwhile the many Corsicans who reject a violent revolution, operate the new institutions and procedures quite effectively although they have not come forward with a convincing programme for extending autonomy or accommodating the differences with the centre. Those who have most successfully adapted to the new arrangements have been the clans and their representatives. They function in the new system quite as comfortably as within the old centralized order. This has been a disappointment to many but is a result of the nature of Corsican politics and the confined world in which it operates.

## Notes

1. The French had first sent troops to Corsica in support of the Genoese and against the rebels in 1738. The Treaty of Versailles allowed France to exercise the sovereign rights over Corsica. The French government was to pay Genoa an annual subvention of 200,000 *livres* for ten years.
2. Paoli did not create this measure of independence; this had been achieved by his predecessor as leader of the Corsicans, Gian Pietro Gaffori, in 1753. Gaffori was almost immediately assassinated in October 1753.
3. The declaration integrating Corsica into what the Assembly called 'the French Empire' was made on 30 November 1789. Genoa reclaimed the sovereignty, but this was rejected by the French Assembly.
4. The autonomist movement began to develop its critique of the French state and policies in 1967 with the creation of the *Action régionaliste corse*, although there had been several earlier groups. This major organization, led by the brothers Edmond and Max Simeoni, changed its name during the next twenty years but remains the most prominent autonomist element in the movement. It was the spearhead of the denunciations and sustained a fierce campaign through its weekly newspaper *Arritti*. The criticism covered events from fraud and corruption to pollution and attempts to close the railway. The leaders have been imprisoned. Demonstrations in support of their

cause have numbered hundreds, and they have representatives in the Corsican Assembly. The clearest accounts of these events are Jean-Paul Delors & Stephane Muracciole, *Corse, la poudrière*, Paris, (1978) Pierre Dottelonde, *Corse, la métamorphose*, Levie, (1987) Paul Silvani, *Corse des années ardentes*, Paris, (1976) P. Savigear, 'Corsica and the French state', in C. R. Foster, (ed), *Nations without a state*, New York, (1980) pp 116–35.

5. See Alistair Hennessy's chapter on Spain for a discussion of a similar phenomenon.

6. Corsican is variously regarded as a distinct language, related to others including Catalan, or as an Italian dialect, a kind of Tuscan *patois*. There is little written material but a great oral tradition. In the twentieth century there has been a lively attempt to publish in Corsican and the local press is very active. Paoli had created a university at Corte (or Corti as the Corsicans prefer) which was abolished by the French.

7. Funds from the central state have been the largest element in the total subsidy for the Corsican economy. During the last two decades they have been regularly increased, e.g. 206 million francs additional support from central government in November 1987. The large annual sum (500 million francs) includes all types of state aid and investment. Some of this goes directly to the two departments, the communes and the regional administration. Other support goes to transport, air and sea links, military bases, agricultural subsidies and many particular grants, e.g. university support, roads and port development. In addition the state provides for the pension and social security benefits.

8. Article 1: *organisation administrative*, law of 2 March 1982.

9. The figure has risen steadily through the 1980s. It is misleading because many Corsicans, especially the young, leave the island and if they fail to find work on the mainland are not included in this figure of 11 per cent. Moreover the figure disguises the serious rural decline. In many villages there is both unemployment and depopulation.

10. *Economie corse*, No 41, 1987, 'Les budgets des collectivités territoriales', pp 12–17.

11. 'Faire l'analyse que rien de fondamental n'a changé dans ce Pays en ce mois d'août 1982 serait nier la réalité: le clanisme, allie structurel historique du colonialisme, est entré dans la phase finale de son agonie', *Arritti*, No 805, 26 August 1982, p 1.

12. In November 1987 the autonomist representative Dr Max Simeoni resigned his position as chairman of the Assembly's committee for the investigation of electoral fraud. His reasons were the inertia of Corsican political class and the clans, what he called the 'système clan-colonialisme'. Certainly the Assembly has been dominated by the 'old' interests, M Prosper Alfonsi of the MRG in 1982, Dr Jean-Paul de Rocca-Serra of the RPR in 1984 and 1986 with the largest number of seats for his list, nineteen in each case.

13. *Tableaux de l'économie corse, 1986*, INSEE, Ajaccio, 1986, p 19.

14. Article 65, *Journal officiel de la République française*, 3 March 1982.

15. 'Quand l'Etat français encourage le séparatisme "rhônalpin" ', first published in the *Peuple Breton*, reprinted in *Arritti*, 3 December 1987, p 9.

## Part Two

# Federal systems and the problem of ethnic cleavage

# 5 Federalism, nationalism and socialism in Yugoslavia

*Christopher Binns*

The Socialist Federal Republic of Yugoslavia (SFRY) is the most highly federated of all communist-party states; indeed, it can be said that it is the only genuine socialist federation.[1] This in itself raises interesting questions. The Marxist–Leninist tradition has been deeply suspicious of federalism, since it involves the separation of powers, whereas the 'communist' view has emphasized the unity of power under the leadership of the communist party. The unity of the working class, expressed in its central vanguard and transcending national and cultural barriers, and the centralized control of the economy and all levers of state power are fundamental ideas in Marxism–Leninism.

The 'federation' which was created as the 'Soviet Union' in 1922 represented Lenin's temporary concessions to the aspirations to self-determination amongst the non-Russian peoples of the former empire which Lenin had used to further the revolution by weakening the Tsarist state. The ultimate goal was still the 'assimilation' of these peoples into an international 'Soviet' culture.[2] In any case the resultant 'federation' involved no real devolution of political or economic power; what little autonomy the federal units were granted was largely linguistic and cultural: 'national in form, socialist in content', as the favourite formula had it. Indeed, it can be argued that in many respects the federal structure of the USSR was designed to increase central control over unruly sub-state nationalism.[3]

Under Stalin the USSR became a highly centralized and authoritarian state in which even linguistic and cultural autonomy was infringed by policies of Russianization masked as 'Sovietization'. When 'communism' spread after the Second World War it was only Yugoslavia which adopted a federal structure and this was of a type similar in form and aims to the Soviet model. More recently, in 1969, Czechoslovakia adopted a Soviet-type federal system. No other multi-national socialist state has adopted a federal structure, although arguably at least two,

Bulgaria and Romania, have intractable national minority problems which might have been alleviated by federalization; but instead they adopted policies of repressive centralism.[4]

Yet, despite the fact that the SFRY initially adopted the Soviet model of nominal federalism, today it appears to be more like a loose confederation. So the first question which needs to be discussed is a historical one: for what reasons and by what stages has this transformation from a Soviet-type federation to a loose confederation taken place?

The second major question we have to address is one more closely related to the main concerns of this volume. Undoubtedly one of the main reasons behind the increased federalization of the SFRY has been the attempt to accommodate strong centrifugal pressures from its highly diverse regions and nationalities which could otherwise be dealt with only by Stalinist-type centralized repression. Yet the post-1981 crisis in the Albanian-dominated 'autonomous province' of Kosovo, following on a similar crisis in Croatia ten years earlier, has shown that the SFRY's nationality problems have not been solved by federalization. Indeed, the last few years have seen a still unresolved debate amongst the interrepublican elite of the League of Communists of Yugoslavia (LCY) between those who believe that federalization and workers' self-management have gone too far and that the country's economic and political problems can only be solved by re-centralization, and those who for ideological or pragmatic reasons still jealously guard the devolved character of the SFRY. So the second major question is why is it, that the Yugoslav federalization process has apparently failed to realize its main aim. We may further speculate as to whether this failure is caused by specifically Yugoslav factors or whether the Yugoslav experience offers useful lessons for other European, including non-socialist, states which are in the process of federalization.[5]

However, part of the explanation both of the SFRY's increasing federalization and the ultimate apparent failure of this process may lie in the country's pre-socialist inheritance and, more generally, in the state-building problems faced by a new state only formed in 1918. So we turn first to a brief survey of these problems.

## Centralism and sub-state nationalism in pre-socialist Yugoslavia

In July 1917 a group of South-Slav ('Yugoslav') exiles, claiming to speak on behalf of their various national movements, issued the 'Corfu Declaration' which recommended the setting up of a 'Kingdom of Serbs, Croats and Slovenes' in the form of a 'constitutional, democratic and parliamentary monarchy headed by the Karadjordjević dynasty'. This

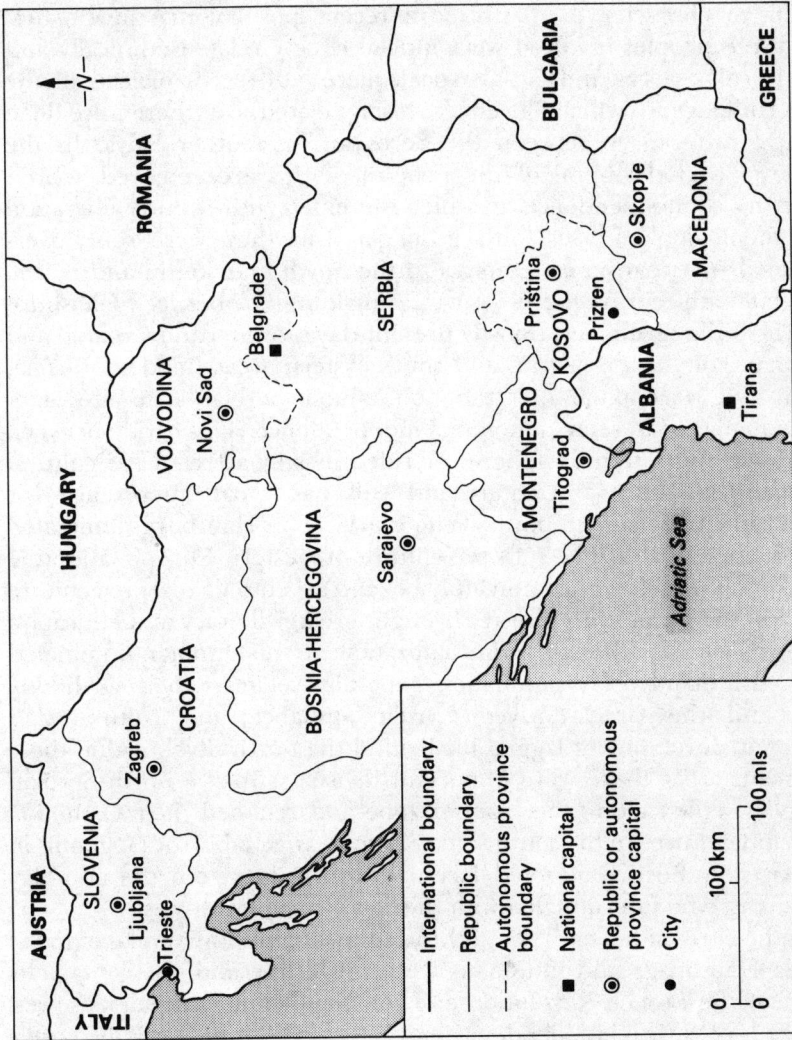

Yugoslavia, showing boundaries of republics and autonomous provinces

proposal was supported by the allies since it suited their wish to stabilize the Balkans area by breaking up the power bases of the former Ottoman and Austro-Hungarian empires. The new kingdom was duly proclaimed, with Alexander initially as regent, on 1 December 1918.

However, the new state was a very artificial and problematic construct, similar in character to many more recent post-colonial new states. The three peoples involved were indeed closely related ethnically and linguistically: Serbs and Croats speak merely different dialects of the same language, to which Slovene is closely related. But there were deep cultural differences between the Serbs and the other Slavs. In the medieval period several of the peoples of this area enjoyed a brief flowering of independence, to which the nineteenth century liberation movements looked back with nostalgia. But they were soon overwhelmed by expansionist empires to the north and south, and by the mid-sixteenth century there was a clear dividing-line between Habsburg control in the north-west (mostly present-day Slovenia and Croatia) and Ottoman rule in the central and south-eastern areas (modern Bosnia, Serbia and Macedonia); only the mountainous Serbian state of Montenegro managed to retain a nominal independence. This divide between Habsburg and Ottoman spheres of rule crucially affected the cultural character of the two regions and still has great importance for the problems of contemporary Yugoslavia. The Habsburg-dominated region became absorbed into the culture of western Europe, adopting the Catholic religion, the Latin alphabet and a Teutonic-oriented culture which in the nineteenth century brought greater literacy and education as well as industrialization and urbanization. In the Ottoman-dominated south the mainly Slav population generally retained their Orthodox faith and the Greek-derived Cyrillic alphabet, and cultural and economic development lagged far behind the north. Even within these two main areas there were important divisions. In the north Serbian refugees settled along the frontier zone and retained their Orthodox faith and culture. In the south some Slavic sects, notably the Bogomils in what is now Bosnia, adopted Islam, as in the main did the non-Slav Albanians, who intermingled with the Slavs in the south-west.

By the early nineteenth century the sprawling multi-national empires of the Habsburgs and Ottomans were in decline and the contagious effect of the French Revolution and the Napoleonic campaigns sowed the seeds of future independence movements which mushroomed after the success of Greece, as an immediate result of which Serbia gained autonomy from the Ottomans in 1830. Under the Obrenović dynasty the power of Serbia, under the patronage of Russia, steadily increased with its economic, cultural and political development until in 1878 its full independence (together with that of Montenegro) was internationally recognized by the Congress of Berlin. Hence, inevitably, it was Serbia

that became the main focus for pan-south-Slav independence movements in the later years of the century. In the Habsburg area the
institution of the Dual Monarchy in 1867 brought Croatia under
Hungarian rule, and the subsequent Magyarization policy stimulated
Slav nationalism. By the turn of the century the Balkans became a
notorious focus of world conflict as Britain, Germany and Russia strove
to increase their influence in areas in which the Habsburg and Ottoman
empires were weakest, and subject peoples took advantage of the
conflicts to push their claims for statehood. A general crisis in the region
ensued with the Austrian annexation of Bosnia in 1908 and the resultant
Balkan wars. A settlement was patched up in 1913, but it was symptomatic that it was the assassination of the Austrian Crown Prince Franz-
Ferdinand by a Bosnian Serb which sparked off a generalized European
conflict in 1914.

After the war the new state faced major difficulties in establishing
itself. It took two years of tortuous negotiations with neighbouring states
under the aegis of the allies to establish its borders. Since the pattern of
ethnic settlement in the Balkans region is extremely complex, the
establishment of fixed state borders, let alone nation-states, in the area
inevitably split many ethnic groups and created problems for the future.
A large group of Slovenes were stranded in Austria (in the province of
Carinthia); many Hungarians remained in eastern Yugoslavia (in the
Vojvodina area); a third of the Albanian population became part of
Yugoslavia; and the Macedonians, a Slavic group, were split between
Yugoslavia, Bulgaria and Greece. These were just the most notorious of
the problems which the mess of the Versailles settlement created in the
Balkans.

Only in 1921 did a constituent assembly approve a constitution for the
new Yugoslav kingdom. Significantly, this 'Vidovdan Constitution' was
promulgated on the Serbian national day, 28 June (sacred to St Vitus
and so called 'Vidovdan'). From the start the new state was dominated
unfairly, if inevitably, by the Serbs who nevertheless (if the Macedonians
and Montenegrins are not included in their number[6]) formed only the
largest minority of the population. Not only was the Karadjordjević
monarchy Serbian[7] but the constitution was modelled closely on the
highly centralist Serbian constitution of 1903, and in any case was passed
by only a narrow majority of Assembly delegates (223 out of 413), with
the Communists (who were soon afterwards outlawed) and the Croat
Peasant Party absent from the vote. The king was dominant in the
new regime: the Council of Ministers was responsible to him and
he appointed ministers and senior civil servants. The parliament
(*Skupština*), largely a talking-shop, became an arena for highly
acrimonious debates. However, it should be noted that local government
was carried out through a diversity of local traditional forms.

With the banning of the main party of the left (the Communists had 14 per cent of the Assembly delegates, with the Social Democrats being very weak) and the systematic exclusion from real political influence of several ethnic groups it was inevitable that political life should become polarized around linguistic-religious rather than class cleavages and that the parliamentary system should become unworkable. Matters came to a head in 1928 when a Montenegrin shot dead the leaders of the Croat Peasant Party during a debate in the Skupština. This led to a Croat boycott and the establishment of a rival parliament in Zagreb agitating for a federal state. Eventually on 6 January 1929 King Alexander abrogated the Vidovdan Constitution and declared a royal dictatorship, renaming the country the Kingdom of Yugoslavia. In 1931 he introduced a new façade constitution with a weak assembly and a senate consisting partly of his nominees and partly of delegates from local assemblies. Local government was completely re-organized along non-ethnic lines in a standardized and centrally-dominated system, with ten new artificial units (*banovine*) designed to break up local loyalties. The latter aim did not succeed, despite a brutal suppression of non-Serb and leftist political activity. Terrorism developed and in October 1934 Alexander was murdered by a Croat-hired assassin. He was replaced by Prince Paul as regent for the young Peter, and there followed a period of relative stability under the premiership of Stojadinović who attempted a reconciliation with the Croats. However, he fell from power in 1939 and conciliatory policies ended. As the war closed in on Yugoslavia Paul's collaborationist manoeuvrings became increasingly impossible and in March 1941 he was replaced by Peter in a military coup. The next month the German invasion swept the country and the King and his government went into exile.

If the experience of constitutional (and unconstitutional) monarchy had been disastrous for Yugoslavia, the years of occupation left even deeper scars. Inter-ethnic relations declined catastrophically with the setting up during the German invasion of a Croat puppet fascist state, the infamous NDH (*Nezavisna Država Hrvatska* or Independent Croat State) under Ante Pavelić, the *Ustaše* ('freedom-fighters') leader, which became an Italian protectorate. The fascist Croats proceeded to implement a horrific 'racial purification' policy resulting in the deaths of up to 750,000 Serbs in the region (not including other minorities), in addition to forcible deportation of others to Serbia and forced conversion of others to Catholicism. The Serbs responded in kind and in Bosnia Serb-Croat conflict was especially severe. Of Yugoslavia's 1,700,000 war deaths (11 per cent of the population) about a million were due to inter-ethnic strife.

However, the horror of this ethnic hatred may have produced a positive effect in a revulsion against particularist nationalism. Certainly the star of the communist Partisans, led by Josip Broz (Tito), rose rapidly under the occupation partly because they were seen to be ethnically neutral to all Yugoslavs as well as being the most consistent and efficient force of national resistance, whereas the Serbian-based Četniks, led by Mihailović, declined in popularity through their association with the discredited Serbian government-in-exile, and ended by collaborating with the Germans. In 1942 the Partisans set up a more broadly-based Anti-Fascist Council for the National Liberation of Yugoslavia (AVNOJ). With British help they went onto the offensive in 1943 and in November proclaimed AVNOJ the provisional government of the country.

What were the lessons of Yugoslavia's first quarter-century for the balance between centralism and sub-state nationalism in the new state? Firstly, it was clear that a centrally-imposed political structure based on Serbian domination could never gain the acceptance of a majority of Yugoslavia's population, and this ruled out the revival of the monarchy after the war (since it was Serbian and there was no rival non-Serbian dynasty). Secondly, Yugoslavia had had only a brief and disastrous experience of parliamentary democracy and in particular had come to associate political party pluralism with ethnic division and strife (an argument still used with effect against the proposed revival of a multi-party system). Thirdly, ethnic particularism amongst both Serbs and Croats had been seen to end in civil war and collaboration, and this predisposed much of the population towards the new approach of the communist Partisans. When this factor was combined with their role as leaders of the national resistance and their espousal of socialist concerns which had been so long suppressed in the country, we can see how there were no serious rivals to the communists as a national government after the war.

## Socialist Yugoslavia: the Stalinist phase

Nevertheless, the 'national question' had long been a thorny issue for the Communist Party of Yugoslavia (CPY).[8] In the early years after its formation in 1919 from pro-Bolshevik groups centred around the Serbian Social Democratic Party the dominant centralist philosophy in the party favoured the retention of a unitary Yugoslav state in a broader Balkan federation, ultimately as part of an international federation of 'Soviet' republics (see note 2). But from 1924 the Comintern (to which the CPY was affiliated), critical of the Versailles settlement of the Balkans, put pressure on the CPY to allow the self-determination of the Yugoslav peoples in a broader Balkan federation; it insisted particularly on the autonomy of Macedonia, where IMRO, a terroristic revolutionary independence movement straddling Yugoslavia, Bulgaria and Greece, was very effectively de-stabilizing the region during this period. So from 1928 the CPY advocated the immediate break-up of the Yugoslav state. However, in 1934, as the Comintern line changed in favour of broader 'Popular Front' co-operation against fascism and the Soviet government sought 'collective security', the CPY came to stress Yugoslav unity and reject secession of nationalities. Soon after the Moscow-trained Tito was sent back to Yugoslavia to re-organize the party, which he proceeded to do very effectively when he became leader of the CPY in 1937, stressing the need for a Yugoslav solution to the national question and the unity of the Yugoslav peoples in the face of fascist aggression.

In the initial occupation period there was much inter-ethnic tension in the CPY since they were forced to rely heavily on the more unitarist Serbian communists. But with the formation of AVNOJ Tito once again emphasized the right of self-determination and proposed a federal solution.[9] Yet soon afterwards the party leaders were dampening nationality enthusiasm by stressing the unity of the Yugoslav liberation movement. Like Lenin in 1917, Tito had a difficult task in manipulating the 'dialectic' between exploiting the revolutionary potential of nationalist aspiration in the short term while stressing the CPY's credibility as a unified national government and the ultimate unity of working class interests.

After an initially cautious approach designed to please the allies the CPY by late 1945 abandoned the fiction of co-operation with non-communist forces. Šubašić, the peasant leader, resigned from the Provisional Government, advising his party to boycott the Constituent Assembly elections. When these were held in November the result was a 90 per cent vote for the People's Front, an AVNOJ-derived organization totally dominated by the CPY. The Assembly met on 29 November and proclaimed the abolition of the monarchy and the creation of the Federative People's Republic of Yugoslavia (FPRY). On 31 January 1946 a new constitution was promulgated.

What was the nature of the federal settlement of 1946? Essentially it was closely modelled on the Soviet 'federal' constitution of 1936. On paper it presented a picture of six free and sovereign nation-states (Serbia, Croatia, Slovenia, Bosnia-Herzegovina, Montenegro and Macedonia) exercizing their right to self-determination by coming together in a federation. The republics apparently had extensive powers of legislation and administrative supervision in areas not specifically reserved for the federation. The latter's powers were, however, considerable: defence and foreign policy, economic planning, the currency and banking system, communications, law and the 'maintenance of the social system'. There was little left in practice for the republics but cultural and linguistic autonomy. The Federal Assembly, based in

Belgrade, consisted of two houses, like the USSR Supreme Soviet, one directly elected and the other formed from representatives of the assemblies of the republics; it met rarely and exerted little power. Real power lay outside the constitution, with the CPY, which, though on paper divided into separate parties for each federal unit, remained in fact highly centralized and hierarchical. The dominant ethos of this period is known as 'revolutionary statism', i.e. the dictatorship of the proletariat (i.e. of the CPY) behind a façade of constitutionalism.

While the centralist and fictive character of the federation of 1946 was largely superseded by later reforms, we should stress here the geographical structure of the federation, which is still in place and has given rise to many subsequent problems. The basic difficulty with this structure is that the design of the six republics, which purported to be nation-states, did not correspond to patterns of homogeneous ethnic settlement but to traditional historical territories and the bargaining-power of particular groups. This did not really matter when the republics had little power and centralist policies predominated. After all, it was expected that all Yugoslavs would soon develop unified socialist loyalties which would make national allegiances outmoded. But when, as we shall see, in later years substantial powers were devolved to the federal units, the anomalies of this makeshift solution became readily apparent. However, the Yugoslav government, like the contemporary Soviet leadership, have shrunk from the awesome task of re-negotiating the whole federal structure. Yet, while one sympathizes with the dilemma of both countries, the fact remains that where ethnic settlement is as complex and diffuse as in the Balkans area, the claim to be making a federation out of sovereign nation-states should not be made if it cannot be fulfilled.

Only the claim of Slovenia looked convincing as a nation-state: it was, after all, 95 per cent Slovene, even if a large number of their nationals remained outside it in Austrian Carinthia. Montenegro is also relatively homogeneous (except for its Albanian minority) but can its claim to be a 'nation' be taken seriously? Montenegrins are often jokingly, and enviously, referred to in Yugoslavia as 'first-class Serbs', because, while they are indistinguishable in ethnicity, language and religion from Serbs, by an accident of history their traditional autonomy and the influence of prominent Montenegrins in the CPY managed to secure for them a federal bargaining-status out of all proportion to their numbers (about 2½ per cent of the population), rather like the status of Luxemburg within the EEC. The Macedonian claim to nation-statehood looks weak in that they have only recently developed a literary language (in the inter-war period they were classified as 'South Serbs'), their republic is substantially multi-national (containing in particular a large Albanian minority) and many of their 'nationals' live in Bulgaria. They were given a republic largely to pacify the IMRO movement which had such strong links with the CPY. Bosnia is a multi-national historical accident with no serious claim to nation-statehood except in the controversial form of an Islamic state, a large minority of its 'nationals' being Islamized Slavs.[10] Croatia, with its majority Croat population and its clear, if controversial national tradition, seems to have a better claim, but is in fact multi-national with large Serb and Slovene minorities.

Serbia, as we have seen, had, with Montenegro, the longest and most developed recent experience of statehood. Like the Russian Republic in the USSR, it is the largest and most heterogeneous of the republics, and was treated as a special case, since within its territory there were denominated one autonomous province (Vojvodina) and one autonomous region (Kosovo-Metohija), in order to facilitate the treatment of important ethnic groups in these areas, both of them non-Slav and 'external', i.e. having their main population outside Yugoslavia: the Hungarians, forming at that time about a quarter of the Vojvodina population (where Serbs were about 55 per cent), and the Albanians, forming about two-thirds of the Kosovo-Metohija (Kosmet) population. The Serbs formed about two-thirds of the total population of Greater Serbia (including the autonomous areas). It is significant that both these non-Slav peoples had been in major conflict with the Partisans in the war, indeed the Albanians had actually staged an armed rebellion against the socialist state at the end of the War, and had been severely suppressed. Nevertheless, from the viewpoint of a supposedly federal system, both can count themselves hard done by. The Hungarians were not much less numerous in population than the Montenegrins, but had virtually no recognition in that they were totally outnumbered in a Serb-dominated province. The Albanians formed a larger proportion of the Yugoslav population than the Montenegrins or the Macedonians and almost as many as the Slovenes. While they dominated their 'autonomous region' numerically, for many years the small minority of Serbs provided a clear majority in party and state posts in the area, and in addition their 'region' was lower in status than the 'province' of Vojvodina. Also there were other significant Albanian minorities in Macedonia and Montenegro. One of the problems here is that the Serbs regard the Kosovo area as the historical heartland of Serbia, scene of Tsar Dušan's medieval kingdom, before Belgrade rose to prominence. Basically the federal structure of Serbia was designed to control rather than to give statehood to what were regarded as two unreliable foreign elements. We should also note that there were many other small national groups which were quite reasonably regarded as being too small to warrant any form of statehood.[11]

In the case of the Hungarians and Albanians, and also of the Macedonians, the obvious solution would appear to have been the uniting of their dispersed nationals into reasonably homogeneous federal units within some broader socialist federation. This had long been under discussion, as we have seen, and was seriously discussed again after the war. The failure of this idea was ultimately due to Soviet opposition and contributed to the escalation of a dispute which changed the political character of the FPRY.

## The Balkan federation project and the 'Cominform Dispute'

Schemes of international federation were as much in the air in Eastern Europe at the end of the Second World War as they were in Western Europe. The Balkan Federation idea had been around a long time, but Tito brought it up again in very concrete terms towards the end of the War. The USSR opposed Tito's suggestion of a unified Balkans military command under his leadership in 1943, but in the following year approved the start of Yugoslav-Bulgarian negotiations on the formation of a South-Slav Union as the first step to a larger Balkan federation. Tito's idea was that Bulgaria would be absorbed into the Yugoslav federation as a seventh republic, with the existing republic of Macedonia being expanded to include the Macedonian-settled Pirin district of Bulgaria, which the Bulgarians would cede to Yugoslavia as a first step towards federation. But this the Bulgarians were unwilling to do before agreement on the broader federation of the two countries.[12]

Meanwhile negotiations also started in 1944 on a merger between Yugoslavia and Albania, in which an enlarged Albania (merged with Kosmet and part of Macedonia) would form an eighth republic in the Yugoslav federation. Most East European socialists regarded this merger as a foregone conclusion, since Hoxha's Albania was virtually a Yugoslav protectorate at this time. The Yugoslavs had been deeply involved with the Albanian revolution from the start: the actual formation of the Albanian communist party had been aided by Yugoslav emissaries and Tito's military advisers were active in directing the Albanian liberation struggle. After the war the Yugoslavs directly intervened, even militarily, in Albania, once to purge the party of anti-Yugoslav elements and again to hasten the expropriation of large landowners' estates. Joint-stock companies were formed (on the Soviet model of disguising exploitation under co-operation); the Albanian armed forces were standardized along Yugoslav lines and preliminary reforms were carried out to prepare for the merger of the currencies of the two countries.

Thus at one stage, say in 1946, it seemed likely that the Yugoslav federation would soon be expanded to include Albania and Bulgaria, all under the dominant leadership of an extremely confident Tito. But Tito was over-confident, underestimating the suspicion and jealousy which his hegemonic, if no doubt entirely sensible and socialist, designs would cause amongst his proposed federal partners and, more particularly, with Stalin. There was also the problem of Greece's relation to the South Slav federation. Yugoslavia had been actively aiding the Greek communists' bid for power, which still looked quite possible in 1946. Since northern Greece was also part of the Balkan minorities jigsaw (notably with the Macedonians), why not bring a socialist Greece into the federation as well? This was probably the last straw for Stalin. The Yugoslav Milovan Djilas reports him as saying that the Greek communists had no prospects of success since the UK and USA would never allow it because it would undermine a vital sphere of influence agreed at Moscow with Churchill in 1944 and confirmed at Yalta.[13] Stalin was determined not to get involved with a conflict with the West at a time when the Soviet economy was still so weak. He was even clearer about this after the announcement of the 'Truman Doctrine' in March 1947 when the US promised support for states (with Greece and Turkey in mind) 'resisting internal subversion or external aggression'. After this Stalin abandoned the Greek communists to their fate.

By early 1948 Tito's federationist plans seemed to Stalin, to be getting out of hand. He saw Tito as being potentially dominant in an uncontrollably large Balkan federation which might become a rival power centre, undermining the USSR's southern flank. His suspicions were confirmed by the highly secret negotiations between Tito and the Bulgarian Dimitrov in late 1947 and early 1948 on 'creating the conditions' for a Yugoslav–Bulgarian federation. The details of these talks have never been divulged, but they appear to have agreed on a customs union, close economic ties and some mutual territorial concessions. What really annoyed Stalin was not the merger itself (which he still supported) but the fact that 'horizontal' negotiations were going on between two of his East European allies without his knowledge or supervision, and he came to see Tito as a dangerous contagion spreading centrifugal tendencies in the Balkans just at a time when East–West relations were tense and when, with the setting up of the Cominform in September 1947, he was starting to demand monolithic discipline from Eastern Europe in the face of the perceived threat from the West. In these circumstances Tito, who had enormous authority due to the fact that his was the only truly autonomous revolution in Eastern Europe, might become a real obstacle to Soviet control.

The Balkan socialist leaders were summoned for urgent talks with Stalin in February 1948. Significantly, Tito did not go, sending his deputies Kardelj and Djilas. Stalin told them he was still in favour of Yugoslavia 'swallowing' Albania (as he put it) and of the Yugoslav–Bulgarian merger. But the Greeks were to be kept out and a Bulgarian–

Romanian merger (which Dimitrov had started to discuss, possibly as a way of mitigating Tito's influence) was out of the question. Essentially Stalin wanted to know exactly what was going on between his allies and to retain the initiative.[14]

The Yugoslav leaders resented Stalin's peremptory tone in these talks, which they took as symptomatic of a hostile and domineering attitude towards Yugoslav socialism which they were not prepared to accept. There were many other differences between Yugoslavia and the USSR at this time: Yugoslav complaints about the behaviour of Soviet troops when 'liberating' Belgrade; apparent lack of Soviet support in Yugoslavia's territorial disputes with Italy and Austria; Tito's refusal to accept Soviet 'advisers' controlling Yugoslav military, foreign and economic policy; and Soviet complaints about the Yugoslav reluctance to push forced collectivization of agriculture and their criticisms of Tito's hegemonism and of the military quality of the Partisans, etc. But essentially the 'Cominform dispute', as the USSR–Yugoslav quarrel came to be known, centred on the Yugoslav refusal to accept the arbitrary and draconian discipline which Stalin now expected from his otherwise compliant East European allies. The result was that in June 1948 Yugoslavia was expelled from the Cominform, in which Tito had been second only to Stalin in prestige. With expulsion came an economic blockade by the Eastern bloc designed to bring Yugoslavia crawling back into the fold, preferably with a new leadership (Stalin was fond of saying: 'I shall wag my little finger and Tito will fall!').

The sudden political isolation and economic blockade were indeed major blows for the CPY leaders. While they resented Stalin's attitude towards their country they still had great admiration for his ideas and his role in world history. Economic isolation was even harder, since the FPRY had orientated most of its trade towards the East and had received significant Soviet aid. Initially, the Yugoslavs did try to get back into the fold, albeit on their own terms. In 1949 Tito resumed the drive for collectivization, abandoned his support for the Greek communists and applied for membership of the newly formed Council for Mutual Economic Assistance (CMEA or Comecon). But all to no avail: their application to the CMEA was refused and the collectivization drive had to be abandoned by 1951 in the face of stiff peasant resistance. The USA baled Yugoslavia out of its economic crisis. Since neither side would give in, the break with Stalin's USSR became permanent.

So it was that all the interesting federalist ideas which might have provided the basis for a much more stable resolution of the national minority problems and state borders of the Balkans region came to nothing. Stalin abandoned multilateralism and federalism and instead imposed a rigid unilateral radial system on his East European empire. The FPRY, after being on the crest of a revolutionary wave, suddenly found itself in a political and economic limbo between East and West. The failure of international federation left it as a truncated state with an awkward national minority structure. More fundamentally, economic and political isolation forced the Yugoslav leaders to reassess their whole domestic and international strategy. In what form could they survive as a socialist state without international socialist support?

## Self-management and the road to federalism

Stalin's treatment of Yugoslavia caused many doubts about his 'statist' socialism. But it soon became clear that in any case Yugoslavia in isolation could not practicably achieve 'socialism in one country' by Stalin's methods of 'revolution from above' and police repression. Yugoslavia did not have the USSR's natural resources or her long tradition of autocratic central control. Neither her peasants nor her workers were so easily cowed. Forced collectivization of agriculture could not be achieved without economic disaster and the alienation of important political support from the peasantry surviving from the Partisan period. At the same time the failure of collectivization deprived the communists of the traditional *Milchkuh* from which what Preobrazhensky had called 'primitive socialist accumulation' could be made for industrial development. This in turn meant that the working class would have to bear the greater burden of financing industrialization, which necessitated their active commitment and support.

The strong practical need to win the confidence of the working class was combined in a typically Yugoslav way with an idealistic reassessment of socialist aims by Kardelj and Djilas based on Marx's early ideas to produce the major change of direction to 'workers' self-management'. After extensive experimentation in 1949 the first law granting apparently wide powers to workers' councils in socialized industry was passed in 1950. At its famous Sixth Congress in 1952 the CPY changed its name to the League of Communists of Yugoslavia (LCY) (to recall Marx's 'Communist League' of 1847–8) and announced that the new party would adopt a 'guiding' and 'arbitrating' role in society rather than the traditional 'leading role' of Leninism. It was 'unalienated labour' which would take the real decisions, not an elitist vanguard.

Whatever the working class made of this 'democracy from above' (and there was something quite Stalinist about the way that the change to self-management was made!), the LCY leaders soon saw in the new slogan an opportunity to restore their hegemonic status in European socialism so rudely swept aside in 1948. They would by-pass Stalin's 'bureaucratic statism' and move directly towards Marx's ideal of a stateless free association of productive communes. These ideas were embodied in the new constitution of 1953, which was a basic charter for self-management.

But it is important to realize that the conversion to self-management did not immediately entail a conversion to federalization. Indeed in 1953 the Chamber of Nationalities was downgraded in the Federal Assembly in favour of the new Chamber of Producers. National affiliation was not of any interest in this period. The model was still one of an international unified working class, but an active, participating working class 'guided' rather than directed by its central vanguard. On this model any mediation between the producers and the vanguard organizing their production, say in the form of substantial powers for republics and provinces, could be regarded as a 'statist' interference. Typical of this period was the Novi Sad Agreement of 1954 which determined that 'Serbo-Croatian or Croato-Serbian' was one language with two scripts and two dialects, thus dismissing Croat national claims to separateness. Even when, at the Seventh Congress of the LCY in 1958 which introduced a new Party Programme, Bićanić pronounced their commitment to the 'Four Ds', i.e. de-statization, de-centralization, de-politicization (i.e. separation of party and state posts) and democratization, the de-centralization involved was largely intended to be to the communes and workers' councils, rather than to the republics and provinces.

The 1950s was, in fact, a period of great confusion and adjustment in Yugoslav politics, both domestic (with the difficulties in implementing self-management and the *cause célèbre* of Djilas) and foreign (the reassessment of relations with the USSR following the death of Stalin in 1953). Economic growth was high but chaotic, and the Third Five Year Plan had to be abandoned in 1962 after the confusion caused by tentative economic reform in 1961. By the early 1960s it was clear that major economic and political reform was necessary in order to create a stable and consistent system. This duly came with the new constitution of 1963 and the major economic reforms of 1965. The 1963 constitution marked a fundamental break with Stalinism and the extension of the self-management principle from socialized industry to all areas of society. Yugoslavia was declared to be a *Socialist* Federative Republic (SFRY) rather than a 'People's Republic', a name associated with East European Stalinism. A complex five-chamber Federal Assembly was introduced with four specialized chambers for various types of decision-making. The chamber of Nationalities was still there, within the Federal Chamber, but, though upgraded in size, its powers were not really increased. This structure did provide during the 1960s a genuinely vigorous political life in Yugoslavia. But, while the powers of the communes and workers' councils were increased, there was no real shift of power towards the republics. The 1965 economic reforms accepted the devolutionary logic of self-management in the abandonment of command planning in favour of indicative plans, the corresponding increase in the powers of enterprises, the reform of the price and wage system, the commitment to making the dinar an internationally convertible currency and the liberalization of foreign trade and investment: in short an attempt to introduce 'market socialism'.

It was these economic reforms which finally brought to a head the question of the powers of the republics and provinces. Three main factors increased pressure towards federalization. Firstly, conservatives within the LCY tried to mount a rearguard action against what they saw as dangerous centrifugal trends, taking as their unofficial leader the Serbian LC Cadre Secretary and head of the secret police (the UDBA), Alexander Ranković, who held the new post of Vice-President of the Republic (i.e. number two to Tito). His refusal to adapt the Stalinist and pro-Serbian orientation of the UDBA combined with his lack of commitment to the reform programme brought increased complaints about 'Serbian hegemonism' in the mid-1960s from the non-Serbian areas. After an army investigation, which revealed extensive corruption and illegality in the UDBA, he was forced to resign and was expelled from the party in July 1966. But while this signalled a defeat for the conservative faction in the LCY, the damage to inter-ethnic relations had already been done, producing the beginnings of a nationalist reaction against Serbia in the republics. This was encouraged by the more relaxed political atmosphere which the fall of Ranković introduced, in which the pent-up frustrations of the past twenty years could be expressed.

The other two factors were more direct consequences of the economic reforms. Firstly, the abandonment of central command planning and the granting of substantial economic powers to enterprises created an urgent need for mechanisms of regional co-ordination, and since the republican structure existed, it was the republics and provinces which were the natural candidates for the development of powers of co-ordination of the work of communes and enterprises and mediation between them and the federation. Secondly, the economic growth of the 1960s, combined with the centrifugal effects of the economic reforms, produced a substantial differentiation in the economic performance of the republics: basically, in relative terms, the more developed areas became richer and the less developed poorer, which stimulated selfish and nationalist concerns.

The combination of these three factors caused an upsurge in national feeling which broke the inter-ethnic calm of post-war Yugoslavia. Factors of Yugoslav unification were declining in importance with time: the revulsion against the ethnic hatred of the inter-war and war years, anti-fascist unity, commitment to social and economic development and consolidation in the face of Soviet pressure leading to pride in Yugo-slavia's isolated but distinctive and independent path. It was an awareness of the decline in the salience of these factors combined with an unease about the implications of the economic reforms that prompted Tito to launch his 'Yugoslavism' (*Jugoslovenstvo*) campaign in 1963 with the aim of producing a unified, socialist, pan-Yugoslav consciousness. But in the circumstances of stronger centrifugal trends this campaign backfired, being viewed in the republics as Serbian hegemonism by another name and an attempt to undermine their natural rights.

## The nationalist upsurge and federalization

In early 1967 nationalist problems surfaced dramatically. In January the delegates in the Bosnian Chamber of Nationalities called an unpre-cedented special session to condemn the allocation of central funds by the federation to the republic. Then the Slovene Social Welfare and Health Chamber rejected a federal proposal to reduce social security expenditure, which led to the proffered resignation of the Slovene premier (the first such case in the SFRY) who had in fact proposed the measure in his capacity as an ex-officio member of the Federal Executive Council (i.e. federal government). In March leading Croat intellectuals signed a 'Declaration' stating the autonomy of the Croat language and rejecting the Novi Sad Agreement on the unity of the Serbo-Croatian language. Extensive protests began in Albanian areas of Kosmet against the pro-Serbian policies of the disgraced Ranković.

The result of these events was that a series of constitutional amend-ments was rushed through the Federal Assembly in April 1967. Essentially these gave greater powers to the Chamber of Nationalities in the Federal Assembly and wider powers to the republics, mainly in the sphere of internal security. They also abolished the system of ex-officio places for republican premiers on the Federal Executive Council, which could, as in the Slovene case, cause a conflict of interest. But these amendments only whetted the appetites of the roused nationalists. In particular, they did nothing for the 'autonomous' areas of Serbia, and in 1968 major riots with Albanian nationalist demands occurred in Priština, the capital of Kosmet, centred on the university students. These were all the more serious because of the uncertain international situation follow-ing the Soviet intervention in Czechoslovakia in August. Along with severe repression of 'trouble-makers' political concessions were made, particularly a rapid Albanization of posts in education and, more gradually, in the party and state administrations (which led, as we shall see, to an exodus of Serbian specialists). Kosmet, renamed Kosovo, was upgraded to the same status as Vojvodina, namely that of a Socialist Autonomous Province. In further constitutional amendments in December the two autonomous provinces were given powers more or less comparable with the republics and 'nationalities' were given the same rights as the 'Yugoslav nations'; the Chamber of Nationalities was made the most important federal chamber and its delegates became bound to represent faithfully the views of their delegating republican/ provincial assemblies.

The constitutional amendments of 1967–8 marked a substantial degree of federalization for the SFRY, but they were insufficient to meet nationalist aspirations, particularly in two areas: in Serbia the powers of the republic in relation to its autonomous provinces were not clearly defined and would later give rise to problems, and, more generally, the republics still had insufficient economic and financial powers to meet the logic of the market-oriented economic reforms. It was the question of republican control of essential economic and financial levers which became a major preoccupation of the two most prosperous republics, Slovenia and, particularly, Croatia. Since the economic reforms Croatia had rapidly become the country's leading foreign currency earner (partly through tourism on the Dalmatian coast and partly from the remittances of Croats working abroad, mainly in West Germany and Austria, as *Gastarbeiter*) as well as the main centre for import–export trade. Yet it was not able to make full use of the wealth it generated (for example to develop its poor eastern interior) because major investment and currency control were still a prerogative of the federation (which kept 90 per cent of foreign currency earnings) and Belgrade still dominated banking (increasingly important for the marketized economy) and import–export handling.

In the case of Croatia these economic demands became bound up with a much broader movement of national regeneration which caused the SFRY's biggest crisis in 1971. This national movement had been building up for some time, mainly amongst the intellectuals and middle classes and centred around a cultural organization called *Matica Hrvatska* ('Croat Homeland'). Encouraged by the frustration produced by Croatia's continuing inability to control its own economic affairs and by the resentment felt by Croatian *Gastarbeiter*, many of whom came from the less developed interior, at the fact that their currency remittances were creamed off by Belgrade while the demands of their own un-developed areas were not met, this organization rapidly took on an anti-socialist orientation with echoes of the fascist *Ustaše* tradition. At the same time in the liberalized atmosphere of the later 1960s there arose a ferment of intellectual debate and literary expression which became known as the 'Croat Spring' after the 'Prague Spring' of 1968, by which it was certainly influenced. By 1971 a liberalizing, Dubček-style triumvirate was in charge of the Croat party (Dabčević-Kučar, Tripalo and Pirker) prepared to voice many of the popular demands (especially on the economy) and working closely with the *Matica Hrvatska*.

It was partly in response to the general nationalist upsurge, and partly also because of the worries of an ageing Tito (he was 76 in 1968) about what would happen after his death, that a further series of constitutional amendments were passed in June 1971. It is these amendments which allegedly transformed the SFRY into virtually a confederation. Certainly they amounted almost to a new constitution. It was now held that primary sovereignty rested with the republics and provinces. The federation still held important 'reserve' areas: defence and foreign policy, the ensuring of a unified Yugoslav market, monetary and foreign trade policies, ethnic and individual rights and the 'principles of the political system'. This was, apparently, not a greatly changed list, but there was this important difference from previous practice, that even in these areas any decision affecting the interests of the republics (the definition of which was endlessly interpretable) had to be made by a process of inter-republican consensus-building. This process was institutionalized in all the leading organs of party and state, which became, in effect, forums for inter-republican conflict-resolution and bargaining based on the principle of parity of representation for each republic (rather less for the provinces). Already in 1969 the LCY had created a collective Presidency with balanced republican/provincial representation and a rotational chairmanship based on a 'national key' (Tito, however, was the exception, being made life president). In 1971 a collective State Presidency was created along the same lines as the LCY Presidency (with Tito again the exception). In the same way the Federal Executive Committee and its ministerial staffs, the Federal Assembly (now reconstituted into just two chambers, Federal and Republican/ Provincial) and the new Constitutional Court were all constructed on the proportionate 'national key' system.[15]

These institutional innovations appeared to legitimize the virtual veto by republics over any legislation harming their interests which had been operating in practice since 1968, resulting in the stalemate in federal decision-making between 1968 and 1971. However, after June 1971 a major change became apparent in the operation of this confederal bargaining system in comparison with the paralysis of the preceding period. In order to achieve smooth and speedy consensus-building at the federal level the amendments provided for the setting up under the aegis of the Federal Executive Council of five specialized inter-regional committees of only nine members (one from each federal unit and one FEC chairman). These received only incidental mention in the amendments[16] but soon gained overriding practical importance. Moreover, when these committees failed to produce a resolution of conflict the problem was remitted to a general Co-ordinating Committee of federal and republican/provincial government leaders, which was not envisaged by the amendments. So in effect the larger and more public federal bodies were by-passed in a typically Titoist way by smaller, private committees of the leading members of the republican/provincial elites. This practice matched the new mood of party consolidation which Tito had enjoined on his republican colleagues at the Brioni meeting of April 1971 and did in fact result in the effective expedition of much federal business in the ensuing months.

However, these developments did not please the nationalist-oriented leadership of the Croatian LC. They were faced with the prospect of being continually outvoted in these committees by the less developed republics and with the undermining of their veto. In response to mounting unrest at increased problems of inflation and unemployment which were expressed in strikes and an increasingly strident *Matica Hrvatska*, the Croat Triumvirate became dragooned into an intransigent public position on fundamental demands for Croatian economic autonomy: reform of the banking and foreign currency systems, abolition of the Belgrade-based import–export firms and redistribution of former federal assets. The uncompromising nature of these demands alienated the support of the Slovenes and left the Croats isolated. Yet the leaders stuck to their guns even after being called to task by Tito in July. For several months the working of federal institutions was paralysed by a virtual Croat veto. Meanwhile conservatives in the Croat LC were becoming increasingly concerned at the effect on the federation as a whole and at the influence of *Matica Hrvatska* on the LC leaders. In November Dabčević-Kučar praised the 'unity between the party and the national movement'. Yet soon afterwards the *Matica*, in a critique of the constitutional amendments, proposed that Croatia should be declared a sovereign national state with Croat as its official language and with full control over tax revenues, foreign currency earnings, banking and even armed forces and foreign policy. There was also talk of the revision of the 'state' frontiers.

At this point the conservatives appealed to Tito to intervene, which he had decided to do anyway, whereupon the university students called a general strike and appealed to the workers to join them, which, significantly, they did not. On 1 December the Croat LC leaders were summoned to a meeting with Tito at his retreat at Karadjordjevo (ironically this was the same place and date that the proclamation of the Kingdom of Serbs, Croats and Slovenes had been made by Alexander in 1918!). He accused them of ideological failings and lack of party discipline and of pandering to liberal and counter-revolutionary nationalists and told them to put the Croat house in order. The old magic worked. The chastened leaders resigned within a few days, realizing that their position was impossible, and the mass movement was suppressed. The new leadership under Milka Planinc proceeded, with the help of the federal army, to carry out a thorough purge of leading party and state officials. *Matica Hrvatska* was banned. The whole dramatic change was carried through with remarkably little disturbance.

The Croat 'rebellion' collapsed for two main reasons. Firstly, it had little support among the 'domestic' working class (it was fortunate, however, for Tito that at the point of crisis the *Gastarbeiter* had not yet returned home for the Christmas holiday). Secondly, the violence of the preceding months (particularly in terms of Serb-Croat clashes, often recalling *Ustaše* activity), the extreme character of the leaders' demands and the federal paralysis resulting from them, and the increasing power of a non-socialist movement convinced many in the party (and outside it) of the futility of the Triumvirate's position. Many accepted Tito's view that civil war would have ensued if drastic action had not been taken.

Tito wisely decided against a major witch hunt in Croatia, and surprisingly, there was no reversion to a centralized system of control. Indeed some of the main demands of the Croat Triumvirate, to which the new leaders remained committed in a modified form, were in fact partially met in the next year or two: the 'retention quotas' for foreign currency were more than tripled and, more significantly, in 1972 Tito took action against 'liberals' within the Serbian LC leadership who had connived at the growth of 'centres of alienated financial power', i.e. Serbian-dominated banks and foreign-trade agencies, which had become a law unto themselves. The constitutional amendments remained in place, 'normalization' was aided by the general mood, especially in the party, of unification in the face of the risks involved in excessive pluralism on the part of the republics.

It was in these circumstances that a general constitutional revision was undertaken. The new constitution, proudly announced as being the longest in the world, was duly promulgated in February 1974, followed by the Tenth LCY Congress in May. Much of this revision was a tidying-up process, adapting the 1963 constitution to the amendments of 1967–8 and 1971. The institutional innovations of 1974 mainly concerned the assembly system, for which an elaborate system of indirect election from 'delegations' was introduced. The apparent aim of this was to develop 'direct democracy', but its operation, in which elections would be dominated by the LCY-controlled Socialist Alliance, suggests that the real underlying change behind the 1974 constitution was a revival of the unifying role of the party in state bodies. The Chair of the Party Presidency became an *ex officio* member of the State Presidency. Perhaps even more significantly, the military were given separate representation for the first time on the party central committee, reflecting their crucial role in backing the party purge of the Croat nationalists in 1972, and in the assembly system. At the party congress there was renewed talk of 'democratic centralism' and the 'dictatorship of the proletariat' (i.e. typical Leninist terms) and criticism of the 1952 Congress which abandoned Lenin's concept of the 'leading role of the party'.

But most of this 'Cominformist' talk remained talk. For most of the party too much was at stake in the confederal and self-managed system to give it up. There would be no return to Stalinist 'statism'. The confederal structure was retained with even more constitutional guarantees for the federal units, but the idea was that, to compensate, the whole structure would be infused by a tighter control from a more centralized and disciplined party elite backed up by the federal armed forces. However, in practice this rather dialectical, if typically Yugoslav, concept of 'unity in diversity' proved very difficult to maintain.

## Tito's death and the crisis in Kosovo

In the six years between the promulgation of the 1974 constitution and the death of Tito in May 1980 the SFRY was dominated by two overriding issues: economic crisis and fears about what would happen to the country, both internally and externally, after Tito's death. In both cases the general effect of these problems was to promote consolidation and unity, at any rate amongst the party elite. In the case of the economy, Yugoslavia's inflation and trading balance with the West had become so bad by the mid-1970s, partly under the impact of the OPEC price rises and subsequent Western recession, that it was forced to seek help from the IMF and western banks. These creditors attempted to exert, with mixed success, some financial discipline on Yugoslavia's economy, which suited her leaders well since they could always claim that any unpalatable measures represented the requirements of international creditors. The inevitability of the impending loss of the dominating figure of Tito prompted a general attempt to try to make the complex system of conflict-resolution work and the preoccupation with federal and party unity was reinforced by fears about Soviet intentions after the invasion of Afghanistan in 1979 showed that the USSR had not lost its hegemonistic and interventionist tendencies.

Nevertheless, the intended recentralization and de-federalization of the LCY and its increased control of the country never really took place. The LCY has remained a federated party and there has been little attempt to put flesh on the bones of talk of 'democratic centralism'. This fact probably made the transition to the post-Tito situation easier, though in his last couple of years Tito was only nominally in control anyway. The improbably complex system of rotating and nationally-balanced state and party hierarchies moved into operation smoothly after Tito's death and is still in place without any 'dominant leader' having yet emerged (1989). But while the inter-republican elite have been quite successful in preventing the dominance of any one republican group, they have been rather less than successful at running the country. One of the features of the post-Tito situation has been the increasing stalemate at federal level in the face of economic crisis and national tensions. Two reasons for this have been the absence of an authoritative figure (resulting from the rotational leadership system) capable of knocking heads together at crucial times, as Tito was, and the fact that since 1980 the *in camera* conflict-resolution procedures which he preferred have turned into acrimonious public wrangles.

But the biggest test of the post-Tito leadership undoubtedly came in 1981 with the serious disturbances in Albanian-dominated Kosovo. We have seen that the troubles in this province started in the 1960s, but it is no accident that the worst outbreaks of unrest have occurred there in recent years.[17] The basic problem is that as the Yugoslav system has become more confederal and the republics more autarkic, the poorer areas have benefited less from central redistribution of resources and the impact of world recession and internal economic crisis has been hardest on them as the richer areas become less willing to bale them out. In addition there is the problem, which we have discussed before, of the basic unfairness of the federal structure with regard to the Albanian population. While the status of Kosovo was upgraded in 1968 and its cadres Albanized, and while it is true that the difference between the powers of republics and provinces has been lessened, the fact remains that the Kosovo Albanians have less weight at the federal level than smaller national groups and substantial numbers of their nationals are in other republics. Finally, they remain ultimately a part of Serbia, which retains rather vaguely specified powers of control over economic life and security in the province, as has been demonstrated since 1981. It is said that the main reason for not granting Kosovo republican status, which the nationalists demand, is that in this case it would have the right to secede from the federation. It is in fact very doubtful whether this option would be taken up, partly because few sensible Yugoslav Albanians would seriously want to join their even less developed and still rigidly Stalinist 'motherland', and partly because of the harm secession would cause the Albanians in Macedonia. In any case it is the continued lack of action in rectifying the anomaly which makes the nagging sore of unrest as dangerous as the possibility of secession and makes the negative use of increased status more likely.

Rusinow has termed the crisis in Croatia in 1971 a 'crisis of modernization'.[18] The term is even more appropriate to describe the crisis in Kosovo. It is typical of nationalist movements generally that the Kosovo troubles started amongst the middle classes and, in particular, the students. In March 1981 a demonstration over living and working conditions by students at Priština university led to extensive and increasingly nationalist-oriented protests which were heavily suppressed by police. These were followed by outbreaks of violence and more extensive unrest throughout the province and in Macedonia in April. Following the Albanization of the university in 1968, including the employment of a number of lecturers from Albania itself because of the shortage of qualified Albanians, it was inevitable that the university would become the focus of national assertion. The students are forming a classic type of frustrated 'modernizing elite', educated but with little political influence and, because of the continued under-development of the province, with few career opportunities. At the same time the non-Slav language imposes an obstacle to extensive migration to work elsewhere in Yugoslavia or abroad.

Albanian Kosovo exhibits the typical problems of developing countries. It has maintained a very high birth rate (25/1000) which, when combined with a reduced death rate, results in enormous population growth and surplus especially in rural areas, which causes an outflow to the towns, increasing pressures there. Unemployment is very high (about 50 per cent in early 1989) and there is a high illiteracy rate (about 18 per cent) and low educational level. The general level of per capita income declined from 48 per cent of the national level in 1954 to 28 per cent in 1980. In addition the republic has become more homogeneously Albanian, due to several factors: the population growth amongst Albanians; the inflow of Albanians from Macedonia and Montenegro; and the outflow of Serbs and Montenegrins because of the Albanization of cadres and, more recently, violence inflicted on non-Albanians. In the 1940s the province was about two-thirds Albanian; now the proportion has risen above 85 per cent.

The disturbances of 1981 were followed by extensive purges of 'nationalists' from the party and state administrations and show-trials of key 'trouble-makers'. In addition the LCY and FEC developed an 'Action Programme' for the development of the province which goes some way to recognizing, if not remedying, the special economic problems of the area. But there are no signs of weakening on the demand for republican status; indeed, recently there seems to have been a hardening of Serbian attitudes to the Albanian problem. There was further unrest in the province in 1983 and it has rumbled on sporadically ever since. It is clear that, whilst Albanian unrest started amongst the students, the seeds of discontent have a much wider base among the broader population and are therefore much more difficult to eradicate than the Croat unrest of 1971.

## The current situation

At the time of writing (early 1989) the SFRY is going through a crisis potentially worse than any in its existence. Matters came to a head with the announcement of a series of constitutional amendments which were due to be implemented by the end of 1988.[19] These were elaborated by an FEC commission on the recommendation of the Thirteenth Congress of the LCY in 1986 and are basically designed to give federal bodies (such as the Federal Executive Council and the Federal Assembly to which it is responsible) sufficient authority *vis-à-vis* the republics/ provinces for them to carry out the macro-economic policies which are required by Yugoslavia's mounting economic crisis. The changes include the abolition of the right of veto on federal legislation which had been so frequently used in recent years to block decision-making in the Chamber of Republics and Provinces. It should be noted that one reason why Yugoslavia's economic crisis has gone from bad to worse (inflation in early 1989 is nearly 200 per cent) is the difficulty in obtaining consensus in a confederal system on unpalatable economic measures, stemming from the Stabilization Programme of 1983, of pan-Yugoslav application, such as currency devaluation, wage freezes and credit squeezes.

These constitutional amendments seem to be an indication that the 'centralizers' have been winning the argument over the 'confederalists' in the general debate about the future of the Yugoslav federal system which has raged in the LCY ever since Tito's death. However we interpret the current alignments in this debate[20] there does seem to be an emerging consensus on the need for limiting excesses of confederal pluralism. But this does not imply a return to some form of neo-Stalinism: for non-Serbs Stalinism is so closely associated with Serbian hegemonism of the Ranković variety as to rule out that option. The modern 'centralizers' are predominantly Serbian monetarists, strongly pro-market but determined to control national monetary and credit policies. However, the current situation amongst the nationalities seems to be giving encouragement to people of a more Stalinist orientation in Serbia. The federation has indeed been wracked with problems recently. In 1987 Bosnia was rocked by a major financial scandal which caused the resignation of the federal vice-President and an extensive anti-corruption purge. There have also been trials of Islamic fundamentalist nationalists, though the significance of these has probably been exaggerated, despite the high population growth of Bosnian Muslims. Also in 1987 violence in Kosovo erupted again directed against Serbs and Montenegrins in the province to which these groups reacted with counter-demonstrations demanding protection from the Serbian republican authorities. A new hard-line Serbian LC leadership under Slobodan Milosević has managed to have some prominent officials removed (notably the Chair of the Serbian Presidency, Ivan Stambolić) for being too soft on Albanian nationalists. In a controversial move Milosević has used Serbian reserve powers to suspend the provincial police and judiciary as being unable to cope with the crisis and has sent in special Serbian police units 'to prevent anti-constitutional and illegal acts by nationalists and separatists', exercising Serbia's 'legitimate right to prevent the total annihilation of non-Albanian nationals in Kosovo by Albanian irredentists'.

This action, combined with the current constitutional amendment proposals, has brought to a head a dispute between Serbia and its other province, Vojvodina, since one effect of the amendments is to increase the reserve powers of Serbia *vis-à-vis* both its provinces. In January 1988 the provincial and republican leaderships came to an agreement on the jurisdiction of the republic, but the action of Milosević in Kosovo has re-opened controversy on the details of the agreement. The combination of a Serbian nationalist backlash and a corresponding resistance in Kosovo and previously quiescent Vojvodina makes the current crisis very serious.

The passing of the constitutional amendments by the Federal Assembly in November 1988, and the use of the greater powers given to Serbia over its provinces by the suspension of local control over police and judiciary in Kosovo by Milosević, have generated a violent public confrontation between Serbs and Kosovars. There have been major public protests by Serbs against the alleged terrorism by Kosovars against the Serbian minority, and the use of special police units and courts to purge nationalist elements in Kosovo has led to a general strike in the province and the risk of increased violence, despite the ban on all public protests. The chair of the state presidency (which heads the armed forces), Raif Dizdarević, has hinted at the use of martial law in Kosovo if the situation does not improve.

### Assessment of Yugoslav federalism

The current situation of Yugoslav federalism is clearly so fraught that it is difficult to make a detached and measured assessment of its development. Nevertheless, some tentative comments may be made. Let us return to the two questions we posed at the start of this chapter. The first, historical, question was why and how socialist Yugoslavia embarked on the road to federalization. We have seen that initially the CPY had only a nominal commitment to federalism of the cultural type. Its largely centralist policies up to 1949 were encouraged by the need for economic development and re-distribution, reaction against Serbo-Croat ethnic hatred and the need for national consolidation in the face of foreign pressure. These factors continued to be influential even after the break with the USSR, since the change to self-management did not at first involve any move towards federalism. It was the economic and political liberalization of the 1960s which produced both the conditions and the opportunity for the rebirth of sub-state nationalism and the federalizing response in the constitutional changes of 1967–71. The federalizing momentum was maintained even after the Croatian crisis in the constitution of 1974. Tito's hopes for a re-centralized LCY acting as a unifying force in a confederal structure did not really materialize, and since his death in 1980 the country has been precariously held together in the face of nationalist pressure and economic crisis by an inter-republican party elite prevented by their mutual jealousies from taking any effective governmental action at the federal level.

On most counts Yugoslavia's record on federalization does not seem to have been very successful. This brings us to our second question: what have been the main problems faced by the SFRY and how far are these specific to Yugoslavia or do they carry warnings for other federalizing states?

Firstly, there are problems which concern the pre-socialist heritage of the SFRY and its international context. The linguistic and cultural diversity combined with the generally low and highly uneven economic development of the new state created in 1918 meant that nation-building would be problematic under any political system. Parliamentary democracy hardly got off the ground before constitutional monarchy degenerated into Serbian autocracy, and the fascist wartime occupation actively stimulated ethnic hatred. This inheritance of division and conflict cannot be easily overcome. It must be remembered that most European 'nation-states' only achieved cultural homogeneity after centuries of development, usually involving the systematic suppression of minorities by the dominant ethnic group, and even here the 'homogeneity' seemed rather fragile by the 1960s. Even the sweetness and light of Swiss federalism was not achieved without many periods of acute conflict over the centuries. So it is unreasonable to expect the SFRY to solve its problems of state-building in a couple of generations. In addition, as regards Yugoslavia's international context, the failure of post-war boundary negotiations and, especially, of schemes for a socialist Balkan federation added greatly to the SFRY's problems. If the socialist governments of the area had been willing (and permitted) to seriously re-negotiate their state boundaries and co-operate in an international federation (producing, e.g., a greater Albania, Macedonia and Hungary), so many of Yugoslavia's problems would have been mitigated. But the failure of these negotiations and Yugoslavia's subsequent isolation from its natural allies in Eastern Europe left it with severe internal structural problems.

Secondly, there are problems which concern the SFRY's own policy decisions on the structure and methods of federalization. As we have seen, the 'federal' structure of 1946 was fundamentally flawed in that it claimed to be based on the 'nation-state' idea whilst in fact deriving from vague historical boundaries which no longer corresponded to ethnic settlement and ignored the just claims of ethnic groups outside the five 'nations'. This might not have been important if centralist, redistributive-developmental policies had been maintained with a minimum of central-ized repression and plenty of foreign aid in the context of a Balkan federation. But when economic and political devolution in circum-stances of international isolation brought real power to the federal units the inadequacy of the structure became manifest. Until the worst anomalies of this structure are rectified the SFRY will never solve its federal problems.

Next, there is the problem of economic reform and performance. Under conditions of economic prosperity and a reasonable distribution of benefits structures of administration assume less importance. In the case of the SFRY economic crisis and structural crisis seem to have reinforced one another: economic and political reform generated federalization, but federalization seems to have ultimately inhibited the success of economic reform, increasing uneven development and inter-republican tension. Yugoslavia's economic crisis makes the federation increasingly difficult to operate, and the failure of the federation to produce decisive government compounds the economic crisis. Finally, there is the question of political reform. Yugoslav official pronounce-ments always maintain that self-management and federalism are integrally related in the political system of the SFRY. But in practice they have operated separately or in conflict. For most of the country self-management is a sham which has greatly added to the complication of political decision-making and the inefficiency of Yugoslav industry, making the successful operation of a federal system even more difficult. The fact is that the imposition and maintenance of 'self-management' under the control of the albeit-federated LCY has as little to do with genuine democracy as the original imposition of Stalinist 'statism' in the 1940s. A federal system, based as it is on voluntary co-operation and conflict-resolution, cannot be made to work in the absence of unrestricted political choice. Some form of political pluralization involving a challenge to LCY elite control is increasingly demanded by Yugoslav dissidents and is now perhaps starting to be implemented in Slovenia. It would seem to be a precondition for the successful operation of a Yugoslav federation.

Nevertheless, to end on a brighter note, the Yugoslav experience of federalization is not all negative. In contrast to the communist leader-ships of the USSR and Eastern Europe the LCY elite has shown a far greater readiness to re-think its aims and to develop and consistently maintain new political institutions and structures. In particular, its consistent application of the principles of national proportionality and office rotation in all federal and republican political institutions is very impressive. The SFRY has developed in its federal institutions 'consociational' structures of conflict-resolution which have enabled it to survive the death of its founder and economic and political crisis. In view of Yugoslavia's structural problems this represents a genuine achievement worthy of consideration by other federalizing states. What is necessary for the federation to survive and flourish is that these consociational mechanisms should cease to be a means of preserving LCY control and become an expression of the democratic choices of the whole population.

## Notes

1. The term 'socialist' is used in Eastern Europe to refer to states aspiring to create the ultimate classless society, 'communism'. 'Socialism' is the transitional stage between capitalism and communism in which the means of production are socialized and the state's development is controlled by the 'communist' party. Therefore such states are only loosely to be referred to as 'communist'.

2. The term 'Soviet' is a Russian word originally meaning 'Council', referring to the workers' councils created in 1917; these were intended to be the main mediators between party and people, an expression of direct democracy under socialism. It was only under Stalin that the word took on a national rather than a class character, being associated with a Russian-led state rather than an ever-expanding class-led republic.

3. On the creation and operation of the USSR 'federation' see R. Pipes, *The Formation of the Soviet Union*, New York (rev ed 1968); E. H. Carr, *The Bolshevik Revolution*, vol 1, London (1950); R. Conquest, *Soviet Nationalities Policy in Practice*, London (1967); J. Azrael (ed), *Soviet Nationality Policies and Practices*, New York (1978).

4. On the broader question of the relationship between nationalism and Marxism–Leninism see W. Connor, *The National Question in Marxist–Leninist Theory and Strategy*, Princeton (1984); on Bulgaria and Romania more specifically see O. Nissan, *Revolution Administered: Agrarianism and Communism in Bulgaria*, Baltimore (1973); R. J. Crampton, *A Short History of Modern Bulgaria*, Cambridge (1986); G. Schöpflin, *The Hungarians of Romania*, London (1978); M. Shafir, *Romania*, London (1984); and more generally, R. King, *Minorities under Communism*, Cambridge, Mass (1973).

5. For a general historical account of the relationship between nationalism and state structure in a crucial two decades of the SFRY see P. Ramet, *Nationalism and Federalism in Yugoslavia, 1963–1983*, Bloomington (1984). There is no good thematic discussion of Yugoslav federalism in the

literature. The best general historical accounts of Yugoslavia are F. Single-
ton, *A Short History of the Yugoslav Peoples*, Cambridge (1985) and, in more
detail on the SFRY, D. Rusinow, *The Yugoslav Experiment, 1948–1974*,
London (1977); also useful are F. Singleton, *Twentieth Century Yugoslavia*,
London (1976) and, on the more recent period, S. Burg, *Conflict and
Cohesion in Socialist Yugoslavia*, Princeton (1983).

6. In the statistics of this period Montenegrins and Macedonians were counted
as Serbs; in the census of 1921 'Serbo-Croats' constituted 74.4 per cent and
Slovenes 8.5 per cent of the population.

7. Peter Karadjordjević had ended the Obrenović dynasty by a bloody coup in
1903.

8. On this and the early post-war debates see P. Shoup, *Communism and the
Yugoslav National Question*, New York (1968).

9. For the text of the 1943 AVNOJ Decision 'On the development of
Yugoslavia on the federal principle' see *Socialist Thought and Practice*
(Belgrade, in English), No 58 (November 1973), pp 51–2; this recognized
the 'sovereignty' and 'full equality' of five peoples (Serbs, Croats, Slovenes,
Macedonians and Montenegrins) within six republics (i.e., including Bosnia-
Herzegovina, which was multi-national) and, in addition, declared that 'all
national rights will be guaranteed to national minorities in Yugoslavia'
(para 4).

10. During the war several Moslem groups had sided with the Ustaše and had
clashed with the partisans; the creation of Bosnia-Herzegovina was probably
intended to appease Moslem nationalist aspirations, though the legitimacy
of their claim for an Islamic Republic has never been conceded; Moslems
formed about 30 per cent of the population of Bosnia in 1946, now over 40
per cent. During the 1960s the Moslems were recognized as being an ethnic
as well as a religious grouping and now constitute one of the major 'ethnic'
groups. Another new grouping recognized in this period was that of
'Yugoslavs', a category for those of mixed ethnic affiliation, which increased
to 5.4 per cent of the population by 1981, mainly consisting of Bosnian
Moslems reluctant to associate their religion with their ethnicity, and
Hungarians in Vojvodina. (See Table 5.1).

11. For a complete list of ethnic groups see Table 5.1.

12. On the general negotiations on federation see Shoup, op. cit. (note 8)
chapters 2–3.

13. See M. Djilas, *Conversations with Stalin*, London (1963), p 141, and, in
general, chapter 3.

14. See Djilas, op. cit. (note 13), pp 111 ('swallowing' Albania) and p 137, where
Stalin is also said to have advocated a federation between Romania and
Hungary, and between Poland and Czechoslovakia. Djilas maintains that the
Yugoslav military intervention in Albania without consulting the USSR was
the initial cause of the Soviet–Yugoslav rift.

15. The *LCY Presidency* consists of three members from each republic and two
from each province (plus one from the armed forces), with a one-year
President and a two-year Secretary elected on a national-rotation basis; the
*State Presidency* consists of one member from each republic and each
province plus the LCY President *ex officio*, with one-year President and Vice-

President; in the *Federal Assembly*, the Federal Chamber consists of thirty delegates from each republic and twenty from each province, the Chamber of Republics and Provinces of twelve from each republic and eight from each province; the *Constitutional Court* consists of a President and thirteen judges, two from each republic and one from each province; the *Federal Executive Council* is not exactly proportional, consisting of twenty-nine members, *at least* three from each republic and two from each province.

16. In the subsequent 1974 Constitution, which adhered closely to the wording of these amendments, Article 357 states: 'In order to ensure the participation of the competent republican and provincial agencies in the adoption of statutes and other enactments of the SFRY Assembly ... the Federal Executive Council and the competent republican and provincial agencies shall by mutual agreement set up inter-republican committees for individual spheres ... according to the principle of equal representation of the Republics and corresponding representation of the Autonomous Provinces.'

17. See V. Meier, 'Yugoslavia's National Question' and M. Baskin, 'Crisis in Kosovo' in *Problems of Communism* March–April 1983.

18. Rusinow, op. cit. (note 5) p 266.

19. For recent developments in Yugoslavia see the discussion by D. Rusinow, 'Nationalities Policy and the "National Question" ' in P. Ramet (ed), *Yugoslavia in the 1980s*, Boulder and London (1985), pp 131–65; a convenient summary of events is to be found in *Keesing's Contemporary Archives* (London) pp 35730–4 and 35795–7, etc.

20. Rusinow, in op. cit. (note 19) (1985) accepts and develops the analysis of S. Burg (unpublished paper quoted by him) of the LCY leadership as consisting of three groupings: 'confederationalists', 'ideological conservatives' and 'liberal reformers' more or less equally balanced and effective blocking action by the others, though there is a recent tendency for the second and third groups to form an uneasy alliance against the first. Rusinow seems rather too optimistic in his assessment of the post-1981 situation; since he wrote the crisis has undoubtedly got much worse.

*Table 5.1: Nations, nationalities and ethnic groups in Yugoslavia (1981 Census)*

|  |  | % |
| --- | --- | --- |
| Population of SFRY | 22,427,585 | 100 |
| *Nations of Yugoslavia* |  |  |
| Croatians | 4,428,043 | 19.7 |
| Macedonians | 1,341,598 | 6.0 |
| Montenegrins | 579,043 | 2.6 |
| Moslems | 1,999,890 | 8.9 |
| Serbs | 8,140,507 | 36.3 |
| Slovenes | 1,763,571 | 7.8 |
| *Nationalities of Yugoslavia* |  |  |
| Albanians | 1,730,878 | 7.7 |
| Bulgarians | 36,189 | 0.2 |
| Czechs | 19,624 | 0.1 |
| Hungarians | 426,867 | 1.9 |
| Italians | 15,132 | 0.1 |
| Romanians | 54,955 | 0.2 |
| Ruthenians | 23,286 | 0.1 |
| Slovaks | 80,334 | 0.4 |
| Turks | 101,291 | 0.5 |
| Ukrainians | 12,813 | 0.1 |
| *Ethnic groups* |  |  |
| Romanies | 168,197 | 0.7 |
| Vlachs | 32,071 | 0.1 |
| Yugoslavs (persons not claiming any national affiliation) | 1,219,024 | 5.4 |
| Others (no national affiliation, unknown, under 0.1%, etc) | 254,272 | 1.1 |

Reproduced from K. Jončić, *Nationalities in Yugoslavia*, Belgrade (1982), pp. 5–6 (in English).

# 6 Canadian federalism: a working balance

*Alain Gagnon*

Does the establishment of a federal system resolve political antagonisms, or preserve and perhaps even exacerbate them? The question is a fundamental one, and is of particular concern to students of Canadian federalism. Since its inception in 1867, the Canadian federal system has endured tremendous pressures born out of deep-rooted conflicts, not least of which has been the French–English rivalry. During recent years, issues in Canada such as the patriation from Britain of the constitution without Quebec's consent, the need for province-building, the threat of federal unilateralism, the fiscal imbalance in favour of the central government, and controversy over free-trade with the United States, have accentuated conflict in the political system and have thereby suggested to many analysts that the federal structure is failing.

It is not the intention here to make a protracted analysis of these specific issues facing Canadian federalism. They have been examined elsewhere.[1] Rather what follows is an attempt to account for the continuing vitality of the Canadian federal system, despite a milieu laden with such powerful conflict-generating components. In surveying the nature of contemporary Canadian federalism, I shall maintain that the Canadian system has been successful, not so much in resolving conflict, as in managing it, and striking a flexible balance between the divergent views of the initial bargain.

It is argued here that the principal means of preserving the Canadian polity has been the evolution of instruments of conflict management, and the tremendous flexibility allowed in the political system, permitting a pendulum movement between centripetal (centralizing) and centrifugal (decentralizing) federalism.[2] The central contention of the chapter, however, is not that centralization or decentralization constitutes the solution for achieving some obscure notion of success or the avoidance of failure, but rather that whatever the political setting, the commitment to achieving a 'working balance' has been, and must be, the key to keeping whole and parts together. As a result of this commitment, Canadians have generally been able to enjoy the fruit of membership both of a healthy and prosperous country, and of provincial societies wherein their respective provincial governments work and periodically even fight to preserve their distinct linguistic, cultural, social and economic characteristics.

The work of Elazar is particularly relevant to the Canadian situation. In his view only in those polities where the processes of government reflect federal principles is the structure of federalism meaningful.[3] In other words, the accommodation of diversity must exist in practice as well as in law. Wheare arrived at the same conclusion a few decades earlier. In his view the importance of the initial political bargain, and the accompanying written agreements often cause too much attention to be paid to the structural dimension of federalism.[4] Friedrich concurred that the strict legal position, both in analyses and in the practice of federalism, does not account for the importance of the political process.[5] Friedrich also adds that federalism cannot be merely a legal structure but must be defined as an active process, an adaptable mechanism which governs the people of a federal state: 'Any particular design or pattern of competences or jurisdictions is merely a phase, a short run view of a continually evolving political reality.'[6] To accommodate effectively the strength and potential danger of this diversity requires some flexibility so as to be able to address continually changing manifestations of the political formula.

This flexibility is well exemplified in Canada by the recent Meech Lake Accord (1987) which came about as a result of Quebec's refusal to sign the Constitution Act of 1982 and which attempted to meet some of Quebec's demands. However, it should be noted that in this instance Ottawa gave in to Quebec's demands, but refused to allow Quebec to claim a distinct status, in that it provided the other provinces with exactly the same benefits.[7] The intention was clear: the federal government 'sought ways to restore the balance among provinces'.[8] A balance theory oriented more towards equality among provinces than between the federal and the provincial government(s) has been developed in Canada.

**The politico-economic setting**

Donald Smiley, writing in the early 1980s, provided an accurate and concise picture of the federal setting by defining what he termed the 'compounded crisis' of Canadian federalism.[9] While not ignoring other factors, Smiley contended that the crisis is the compounded product of the problematical relations between the French and the English, between central Canada and the outlying regions, and between Canada and the United States. Although issue can be taken with Smiley's diagnosis of these three relationships, there can be little doubt that they weigh heavily upon the Canadian political system. It is these relationships and the accommodations which they demand that provide Canadian federalism with its unique character. The very power of these forces create simultaneously incessant pressures and strains, and reinforcement of the federal system.

Only a brief discussion of these relationships is necessary here. They date back to the establishment of Confederation, and the fact that they still persist gives credence to the view that they are not problems to be solved or 'cured', but rather conflict-generating issues which must be accommodated in order for the divergent interests involved to benefit as members of a larger and stable polity.

Since the compact of 1867, the growing dominance of the Ontario–Quebec core over the periphery – the Atlantic and Western provinces – has been particularly important. This dominance by the core region, fostered by its large population base and its extensive political and economic power, has provided continued strains on the fabric of the political structure. In the Atlantic provinces, one finds an overwhelming provincial dependency upon the central government. In the more prosperous West, the long tradition of third political parties or 'protest parties' exemplifies the perceived alienation from the heartland.[10] Given the geographical immensity of Canada, and the related problem of uneven population distribution and, in some cases, even isolation, it is not difficult to understand the inevitability of strains and conflicts resulting from a sense of isolation and neglect in the peripheries.

The regionalized nature of the Canadian political economy clearly exacerbates this problem. The hinterland supplies natural resources while the industrialized core reaps unequal benefits by selling manufactured goods. Canada's economic structure suffers from severe weaknesses related to the pattern of capitalist development. Manufacturing is concentrated in Central Canada and is oriented towards servicing a protected domestic market. The other regions have an economic base that relies heavily on the export of natural resources. Significant regional disparities stem from this division of economic activity, particularly for those regions that do not have valuable natural resources that can be efficiently exploited. Changes in international trading patterns and the lowering of trade barriers, increased international competition, and the introduction of new fields of technology now threaten non-competitive Canadian industries. Moreover, the balkanized nature of the Canadian economy reduces the extent of common economic interest amongst the various regions, and constitutes a major difficulty for the central government's attempts to elaborate a workable national strategy.

The Atlantic region has since the 1920s experienced a continued de-industrialization, and is becoming Canada's poorest area with the highest levels of unemployment. The Maritime economy has been dominated by fishing, lumber, agriculture and mining while the central provinces of Ontario and Quebec have been the main beneficiaries of industrialization. Quebec, however, has lagged behind in recent years due to its inability to maintain its economic competitiveness by replacing its labour-intensive industries with more capital-intensive ones. Ontario and Quebec also have well developed agricultural regions and extensive lumber and mining resources. The Prairie provinces have agriculture-intensive economies supplemented by other primary resources, e.g. potash in Saskatchewan and oil in Alberta. The Pacific province of British Columbia is dominated by the mining and lumber sectors and has usually generated substantial revenues for its residents.

Both the federal structure of the Canadian state and the regionalized nature of its economy and society have given the provinces a major role in managing and promoting the development of their own economies. This became especially evident during the resources boom of the 1960s, and was carried over into the 1970s with the elaboration of economic strategies by many provincial governments.

Complicating still further the original political bargain is the imposing presence of the United States. As Smiley notes: 'the influence of multinational corporations and the American government over the Canadian economy has weakened and is weakening the capacity of Ottawa to structure the economy.'[11] Continentalism and economic integration, as demonstrated by the current negotiation in favour of a free trade arrangement between Canada and the United States, threaten the very nature of the federal bargain, weaken east–west ties, and hamper an effective, united Canadian position. Each of these relations, in their own right, could prove a formidable obstacle to the preservation and growth of a federal system.

The establishment of the federal bargain did not and perhaps could not resolve the conflicts inherent in these relations which continue to weaken the pillars upon which the federation was established. Rather, true to Friedrich's postulate, federalism in Canada has provided a means of managing these and other conflicts, thereby minimizing discord while maximizing the collective wellbeing.

The longest standing, and surely the most vital, issue is that of French–English duality. This problematic relationship predates Confederation. As Lord Durham remarked in 1837: 'I found two nations warring in the bosom of a single state: I found a struggle not of principles but of races.'[12]

Canada is unique in that it was settled by two different and powerful nations. However, as Monière notes: 'Before it could achieve autonomy as a colonizing element, at a time when it was still dependent on the

mother country, Quebec was conquered and placed under the domination of another country and another social structure with appreciably
similar economic base.'[13]

In Canada, it has always been possible to be 'Canadian' or 'canadien'
and to view Canada from two different linguistic, cultural, and religious
perspectives. The duality is perpetuated by various socializing agents
resulting in further divergence. For instance, the Church in Quebec
long advocated a life on the land while Anglo-Saxon culture glorified the
entrepreneurial spirit. That the British Conquest in 1759 was not
marked by overt oppression or violence could not lessen the fact that the
sizeable French population was subject to English laws. Conflictual
relations were inevitable. More importantly, they are still difficult
to avoid because French Canadian culture and institutions are continuously threatened.

Many Canadians, however, still do not recognize or accept the
importance of maintaining the rights and responsibilities that have
accrued to the French Canadians as a founding people. Accommodation
of Canada's two founding nations is the fundamental principle upon
which Canada was created.


## French–English relations

As McRoberts and Postgate write:

For French Canada, the real benefit of Confederation was the provision of a
range of powers, limited but sacrosanct, over its own affairs. It meant that the
Province of Quebec could serve as a concrete political unit, protected by
the Constitution, in which the French Canadian community could be clearly
dominant and thus have a chance to survive on its own terms. Confederation also
entailed a risk, since, at the federal level, French Canadians were relegated to the
position of a permanent minority, where their rights and powers were subject to
the actions of the Anglo-Canadian majority.[14]

It should be noted here that Confederation was the sixth attempt to
create a framework in which French and English Canadians could live
together peacefully. None of the earlier phases, that is the military
regime of 1760, the Royal Proclamation of 1763, the Act of Quebec
1774, the Constitution Act of 1791, and the Act of Union of 1841, had
provided a satisfying working arrangement. Confederation was the first
constitutional arrangement giving Lower Canada a degree of political
autonomy.

Ramsay Cook, a major Canadian historian, has made the following
caveat:

If French Canadians had been left to themselves to decide the shape of British

North America in 1867, it is doubtful if there would have been a Confederation. It was not that the Union of 1841 provided them with an ideal state that they wished never to change. It was rather that the dangers of the status quo were at least familiar; a broader union of all the British colonies, plus the promise of a vast empire to be added in the west, carried with it dangers unknown, but suspected.[15]

Smiley gives credence to this view in *The Federal Condition in Canada* when recognizing that:

There were increasingly insistent pressures from Upper Canada, which now had a larger population than the other section, for representation by population in the Legislative Assembly, and although the French Canadian politicians were understandably unwilling to concede this, the more perceptive of them, along with their bleu political allies from Upper Canada, knew that such pressures could not be resisted indefinitely.[16]

Nonetheless, Smiley thinks that French–English relations were central to the creation of a Confederation rather than some other form of government, stressing that it resulted from the cultural, linguistic and religious duality prevailing at the time.

Smiley reminds us that the Act of Union of 1841 establishing the United Province of Canada, led to a political impasse, and that Confederation was proposed as a timely arrangement to accommodate both French and English. According to Smiley, dualism was made an essential component of the confederal compromise. For instance, 'the provinces received exclusive legislative jurisdiction over those matters in respect to which the two linguistic and cultural communities differed most markedly',[17] for example, provincial jurisdiction in education, property and civil rights. However, under section 133 of the British North America Act of 1867, minority rights in education were guaranteed to religious denominations, which represented a restriction on provincial rights. (At the time of Confederation French-speakers were mostly Catholic, while English-speakers were predominantly Protestant.)

According to David R. Cameron, later appointed Director of Research for the Task Force on Canadian Unity (Pépin-Roberts Commission), writing in 1978, dualism is essential to a fundamental understanding of Canadian politics.

Dualism in Canada may be generally described as the view which holds that the most significant cleavage in Canadian society is the line dividing English from French, and which identifies as the major challenge to domestic statecraft the establishment of harmonious and just relations between the English-speaking and the French-speaking communities of Canada.[18]

It should be added that the line of division between Francophone and Anglophone to which dualism refers does not only characterize Canada as a whole, but is reproduced in the province of Quebec, albeit in inverse numerical proportions.

The French–English line of cleavage is revealed by a succession of crises in Canadian history, beginning with the 1837 Rebellion, Lord Durham's Report (1939), the Riel Rebellions (1869, 1884–5), the Manitoba (1890) and Ontario (1912) schools question, the two conscription crises (1917, 1944), the air traffic controllers' crisis (1976), and the refusal in 1980 of Quebec to give its approval to the patriation of the British North America Act from Britain. The setting up of the Royal Commission on Bilingualism and Biculturalism in 1963, with the mandate

to inquire into and report upon the existing state of bilingualism and bicultural-ism in Canada and to recommend what steps should be taken to develop the Canadian Confederation on the basis of an equal partnership between the two founding races, taking into account the contribution made by other ethnic groups to cultural enrichment of Canada and the measures that should be taken to safeguard that contribution

confirmed dualism as the fundamental term of reference for Canadians. It received an official sanction.

The Commission on Bilingualism and Biculturalism was in part the result of the Report of the Quebec Royal Commission of Inquiry on Constitutional Problems (The Tremblay Commission) set up in 1953, and which opposed centripetal federalism on the grounds that it affected Quebec's distinctiveness. The Tremblay Report provided ammunition against federal interventionism in the economy, and pictured the federal government as the defender of English-Canadians.

From the 1960s onwards, all Quebec governments have attempted to maximize the province's autonomy within the federation. In general, they have made five claims:

1.  Recognition of Quebec as a distinct society;
2.  Reform of the constitution that guarantees Quebec a veto power, and maximizes the scope of Quebec's jurisdiction in most policy fields;
3.  Re-apportionment of federal-provincial fiscal resources to reflect Quebec's needs;
4.  A reduced federal role in the development, implementation and financing of provincial policies/programmes; and
5.  An increased role for Quebec both in determining the composition and operation of federal institutions, and also in decisions regarding the development, implementation and financing of federal policies/ programmes.

Within the existing federal system, successive Quebec governments have thus sought to uphold 'dualism'. Not all Quebec governments, however, have agreed about the adjustments that required to be made to the terms of Confederation or even about Quebec's continuing membership of the Canadian federation. The Parti Quebecois government claimed during most of its 1976–81 and 1981–5 mandates that Quebec could not accomplish all of its aspirations under either the existing or the modified terms of Confederation. A step by step strategy (*étapisme*) was elaborated to make sure that full independence would be accomplished.

It does not make a significant difference to Quebec whether Canadian federalism is depicted as a compact between provinces or an alliance between two language groups. In both cases it defines itself either as a founding signatory of the 'provincial compact' or as a legitimate representative of the French-speaking group in the 'linguistic alliance'.[19] Here it must be added that the definition of Canadian federalism as a compact has a long history in Canada, and is shared at present by many of those discussing the constitutional issue. Differences between them tend to be on the precise nature of Quebec's relations with the rest of Canada, as expressed by the concepts of 'special status', 'sovereignty-association', 'cultural sovereignty', and more recently the notion of 'distinct society'.

In whatever way Quebec's relations to Canada are viewed, the province's conception of itself as an original partner remains, as shown by the following excerpt, taken from the July 1968 submission of the Quebec delegation to the Continuing Committee of Officials of the Constitutional Conference.

Canadian federalism owes its originality to the fact that its components are of two different kinds. The first are territorial or political, that is states or provinces, which now number ten. The second are sociological, that is two nations, societies or cultural communities united by history, one of which has had its roots implanted in Canadian soil for over three and a half centuries.[20]

Without exception, Quebec premiers have presented the vision of Quebec Society as an equal partner in Confederation.

In addition to this ascriptive dimension, it is important to note that since the early 1960s, in particular, Quebec provincial governments have been a powerful force at the forefront of the provincial rights movement. They have been instrumental both in expanding the scope of provincial responsibility in several policy sectors and the provincial share of fiscal resources, and also in blocking federal intrusions into areas of provincial jurisdiction. This last point, however, will be modified if the Meech Lake Accord receives unamimous support from the Canadian provinces.

Recent efforts (after Premier Pierre Trudeau's departure from federal politics in 1984) by the federal government to get Quebec's signature on the Constitution Act of 1982 suggest that it recognizes that

Quebec's objectives cannot be overlooked or frustrated indefinitely. It is significant that secession either with or without some limited form of economic association is no longer considered to be a radical and implausible option. The Parti Quebecois has made most people realize that, even though its costs and benefits for Quebec and Canada remains a moot point, it is a real option.

It is perhaps this 'secessionist potential', which currently is so much stronger in Quebec than in any other province, that gives it its special position, and partly facilitates its ability to attain special powers, resources, roles, and status within the Canadian federation. That ability, of course, is also assisted by the nature and electoral significance of its population, given the dynamics of the federal electoral and party systems. Ironically, while the nature and dynamics of the Quebec political system have provided the impetus and momentum for its successive governments to negotiate a better deal, traditionally those same factors have also generated forces which have divided Quebec and weakened its administration in the intergovernmental bargaining process.

Nevertheless, since 1985 a growing consensus among the major political parties has developed within Quebec on the issue of constitutional reform. Particularly noteworthy is the convergence which occurred in the position of the Liberal Party and the Parti Quebecois during the 1985 electoral campaign.[21]

Following the election of the Parti Quebecois in 1976 in Quebec, a real effort was made by the federal government (abetted by several provinces) to alter the predominant definition of Canada as a compact between the French and the English, and to stress instead the characteristic of regionalism. For instance, the setting up of the Task Force on Canadian Unity in 1977 highlighted the question of regionalism. Dualism and regionalism were represented as issues to be reckoned with equally if Canadian federalism was to survive the crisis through which it was passing. According to the Commissioners:

We believe that the heart of the present crisis is to be discovered in the intersecting conflicts created by two kinds of cleavages in Canadian society and by the political agencies which express and mediate them. The first and more pressing cleavage is that old Canadian division between 'the French' and 'the English' . . . The second cleavage is that which divides the various regions of Canada and their populations from one another. Regionalism, like duality, also has an extended lineage in Canadian social, economic and political life.[22]

In short, it was argued increasingly that French–English relations were losing the prominence they had had since 1867, that the issue of regionalism was coming to the fore, and that Quebec nationalism was being undermined. To consolidate its position the federal government decided to patriate the Canadian constitution from Britain and to append it to a Charter of rights and freedoms. This initiative caused much concern in Quebec because it entailed a diminution of the province's position in the federal bargain. Individual rights were being given precedence over collective rights, resulting in a net loss of power for the Quebec government.

It should be stressed here that from June 1980 to the historic First Ministers Conference in November 1981, where Quebec was the only province not to sign the constitutional accord, the government of the province, with the express support of all political parties in the National Assembly, reiterated its complaints about the federal approach. Premier René Lévesque's efforts to form and to maintain a united provincial front (with the exceptions of Ontario and New Brunswick) against the federal government's constitutional package proved futile. Progress was made, as eight provinces conceded that Quebec was a distinct linguistic and cultural society with a special role and status, including the right to maintain or to sever ties with the Canadian federation.[23] But Trudeau, in accordance with his longstanding reluctance to heighten Quebec's status in the constitution, refused to assign a special role to the province in the Constitution Act that was passed in 1982.

It is worth concluding this section on French–English relations by discussing a little further the way in which the new Charter of rights and freedoms impinged upon Quebec's position. It is well known that Trudeau wanted to patriate the Canadian constitution from Britain with a Charter of rights and freedoms, because he saw it as a means of countering provincialism in Canada. Alan Cairns reminds us very clearly of the potential impact of the Charter on the future of Canada when he writes that:

the citizens of a fragmented society may achieve an integrating collective sense of themselves from their common possession of rights and the availability of a common language of political discourse.[24]

Elsewhere, Cairns defines the Charter as a centralist document:

At a more profound level . . . the Charter was an attempt to enhance and extend the meaning of being Canadian and thus to strengthen identification with the national community on which Ottawa ultimately depends for support. (. . .) The resultant rights and freedoms were to be country-wide in scope, enforced by a national supreme court, and entrenched in a national Constitution beyond the reach of fleeting legislative majorities at either level of government. The consequence, and a very clear purpose, was to set limits to the diversities of treatment by provincial governments, and thus to strengthen Canadian as against provincial identities.[25]

## The management of conflict in Canada

What must be understood at the outset is the inevitability of conflict and indeed its actual value in most federal systems. Insofar as federal systems seek to accommodate diversity, conflict must be recognized as inherent in the federal setting because, despite its appealing strengths, diversity invariably produces some conflict.

In contrast to the American experience where the mobilization of bias emphasizes a search for nation-building, as indicated by the perception that 'too much federalism' endangers the foundations of a country, and therefore constitutes an obstacle to the realization of the one-nation concept, Canadians developed the notion of a 'federal bargain' stressing and accepting as a *fait accompli* the conflictual relationships prevalent at the origin of a federal system.

Canadians have come to understand this diversity to be an acceptable and promotable feature of the system. A single perspective, after all, is not infallible. Although many have argued that former Premier Pierre Trudeau was intolerant of any but his own views, he recognized the value of debates and conflicts by urging Canadians to protect their differences: 'creative tension, after all, gives society its very life and growth'.[26] (Albeit Trudeau's threat to patriate the Constitution unilaterally from Britain in 1980 suggests his actions contradict his rhetoric).

Conflict regulation is obviously a key aspect in any discussion pertaining to federalism and requires special attention. Conflict left unchecked or unmanaged can threaten the political legitimacy of a regime. Events in Argentina, Brazil, Nigeria, Lebanon and Mexico demonstrate that the absence of viable conflict-management instruments can lead to revolution and chaos. So, in analysing the success of a federal system, one obvious criterion is the capacity to manage conflict, that is, to reduce the intensity and effect of conflict so as not to create 'crises' that threaten the social contract and the stability and unity of a particular society.[27] The fact that conflicts have been successfully managed in the Canadian case is a tribute to the instrumentalities established by the federal bargain of 1867, the very flexibility of the original compact, and the will of successive federal and provincial governments to make accommodations, and accept or live with compromises.

That a flexible federalism evident in centripetal and centrifugal tendencies has evolved, however, is a major departure from the intent of 1867. From a strictly legal perspective, the Canadian constitution is clearly centralist or weighted in favour of Ottawa. In fact, in the light of such unitary features as powers of 'reservation' and 'disallowance' and Ottawa's constitutional right to the disproportionate bulk of financial resources, Wheare referred to the Canadian constitution as 'quasi-federal'.[28] Furthermore, insofar as over time and in practice Canada became fully federal, for most of the nineteenth century it was highly centralized.[29]

The fathers of the Canadian Confederation learned from the American experiment. The American federal structure, as established by the constitution of 1787, evolved as a compromise between those supporting a loose collection of sovereign states and those in favour of a unitary national government. Yet, despite the significant contribution of the American model to the formation of other federal systems, the American civil war demonstrated that it was not without imperfections. Significantly, the Canadian fathers accepted the principle of the American model, that is the establishment of separate and autonomous levels of government, but radically, at first, altered the framework supporting this principle. In the opinion of some Canadian observers at the time, the American model was fundamentally flawed due to the conflict over jurisdiction and authority inherent in a system which gave too much power to the states. As Macdonald noted in 1865:

They commenced in fact, at the wrong end. They declared by their constitution that each state was a sovereignty in itself and that all powers incidental to a sovereignty belonged to each state.[30]

The division of responsibilities is largely determined by sections 91 and 92 of the British North America Act of 1867 (a legislative statute of the British Parliament, patriated in 1982). While 'grey' areas exist, these two sections identify different responsibilities for each level of government. The Constitution provided for a powerful central government, for example, it grants the centre the ability to declare its jurisdictional primacy over works and undertakings it declares to be 'for the general advantage of Canada'. The central government has access to all forms of taxation from which stems the pre-eminence of its spending power, and it is given the responsibility for securing 'peace, order, and good government'. The central government also possesses the 'residual' power, i.e. all matters not assigned to either the central or provincial governments by the Constitution fall under federal authority. Furthermore, the central government is empowered to regulate trade and commerce between provinces, and between Canada and foreign countries. As for the provinces, they have authority within their own boundaries 'to provide local services and to regulate relations among individuals and groups. Moreover, the provinces possess important land and property rights.'[31]

The British North America Act of 1867 thus provided the framework for a Canadian federal system which differed initially from the American model by theoretically strengthening the central government. John A. Macdonald remarked that:

We have given the General Legislature all the great subjects of legislation. We have conferred on them, not only specifically and in detail, all the powers which are incidental to sovereignty, but we have expressly declared that all subjects of general interest not distinctly and exclusively conferred upon the local governments, shall be conferred upon the General government.[32]

It was believed that the strengthening of the central power *vis-à-vis* the provinces would serve to avoid all conflict over jurisdiction and authority, and in the event of conflict, would guarantee that the central level of government would prevail.

In the light of this initial centralist approach, how can one explain the centrifugal state of contemporary Canadian federalism which is so far removed from the original intent of 1867?

The answer is that, during the latter part of the nineteenth century, the provinces asserted themselves at the expense of a centralized conception of Canada, and made it a more fully federal system, which has oscillated from that time onward bringing forward a greater balance between the central and the provincial governments. First, interpretations of the British North America Act of 1867 by the British Judicial Committee of the Privy Council (replaced by the Canadian Supreme Court in 1949) tended to be favourable to provincial rights. Second, the presence of strong premiers in both Quebec (Honoré Mercier) and Ontario (Oliver Mowat) gave significance to the provincial rights movement at the end of the nineteenth century. And third, the defeat of the Conservatives in 1896 at the hands of Wilfrid Laurier's Liberals, running under the banner of provincial autonomy, maintained the momentum until his party was defeated in 1911.[33]

After a period of centralization beginning with the 'Dirty Thirties' and consolidated during the Second World War, the expansion of provincial activities and the increase in federal transfers to the provinces were in part made possible because the Canadian economy experienced growth during the 1950s and 1960s. Exports were vigorous, and investment was strong in most economic sectors. In the latter part of the 1970s, Canada experienced difficulties similar to most industrialized countries: lower productivity, high inflation, declining demand for natural resources on the international market, and ageing industrial structure. Consequently, the last decade of federal-provincial relations has reflected the need to equilibrate sources of revenues with expenditures, at a time when federal transfers to the provinces decreased (in relative terms) and became more constrictive while provincial programmes were being rationalized.

Thus, in accordance with Friedrich's view, Canadian federalism is a dynamic and evolutionary process. It represents the accommodation of particular needs of various elements of the society in the light of changing socio-cultural, economic, and political factors. As a dynamic process, a federal system is susceptible to pressures which may significantly alter both its original intent and subsequent configurations. The Canadian experience with alternating periods of centrifugal and centripetal federalism illustrates this point.

## Centripetal versus centrifugal forces

A striking feature of the Canadian political system has been its remarkable versatility in striking varying balances between centripetal and centrifugal forces. Robert Adie and Paul Thomas note seven distinct phases which the Canadian political system has adopted since Confederation, each of which marks a different point on the centrifugal-centripetal plane.[34] The centrifugal-centripetal continuum may possibly be best visualized by comparing it to a see-saw. While a perfect balance is always theoretically possible, dynamic forces throw the balance in one direction or another.

The inequalities of the core–periphery relationship and the persisting French–English duality have contributed to centrifugal positions, as provincial governments deemed it necessary to move away from the centre to protect their interests. Conversely, the central government has from time to time, and especially during instances of national crisis, adopted a centralizing position which has invariably had the effect of infringing upon provincial jurisdiction. Support for centralization has emerged from the belief that decentralization, and greater authority for semi-autonomous provinces, resulting from centrifugal conceptions of federalism, should be reversed to alleviate the consequences of major crises requiring a concerted national effort.

As Premier Trudeau succinctly stated in 1980, there are two opposing views of Canadian federalism:

There is one view which holds that national Canadian politics ... ought to be what results from each province acting independently to maximize its own self interest. The other view is that there is a national interest which transcends regional interests ... That view also goes so far to say that where there is a conflict between the national interest and the provincial interests, the national interest must prevail because Canada is more than the sum of its parts.[35]

These two opposing views of Canadian federalism serve as the central point of contention and source of conflict within the realm of federal–provincial relations. The conflict is real and significant because each side firmly holds a different conception both of the meaning and purpose of Canadian federalism, and what constitutes the best means to achieve successfully various objectives.

Alan Cairns develops this distinction further. He argues that contemporary intergovernmental co-ordination is a contentious process that involves more than just two different conceptions of Canadian federalism: it also includes at least eleven different sets of governmental interests. This diversity of interests, he argues, requires: 'the containment of ineradicable tendencies to conflict between the federal vision of a society and economy and ten competing provincial visions.'[36] Cairns, in fact, disputes René Lévesque's definition of Canadian federalism as 'two scorpions in the same bottle' which stresses the French–English relationship, and prefers instead the image of 'eleven elephants in a maze'.[37]

In the light of these alternative positions, the Canadian system requires that central and provincial governments preserve and enlarge their ambits of power so as to avoid becoming irrelevant in the face of centripetal–centrifugal forces. Consequently, in the face of centrifugal influences in the late 1960s, the federal government expanded its jurisdictions into uncharted territory: urban affairs, environmental protection, consumer affairs, regional development, women, youth, etc. Likewise, in response to the huge and sophisticated federal bureaucracy that existed after the Second World War, the provinces were forced to catch up in order to deal with and counter complex federal government action. Indeed, the federal advantage gained via its large technically trained bureaucracy inherited from the war effort allowed, to a certain extent, a continuation of centripetal federalism for some time. By virtue of its technical superiority, the federal government was able to intrude, for instance, upon provincial jurisdiction to influence the development of social and welfare policies. Partly to counterbalance the ominous federal bureaucratic machine, provincial government employment increased by 40 per cent between 1965 and 1985.[38]

As a direct consequence of the centripetal–centrifugal dichotomy, Canadian federalism requires a level of consensus and collaboration that is either not generally required or encouraged in other federations. This, in itself, is no recipe for disaster. Elazar argues that the true federal process requires negotiated co-operation and consensual decision-making.[39] The importance of bargaining and collaboration cannot be ignored as it implies that neither level of government can dictate policy nor act unilaterally in many areas. Thus, efforts at accommodation, rather than being viewed as a process encouraging indecision or even paralysis, should instead be perceived as a vital means of protecting the collective welfare. In fact, it also provides both better representation of interests and a set of *checks and balances that could foster democracy* in Canada.

Much more than in most other federations, the various governments of the Canadian federation are not, within each of their respective spheres, autonomous. They have penetrated into each other's sphere of power. This has caused jurisdictional problems, but according to the Macdonald Commission, there is no need to remedy this situation, nor should there be:

We see no merit in efforts to restore the classic model of 'watertight compartments' ... Certainly, disentanglement in specific areas might reduce confusion and the costs of decision making; generally speaking, however, overlapping of authority and de facto concurrence are not only inevitable, but also desirable. Shared responsibility opens up the possibility that the federal and provincial governments might compete to respond to citizens' problems. In this competition, the need to win popular support can temper the self-interest of governments.[40]

Accountability rather than division of powers is becoming a central feature in federal–provincial negotiations. This is clearly brought out in another excerpt taken from the Macdonald Commission:

Provinces spend money which they are not responsible for having raised. The federal government transfers money to the provinces, but has little control over the manner of its spending. Citizens cannot hold the federal government accountable because they receive the services through the provincial government rather than directly. And Parliament cannot hold the federal government responsible because the federal government cannot specify how the funds have been used.[41]

A suitable working balance of centripetal and centrifugal forces is an obvious precondition to effective consensus and collaboration. It must be stressed that equality of forces is not essential for effective negotiation between governments. Rather, a suitable harmony implies that the various governments, by respecting the forces which shape Canadian federalism, can co-operate to achieve the common good. That conflict should arise in developing this working balance is inevitable, for neither level of government is likely ever to be satisfied with its respective responsibilities. Thus, each level will continuously compete in maintaining and developing its responsibilities or, more to the point, its power base. Furthermore, given the varied interests of provincial governments, one can expect competition among the provinces themselves for differential arrangements with the federal government. The Quebec case is the most celebrated. Claiming to speak for all French-Canadians, Quebec demands additional powers to protect adequately this group. In sharp contrast, the federal government

will seek solutions to the French–English problems by policies which do not weaken the central government. They will try to make the federal government, and indeed the whole country a more congenial environment for francophones rather than opt for a solution which enhances the power of the government in Quebec city.[42]

This complicates the problem of accommodation.

In his 1983 study of industrial policy in Canada, Michael Jenkin focused on the increasing importance being placed on inter-governmental relations by all governments within the federation by noting that besides the federal government, five of the largest provinces have created separate ministries to supervise intergovernmental relations.[43] Moreover, in an effort to achieve federal–provincial consensus, approximatly 1,000 federal–provincial committees currently exist to co-ordinate co-operative or accommodative ventures.[44] Despite the sharing of responsibilities and power and the resultant interdependencies, competition between governments, rather than co-operation, generally pervades. To reiterate, this is a result of the two different conceptions of Canadian federalism. Contrary to conventional thinking, the institutionalization of specific policy positions and the politicization of issues at top executive meetings does not necessarily minimize conflict. Rather, it can create and foster unavoidable conflict and competition. As Smiley contends, a federal–provincial specialist 'has a single-minded devotion to the power of his jurisdiction and because his counterparts in other governments have the same motivation conflict is inevitable'.[45]

Here lie two of the paradoxes of the Canadian federal system. The first is that Canadian federalism is supposed to accommodate diversities, yet it creates and fosters them. The second one is that while the system is expected to be negatively affected by such diversity, it has had a positive effect in the Canadian case as it does not permit this support of the people to be taken for granted. As we have seen, the virtues of competing for popular support were underlined by the Macdonald Commission.

The position expressed by the Macdonald Commission reinforces the notion of democracy as interpreted by Whitaker:

A functioning federal state must strike some stable balance between regional, provincial or subcultural identities, and an identity of citizens, *qua* citizens, with their national state. The recognition of the principle of the sovereignty of the people is a way of encouraging such attachments over more limited identities.[46]

It remains, however, that the diversity fostered by the federal system is a positive factor as it invites both the federal and provincial governments to represent citizens in a better way. Our view then is that whatever the 'costs' of federalism and intergovernmental collaboration, they are far outweighed by the benefits inherent in a collaborative consensus and accommodative arrangement.

## The dynamics of federalism

It is proper at this point to refer back to J. Bryce when arguing that the principal problem of a federation is 'to keep the centrifugal and centripetal forces in equilibrium'.[47] An appreciation of such forces is important for an understanding of developments in federal states since conflicting demands and forces are continually renewing the workings of a federation; constantly questioning existing arrangements by proposing alternatives which will better suit their goals. As a result, the maintenance of federalism requires 'instrumentalities' to ensure that new demands are met while past ones no longer require attention. Livingston has discussed this point particularly well in his influential study, 'A Note on the Nature of Federalism', where he states:

> as the nature of society changes, demands for new instrumentalities are created and these demands are met by changing or abolishing old instrumentalities and establishing new ones in their place.[48]

Thus federalism should be viewed as an adaptable 'bargain' that will be maintained only if the member states are receiving positive reinforcement. This, of course, reveals the necessity of constitutional and political adaptation to evolving historical circumstances which is essential for the maintenance of the original compromise.

It is in this context that Friedrich's interpretation of federalism proves most useful since he perceives it as a process involving persons, institutions, as well as ideas. He also notes that the initial arrangements between the member states do not eliminate the presence of the forces which resulted in the implementation of such arrangements. To strike a federal bargain does not result in the resolution, but rather the management, of political conflict; it indicates that member states were able to strike an agreement regarding particular demands of the participants at a particular historical juncture. These groups' interests, values or beliefs, however, might at some future point change, rendering the original agreement less acceptable. This explains why the stability of federal systems has been challenged at different phases in their historical development. Friedrich emphasizes the importance of this fact when commenting that:

> Federal relations are fluctuating relations in the very nature of things. Any federally organized community must therefore provide itself with instrumentalities for the recurrent revision of its pattern or design. For only thus can the shifting balance of common and disparate values, interests, and beliefs be effectively reflected in more differentiated or more integrated relations.[49]

Changes might favour centralization at some point, while favouring decentralization at another. Indeed, there is no predetermined course when it comes to political solutions. The constitutional arrangement which was reached in 1987 between Quebec and the other partners in the Canadian federation is a clear illustration of this point. Unlike Trudeau, who held a vision of a federal system with a constitutionally powerful national government in which Quebec could only expect concessions and accommodations at the *de facto* level, but not at the *de jure* level, the Meech Lake and Langevin Accords suggest that Premier Mulroney is quite prepared to accommodate Quebec at the *de jure* level by, among other things, granting that province constitutional recognition as a distinct society. It is important to note as well that the other provinces had their own reasons to support this agreement. In fact, they obtained the same basic 'privileges' that Quebec had just received.

As a political instrument, federalism is adaptable to many ends. As Hoetjes writes:

A federal constitution offers an instrument to political actors, which they can use for their own purposes. Once a federal constitution has been adopted, it becomes a vested interest for certain groups: local and regional interests derive additional protection from it, parties and movements may use the state level as a jumping-board for nationwide activities, for minorities or political losers it offers a place for refuge in times of adversity, and nationwide parties or interest groups may benefit from the federal order in a tactical sense, i.e., for 'try-outs', experiments as well as organizational divide-and-rule tactics.[50]

Alan Cairns has a similar view: 'Federal and provincial governments, federal and provincial parties, and federal and provincial pressure groups reinforce each other and they reinforce federalism'.[51] As this statement suggests, Cairns not only sees federalism as a structural arrangement, but also as a societal quality. The politics of federalism and the dynamics underlying it require an approach capable of accounting simultaneously for changes at the level of power distribution, as well as for the evolution of political ideas, social structures (governmental and societal), and vested interests.

## Conclusion

Canadian federalism should not be viewed strictly as a structural or governmental arrangement. Society is also important.

The continued federal process in Canada requires federal–provincial collaboration which effectively prevents either level of government from becoming too powerful, and fosters a working balance between the two which is satisfactory to all governments. Ultimately, however, success is contingent upon the working attitude or disposition of the various governments themselves. In short, it requires reasonable governments, making sensible demands and accommodations.

Furthermore, as Richard Simeon points out, the policy-making process in Canada must work within a framework which restricts alternatives and innovations. Effective action can only result by limiting discussion to alternatives which have a realistic chance of achieving favourable consensus from the federal government and all ten provinces.[52] This is a distinguishing feature of the Canadian polity; the absence of jurisdictional independence requires consensus through competition to succeed.

As a country, Canada has survived and even prospered under a federal system. It has been argued here both that the federal process represented the only viable means of managing the inevitable conflicts posed by the dynamics of the Canadian political economy, and that it is the flexibility of the federal process which explains and assures the continuing success of federalism in Canada. Canadian federalism should be understood as a federal bargain being continually revived as vested interests are challenged and federal arrangements modified to accommodate them. For too long Canadian political scientists have underestimated the strengths of the 'federal bargain' by assuming that institutions can actually resolve deep-seated inter-regional conflicts rather than simply manage their evolution.

## Notes

1. See C. Beckton and W. A. Mackay, *Recurring Issues in Canadian Federalism*, Toronto (1986).
2. M. Covell, 'Regionalization and economic crisis in Belgium: The variable origins of centrifugal and centripetal forces', *Canadian Journal of Political Science* (1986), XIX, 2, 261–81.
3. D. Elazar, The Ends of Federalism: Notes Towards a Theory of Federal Political Arrangements, Philadelphia (1976) 4.
4. K. C. Wheare, *Federal Government*, London (1964).
5. C. Friedrich, *Trends of Federalism in Theory and Practice*, New York (1968).
6. Quoted in L. A. Jinadu, 'A Note on the Theory of Federalism' in A. B. Akinyemi *et al.*, *Readings on Federalism*, Lagos (1979) 13–25.
7. See A. G. Gagnon and J. Garcea, 'Quebec and the pursuit of special status' in R. Olling and M. Westmacott (eds), *Perspectives on Canadian Federalism*, Scarborough (1988) 305–25.
8. *Report of the Royal Commission on the Economic Union and Development Prospects for Canada* (Macdonald Commission), vol 3, Ottawa (1985) 240.
9. D. V. Smiley, *Canada in Question: Federalism in the Eighties* (3rd edn), Toronto (1980) 252.
10. A. G. Gagnon and A. B. Tanguay (eds), *Canadian Parties in Transition: Discourse, Organization and Representation*, Toronto (1989) 220–48.
11. Smiley, op. cit., 273–4.

12. J. H. L. Durham, *The Report of the Earl of Durham*, London (1922) 8.
13. D. Monière, *Ideologies in Quebec*, Toronto (1981) 20.
14. K. McRoberts and D. Posgate, *Quebec: Social and Political Crisis* (rev edn), Toronto (1980) 32.
15. R. Cook, 'French Canada and confederation: the quest for equality' in R. S. Blair and J. T. McLeod (eds), *The Canadian Political Tradition: Basic Readings*, Toronto (1987) 81.
16. D. V. Smiley, *The Federal Condition in Canada*, Toronto (1987) 126–7.
17. Ibid., 127.
18. D. R. Cameron, 'Dualism and the concept of national unity' in J. H. Redekop (ed), *Approaches to Canadian Politics*, Scarborough (1979) 237.
19. E. Black, *Divided Loyalties: Canadian Concepts of Federalism*, Montreal (1975) 149–202.
20. Quoted in Cook, op. cit., 79.
21. A. G. Gagnon, 'A Tranquil Quebec: The end of conflictual relations?' in R. J. Jackson *et al.* (eds), *Contemporary Canadian Politics: Readings and Notes*, Scarborough (1987) 148–61.
22. The Task Force on Canadian Unity, *A Future Together: Observations and Recommendations*, Ottawa (1979) 21.
23. G. Rémillard, *Le fédéralisme canadien: le répatriement de la constitution*, Montréal (1985) 115–17.
24. Quoted in Smiley (1987) op. cit, (note 16) 193.
25. A. C. Cairns, 'Recent federalist constitutional proposals: a review essay', *Canadian Public Policy*, (1979) **5**, 354.
26 P. E. Trudeau, 'Speech to the Confederation Dinner', October 27 1982.
27. R. Gibbins, *Conflict and Unity: An Introduction to Canadian Political Life*, Toronto (1985) 2.
28. Wheare, op. cit. (note 4).20.
29. See G. Stevenson, *Unfulfilled Union*, Toronto (1982).
30. Quoted in J. M. Beck, *The Shaping of Canadian Federalism: Central Authority or Provincial Rights?*, Toronto (1971) 12.
31. Macdonald Commission Report, vol 3, 255.
32. Quoted in Beck, op. cit. (note 30) 12.
33. Smiley, (1987) op. cit.; R. A. Adie and P. G. Thomas, *Canadian Public Administration: Problematical Perspectives*, Scarborough (1982).
34. Ibid., 228–237.
35. Trudeau, loc. cit. (note 26).
36. A. C. Cairns, 'The governments and societies of Canadian federalism', *Canadian Journal of Political Science* (1977) X, **4**, 695–725.
37. A. C. Cairns, 'The other crisis of Canadian federalism' in *Canadian Public Administration* (1979), 22, **2**, 192.
38. Dominion Bureau of Statistics, *Provincial Government Employment, July–September 1965*, Ottawa (1965) 13; Statistics Canada, *Provincial and Territorial Government Employment, July–September 1986*, Ottawa (1986) 23.
39. Elazar, op. cit. (note 3) 2.
40. Macdonald Commission Report, vol 3, 256.
41. Ibid., 244.
42. Cairns, (1977) loc. cit. (note 36), 705.

43. M. Jenkin, *The Challenge of Diversity*, Ottawa (1983) 103.
44. K. Kernaghan, 'Intergovernmental administrative relations in Canada' in *Public Administration in Canada*, Toronto (1985) 154.
45. Smiley, (1980) op. cit. (note 9), 110.
46. R. Whitaker, 'Democracy and the Canadian constitution', *Occasional Papers* Inst. of Canadian Studies, Carleton University (1982) 58.
47. Bryce, *The American Commonwealth*, London (1888) 348.
48. W. S. Livingston, 'A note on the nature of federalism: federalism as a juridical concept', *Political Science Quarterly* (1952) 67, **1**, 93.
49. Friedrich, op. cit. (note 5), 7–8.
50. B. J. S. Hoetjes, 'Federal systems in the First and Third World: South Asian and comparative federalism', *Colloques internationaux du CNRS* (1978) **582**, 425.
51. Cairns, (1977) loc. cit. (note 36), 716.
52. R. Simeon, 'Studying Public Policy', *Canadian Journal of Political Science* (1976) IX, **4**, 548.

# 7 Federalism in Africa, with special reference to Nigeria

*Martin Dent*

Federalism in its broadest sense is of the utmost relevance to several political situations in Africa including that of South Africa. In situations of cleavage, whether ethnic, religious or historical, or a mixture of all three, such as exist in certain areas of the continent, federalism provides an important element for the mending of the land. In fact, however, in only one instance in Africa, that of Nigeria, has federalism so far taken root. This, I believe, is not because the system is inappropriate elsewhere but rather because its operation has been nullified by too strong a thirst for power by the ruler at the centre of the nation, or by a failure to achieve the exact balance which federalism implies.

Federalism is a somewhat elusive concept. It refers both to a constitutional dispensation and to a means of exercising power. It applies to the decentralized ordering of an existing state where various geographical parts are inhabited by people with a separate ethos and identity which they wish to preserve within a single federal nation. It applies also to the reaching of a certain stage in the search for 'unions of states' (to quote the phrase used by Murray Forsyth) where a critical level of sovereignty has been given up by hitherto independent states, which wish to form a larger governmental unit. This stage is a very difficult one to reach and so far no African state which has enjoyed independence for any appreciable length of time has been willing to give up enough sovereignty to form a federal union.[1]

As a process of government, federalism is essentially a form of power sharing, though it is not the only form that power sharing can take. Furthermore, one can have federal elements in the running of a state even where the constitution is not fully federal. For its efficient operation, however, a federally organized state requires an exact balance. It cannot exist if the dispersal of power is so great as to constitute no more than a confederal union and the dangers that attend such a dispersal were clearly shown in the United States from Independence to the time

169

of the implementation of the Constitution. Furthermore, there is an important difference between an 'outward leaning' federation that tends towards confederalism, like that of Nigeria under the First Republic from 1960 to 1966, and an 'inward lending' federation, like that of Nigeria after the civil war. It is one of the contentions of this paper that only the latter will suffice in the nation-building context of the Third World.

The danger of dissolving into a confederal union on one side of the narrow federal balance is mirrored by the opposite danger of falling into over-centralization, by moving from a federal state to a unitary one through the unilateral action of the ruler at the centre. In such cases, severe discontent will ensue, which will result in armed resistance, as in Eritrea, or in a subdued discontent with excess centralization, as in the anglophone area formerly known as West Cameroon.

We need to chart our course with care. If we define a federal state solely in the lawyers' terminology of a system where a sovereign constitution distributes power between centre and 'states' or 'regions' or 'provinces', with both being, in Wheare's phrase, 'co-ordinate and in no way subordinate one to another', we shall have difficulty in finding any examples to study in Africa. Nigeria is the only approximation and in that case it soon became apparent that the preservation of Nigeria's existence as a state required the federal government to adopt not a co-ordinate but a leading role.

## The federal experience in Africa as a whole

The Nigerian example is of enormous importance and we shall perforce spend a good deal of time analysing its major lessons. There have, however, been a number of other attempts at creating federal systems in Africa, which have failed to last. Often their failure has had dire consequences for the people concerned, for in some situations federalism can be a matter of life and death. Eritrea opted, by the vote of its Parliament, to join Ethiopia in 1952 with the promise of federal status. Ten years later that status was unilaterally replaced by unitary government by the Emperor and in consequence Eritrea rapidly moved to a situation of armed resistance which still continues today in the longest and one of the bloodiest civil wars in Africa.[2] Southern Sudan broke into revolt within a year of Sudanese independence and that civil war continued for fifteen years until the remarkable peacemaking success at Addis Ababa in February 1972 created the substance of federal devolution for the South, although Sudan was not formally made into a federal state.[3] The result was a return of peace to the war ravaged South, and that peace lasted until President Numeiri, in his last despotic

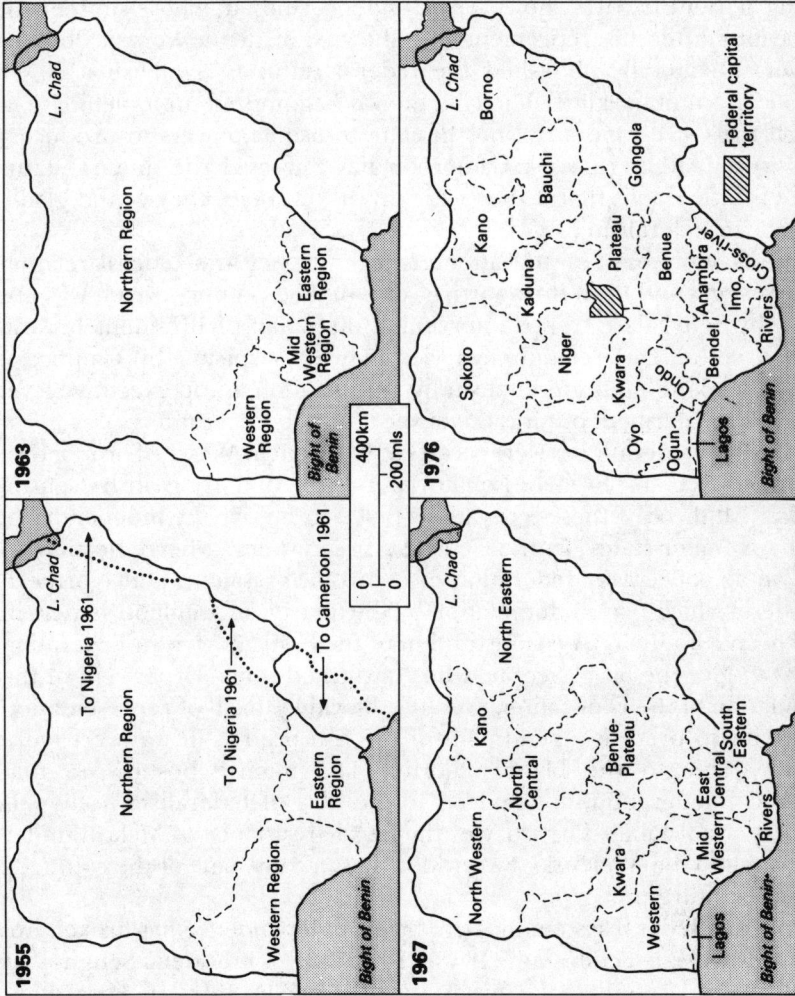

Nigeria, showing the changing boundaries of regions and states since 1955. In 1987 Kaduna state was divided into Katsina and Kaduna, and Cross-River state into Aikwa Ibom and Cross-River.

days of power, destroyed the autonomy he had himself created and civil war began again.

In the Cameroons, the reunification of West and East was achieved by a plebiscite in Western Cameroon in 1961 which at that time was under British mandate rule administered as part of Nigeria. The union was a federal one and federal status was promised by the United Nations for a long period. In 1972, however, President Ahidjou, whose subsequent behaviour after his retirement has shown him to be very jealous of power, unilaterally abolished the federal status to establish a closer union of a unitary kind. The change was 'legitimized' in a plebiscite in which the Government did not hesitate to use its powers to produce a 'Yes' vote. Although West Cameroon has tolerated the unitary status there is little doubt that if they were given the choice they would gladly go back to federalism.

The Gambia has resisted attempts to involve it in a federal relation with Senegal and until the abortive coup in The Gambia, which was put down by Senegalese troops intervening on behalf of President Jawara, even a confederal relation was viewed with suspicion by Gambians. Recently a kind of confederalism by participation at top executive level has been established, but it is as yet short of a federal union.

Abortive federations were created in French West Africa before independence, in French Equatorial Africa, and in British Central Africa. All three of these federations failed to survive the independence of the member states. In the Central African states, a fierce hostility to the whole concept of federation grew up in Nyasaland and Northern Rhodesia which feared domination by the quarter of a million settlers in Southern Rhodesia. The Constitution of the Central African Federation failed to give the black people, who constituted some 97 per cent of the population of the Federation, even the 'blocking third' of representation necessary to prevent amendment of the constitution in ways yet more unfavourable to the black majority. The intense hostility to that particular federation, and indeed to the idea of federalism itself, was entirely predictable. The story of the heroic resistance of Malaŵi under Dr Banda to the 'Welensky Federation' has become part of the country's political culture.

Only one federal system in Africa since independence has broken up, that of the Mali Federation. It was founded by President Senghor of Senegal, who resented the break up of the West African Federation before independence, and by Modibo Keita, President of Soudan (French Sudan), and took the name of the Mali Federation after the great African empire on the Niger bend. But the marriage was of incompatible partners since the Soudan was more radical, more numerous and less sophisticated than Senegal. Modibo Keita, responsive to the ever present African desire for more power, proposed an

Executive Presidency in place of the division of power between himself as Prime Minister and Senghor as President. He also proposed a union of parties. Senghor and the Senegalese took fright, arrested the Soudanese delegates and sent them back across the border. Senghor then appealed to his Senegalese compatriots in the resonant language that De Gaulle had once used over the French Army revolt in Algeria, 'Sénégalaises, Sénégalais, aidez moi, la patrie est en danger' (Women and men of Senegal help me, the fatherland is in danger). The fatherland to which he referred was not the Mali Federation, from which he promptly seceded, but Senegal. Federations need time to become secure.

The only remaining federation in Africa other than Nigeria is that of Tanzania but since the federal relation refers only to about 5 per cent of the Tanzanian population living in Zanzibar and Pemba, it has hardly affected the government of the country as a whole. For a long time President Nyerere treated Zanzibar with great caution, allowing a level of devolution much greater than that normal in federal systems of government. The Zanzibar government retained its own armed forces, and required mainland Tanzanians to ask for special permission before visiting the island. The reign of terror practised under Karume immediately after the Zanzibar revolution of 1964 contrasted strongly with the rule of law in mainland Tanzania and Nyerere underwent the humiliation of returning a wanted person to Zanzibar for trial for treason, only to see him shot out of hand in Zanzibar. Recently however under Jumbe, and later Mwinyi, Zanzibar has moved much nearer to the ordered pattern of government of the mainland and with the choice of Mwinyi as President of Tanzania in succession to Nyerere, the Union has become a close one. None the less, in the last ten years there has been a fairly strong sense of Zanzibarian separatism, based on the slogan of 'Give us back our Islands' and a demand for the use of all the foreign exchange released through sale of Zanzibar's cloves. Zanzibar's political leaders have had to balance loyalty to Tanzania with support for the sense of separate identity, and it was the failure of Jumbe to achieve this that led to his downfall. Zanzibar enjoys a considerable over-representation in population terms in the Tanzanian Parliament and President Mwinyi himself is a Zanzibarian.

The three East African states of Kenya, Uganda, and Tanganyika enjoyed a number of 'common services' under colonial rule. At times colonial governors of Kenya sought to extend this pragmatic co-operation into a 'closer union' of a political kind, but Tanganyika and Uganda, enthused by the 'Spirit of Addis Ababa' after the first OAU conference of 1963, declared that they would establish a full federation within six months. Unfortunately the pressures of internal troubles and the power jealousy of the three Heads of State quickly put an end to the move towards federalism and in due course relations between the three countries became embittered and the common services have gradually ceased to operate. The lesson is clear. Federal unions are hard to create since they require Heads of African states, who are jealous of power, to assume a more subordinate position, but without some form of federal union it is hard to create lasting structures of interstate co-operation. One is, as it were, putting only half a dam into the turbulent streams of interstate politics, and it is soon washed away in political rivalries.

### Features peculiar to the African situation

Before we turn to analyse the Nigeria example, we must look at federalism in broader historical perspective in Africa. A federal state implies giving political recognition of the geographically organized parts of a polity in contrast to the total unitary domination of the power at the centre, through its agents, both political and administrative. It requires a certain legal ordering of society to divide powers upon a geographical basis according to the subject matter concerned. Such a legal ordering on a territorial base did not occur in pre-colonial African society any more than it did in mediaeval or monarchical Europe. In Africa, power centres existed around kinship groups or around kingships and sometimes the political units became quite large. The relation of other authorities in the area to the ruler of the system was however one of subordination. Sometimes that subordination was total where the local ruler was a tool and loyal servant of the central ruler, as in Benin in Nigeria where every citizen was known as an 'Oba's man'. Sometimes the subordination was a more indirect one, typified in relations of feudal allegiance (as in the Hausa relation of '*Chapa*' of a local ruler to a bigger Emir or to Sarkin Musulmi, the ruler of the Sokoto Caliphate). Sometimes the relationship was a loose one symbolized by the rendering of annual tribute, or occasionally by some important ceremonial object.

The main emphasis of the politics of most independent African states in the period immediately after independence has been the establishment of a polarity of power at the centre in order to 'build the nation'. Unless the central authority is emphasized there is a fear that it may be insufficient to hold the nation together. Power is reified and the central power tends to assert (in Humpty Dumpty's words) that 'There is just one question, who is master?' It is for this reason that the word 'federalism' got a bad press from radical leaders such as Nkrumah. It has been seen by most radical African political leaders as something reactionary and even colonial. The action of Tshombe (who was a federalist) in trying to secede from the new state of the Congo, in alliance with 'neo-colonial forces' of big business and former Algerian settlers and other white soldiers of fortune, only tended to reinforce this attitude.

In many instances the unitarist assertion of central power has been successful, particularly if the state is not too large. But almost always this unitary authority has had to rely on quasi-federal elements in the form of recognition of the identity of different geographical, ethnic, or historical, units in the polity and the maintenance of an ethnic or geographical balance in the central cabinet. Not only must the benefits of office be provided for the ethnic power holder at the centre, but it is assumed that he will take morsels from the common national pot, not just for himself and his immediate family, but for his whole ethnic group and perhaps for neighbouring tribes as well in the same area. The local political leader fulfils a role of 'broker' between the central government and the local community.

In the field of administration, also, there often comes a time when the central power feels secure enough to encourage decentralization. Kenya, Zambia, and Tanzania, for instance, have placed great emphasis on this to remedy the excess concentration upon the capital, which had drained resources and political interest away from the provinces. This deconcentration often uses as its lynch pin the centrally appointed omnicompetent official at regional or district level to whom power is delegated from the centre. It is not clear whether he will identify with interests of the centre, or (as so many colonial district officers did on a rural posting) with the people of his district. This is less than full federalism but at least it is a genuflection towards autonomy.

Sometimes, however, these devices are not enough. The central power comes up against a separate historical, ethnic, or religious identity, (or an amalgam of all three), which has enjoyed some separate status under colonial rule and which obstinately refuses to come under purely unitary control. In such situations the alternatives are autonomy of a federal or quasi-federal kind, or civil war. Federalism is not of itself a guarantee against civil war, as the experience of Nigeria and of the United States showed. In both cases 'outward leaning' federal ideas and doctrines of 'states' rights' prepared the way for secession and a civil war of reunification. But without federal or genuine autonomy there is no chance whatever of creating a stable unity in states with great cleavage, as the experience of Sudan and of Ethiopia has shown.

## The premise of inequality

It is reasonably straightforward to apply a federal structure of government to groups who occupy different areas and only overlap on the boundaries or in a few towns. In the South African case and in a few other African cases however the ethnic groups are only partly separated geographically, and often by relatively short distances in fairly small areas of residence of each race. This makes classic federalism difficult to apply. Furthermore, the relation is complicated by the unfortunate psychological 'premise of inequality', or the sense of inherent superiority to others that several African ethnic groups possess as a result of their long tenure of dominant power. The phrase 'premise of inequality' was first used to describe the relationship of dependence and inequality existing between the cattle-owning Tutsi and the Hutu peasant cultivators in Rwanda and Burundi. Just before independence, the Tutsi dominance was overthrown in Rwanda by the Hutu with some help from the Belgian administration and from the Catholic Church. When the Tutsi exiles attempted to return and overthrow the Hutu dominance they were defeated and massacred and most but not all Tutsi were expelled from Rwanda. In Burundi an opposite outcome occurred. The Tutsi made a pre-emptive strike against the Hutu, in the form of a virtual genocide of the elite, and only when they were firmly established in control did they allow Hutu to participate in a subordinate way in the political system.

In Zanzibar the Arab elite was decimated in the Revolution of 1964 but appears to have come back to some positions of influence under the rule of the Afro-Shirazi party (now merged in the all Tanzanian CCM) in Tanzania. In Liberia the 'Americo-Liberian' settler elite held a monopoly of power and position in the country for 140 years, although they only comprised under 10 per cent of the population. Their attitudes were in many ways akin to those of white settlers in Africa, except that they were not exacerbated by racial prejudice based on skin colour. Furthermore, the separation of Americo-Liberian and hinterland peoples was to some extent overcome through the 'unification' policy of President Tubman, himself an Americo-Liberian of aristocratic origin but a man of great charisma and political appeal throughout Liberia. His successor President Tolbert was overthrown and murdered in an army coup headed by NCOs from the hinterland tribes under the leadership of Sergeant Doe in 1980. This coup put an end to the predominance of the Americo-Liberians as a group, and the very use of the word has been forbidden. It is interesting, however, to observe that Americo-Liberian notables, who escaped execution during the coup, quickly came back into senior government positions and into Liberian politics both as supporters of Doe and as his opponents, for their skills are much valued and African society is inclusive enough to overcome many instances of cleavage. Furthermore, there is a strong sense in Africa that 'once a big man always a big man' and this aids the incorporation of fallen groups after dramatic political changes.

In Sierra Leone the contrast between the Creole minority of settler origin and the majority, who are of hinterland origin was not so sharp as in Liberia. Furthermore, the existence of British colonial rule with its presuppositions of equality before the law and democratic one person one vote elections to choose the leadership produced a much smoother change in power relations. At one time the Creoles held almost a monopoly of top governmental and professional positions but that dominance has now ceased. Nonetheless, the Creole heritage and professional skill has enabled them to retain a more than disproportionate share of professional and government jobs, even though they are a minority in the echelons of political power. The intense cultural ethos of Freetown as the 'Athens of Africa' has spread its influence throughout Sierra Leone, and on the whole the Sierra Leonian experience of the Creole 'settler' elite is an encouraging one for other dominant groups in a situation where they have lost their political dominance.

In Nigeria presuppositions of inequality existed in some relations between ethnic groups. The Ibo and the northerners for instance, each regarded the other, at one time, as inferior, the Ibos were looked down upon by northerners because they had not traditionally lived in large political units with prestigious Muslim chiefs, while the Ibos disregarded the northerners because they did not have so much modernization and Western education as they did.[4] Post civil war these presuppositions of inequality have largely disappeared.

## The Nigeria–federal experience: the background

Let us look more closely at the Nigerian case history of federalism, which is unique in Africa, and one of the most significant in the developing world. It is necessary both to recount the main factual outline of Nigeria's federal development, and also to draw out a number of lessons which have hitherto been ignored or too little emphasized, for they are of profound importance for studies of federalism in general and of plans for a possible federal system in post-apartheid South Africa.

The main theme of Nigerian federal development is that of the faltering steps by which the country came to adopt a federal system of government, its reversion to institutions which were contrary to the federal model, and finally the emergence of a Nigerian nation in a strengthened federal form. The first errors sprang from the British colonial heritage. It was characteristic of most British colonial policy making, that it failed to have any long term plans, but rather extemporized and reacted to nationalist or regional pressures. For a long time in its history British government in Nigeria failed to come to terms with the obvious fact that the geographical area of Britain's Nigerian colony would become a nation, the largest in Africa, and that it was incumbent upon Nigeria's British rulers during the colonial period to foster the unity of that emergent nation.[5]

From 1900 to 1914 Northern and Southern Nigeria were treated as entirely separate, although British thought had already recognized the existence of a geographical entity which was called Nigeria, the name being coined by Flora Shaw, later Lady Lugard. In 1914 North and South were 'amalgamated' under the governorship of Lord Lugard and the regional governors were demoted to the status of lieutenant-governor. The amalgamation, however, did nothing to unite the peoples of Nigeria and successive governors of Nigeria in Lagos had the utmost difficulty in persuading the lieutenant-governors of the North to follow their policy.[6] The Northern Region comprised roughly 56 per cent of the population and roughly three-quarters of the area of Nigeria. It was, in fact, more populous than any nation in Africa except Nigeria itself. No wonder that when Nigeria became independent the Sardauna, the Premier of the North, assumed a power most dangerous to Nigerian unity.

In 1939 the South was divided into two regions, so that at independence in 1960 the new federal state of Nigeria was made up of three mighty regions each with a political centre of gravity in its major ethnic/historical group – the Hausa Fulani and their Kanuri allies in the North, the Yoruba in the West and the Ibo (or Igbo as they are sometimes called) in the East. Each of these majority groups comprised some two-thirds of the population of their region while the remainder consisted of a number of different 'minority tribes'. In the North, the Tiv, Idoma, Igbira, Igala and Jukun peoples, together with those of Plateau, Adamawa and Southern Zaria, and a number of Yoruba peoples in Ilorin, all differed from the ethos of the Hausa Fulani empire created by Shehu dan Fodio, in the Jihad of 1804. They all felt more or less restive within the region as soon as political awareness arose in the 1950s. Some identified with regional power and patronage, while some campaigned actively for a Middle Belt Region of Non-Muslim Non-Hausa Fulani peoples in the North.

Despite the internal tensions in the region, the Northern ethos was an attractive one to most of its inhabitants. The empathy between British administrators and Northern Nigerians was considerable and character-ized by mutual respect. All administrators were able to speak Hausa, the *lingua franca* of the region, and had a considerable pride in the North and its rather conservative ethos of indirect rule, which nonetheless allowed for considerable development by native authorities in partner-ship with district officers. At independence Sir Abubakar Tafawa Balewa, the Federal Prime Minister, spoke of the changing relationship between British and Nigerians as being one 'always as friends'. He was drawing on his Northern experience. The sense of Northernness extended even to Middle Belt people who were neither Hausa nor Muslim, and lasted long after the North had been broken up into six states in 1967 by Yakubu Gowon.

It is, however, a sad fact of history that many of the worst quarrels are not between good and bad but between two different sorts of good. The creation of the Northern ethos was a thing of value but the North as a governmental unit had to be abolished and replaced by a larger number of 'constituent' regions or states, if Nigerian federal unity was to survive. The imbalance of size and power was too great.[7]

It would have been very easy for the British colonial power to have broken up the regions into a larger number of smaller states at any time in the 1930s or 1940s, when Nigerian loyalties were local and British authority was dominant. Later, as the tree of political opinion began to grow and to harden it was no longer possible to train it in any direction which the colonial power wished. To change the metaphor, by 1950 the cement had begun to harden and the regional blocks were much more difficult to break, for vested interests both of British regional governors and of Nigerian regional premiers and ruling parties were hard to overcome. The British colonial administration had its last chance to break up the overmighty regions in the Willink Commission which investigated the fears of the minorities in 1957–8, but Lennox Boyd, the Colonial Secretary, deliberately tilted the balance against the creation of new states by saying that this would involve putting off independence for two more years, which nobody wanted to do. The ultimate secession of the Eastern Region in 1967 and the civil war in Nigeria is directly traceable to this colonial error.

The non-Yoruba peoples of the Western Region, the Edo, Itsekiri, Urbobo, Mid-West Ibo, Ishan, Ijaw and other peoples of the Mid-West were likewise attracted to the regional government by ties of power and patronage, but when the opportunity came voted overwhelmingly for the creation of their own Mid-West state three years after independence. In the Eastern Region the non-Ibo peoples, the Ibibio, Calabar, Ijaw, Rivers and Ogoja people looked to the regional capital Enugu for patronage as long as political power was exercized from that regional capital; but when two states were created for the minority peoples of the East in 1967 by Gowon they, for the most part, welcomed this dispensation and identified with the federal side in the civil war.

Thus in the Nigerian case, as in that of India, but in contrast to the federal instances of USA, Canada, Australia, Austria or Switzerland in the developed world, there has been a great and continual pressure for the creation of new federal units. To every minority the prospect of the creation of its own states is both a chance for patronage and government position and also a spiritual enhancement. This was illustrated for me by a Tiv man who approached me in 1966 when I was on a visit to Lagos and asked me whether I thought that the Tiv 'dream' would now be fulfilled. When I asked what dream, he replied 'Our state, of course'.

The irony of Nigeria's successive breakup of regions into states, and of states into more and more states, is that after profound political labour and a destructive civil war, Nigeria now has 21 states which do not differ very markedly from the 22 provinces or sub-units that existed under the regional governors during British rule. How much easier and wiser it would have been if the British colonial government had made Nigeria independent as a federation based on the provincial units, which enjoyed considerable prestige as centres of identity.[8]

## Constitution-making prior to independence

Prior to 1946 the Northern Region had no representation in the Nigerian legislative council. Nigeria was, in theory, more or less unitary for the governor in Lagos had formal authority over all Nigeria, but in practice the degree of suspicion between regional governments was considerable. When the British colonial administration at last woke up after the Second World War and began to decolonize, it produced a series of constitutions which ignored the obvious balances of federalism and were therefore unworkable. The first Richards Constitution failed to provide for a proper federal legislature since its members were to be co-opted from local native authorities or elected by the regional legislative councils. At the same time all regional legislation required approval by the governor of Nigeria and the centre could legislate on any regional matter if it wished. The regional legislature was purely advisory. The Richards Constitution was replaced by the Macpherson Constitution of 1951 which gave more power to the regions, but still failed to provide a proper federal legislature or cabinet since their members were chosen by the regional legislatures. The obvious lack of cohesion resulting from such a system was shown in the 1953 cabinet crisis over the resolution for 'self-government in 1956' sponsored by the Southern members of cabinet and rejected by the Northern members who wished for 'self-government as soon as practicable'. The North which was outnumbered by about ten to one in educational qualifications at every level by the South, was naturally afraid of any close union in which it might lose control over its own administration to better educated southerners. The North's mistrust of strong federal power was at bottom a fear of losing jobs, contracts, government patronage and religious or other identity at a local level.

After the 'self-government in 1956' debate the Northern ministers were booed in Lagos and at every railway station by Southerners as they returned home. Sardauna concluded that 'Lagos is not a place for respectable people' and he and his senior ministers met together in injured silence (for Northerners at that time were 'slow burners', slow to react in words but implacable once aroused). A campaign team of the Action Group, the party of the Western Region, led by Samuel Akintola, at that time a lieutenant of Awolowo, came to Kano and was deliberately waylaid by thugs organized by local leaders of the Northern Peoples Congress (NPC), the ruling party in the North. The resultant riots and two-day war between the traditional city of Kano where the Muslim Northerners lived and the New Town (Sabon Gari) where Southerners or Christians lived caused at least thirty-five deaths, and made it clear that many in the North would react violently if they felt themselves likely to be hustled or despised by Southerners in power in Lagos. This was what happened later in the terrible riots of 1966 under the military government of General Ironsi, when innocent Ibo people living in the North were set upon, beaten up, killed or driven out of the North.

The constitutional response of the Northern Regional Government to the events of 1953 was to produce the 'eight points plan' asking for the Nigerian federal government to be replaced by a mere Common Services Organisation on the model of that in East Africa between Kenya, Uganda and Tanganyika. This perverse plan was first suggested by the British officer serving as second-in-command in the political office in Kaduna.[9] It sought to set up a confederal authority for Nigeria divested of all direct contact with the people and all access to nation building power. Had this model been implemented it would soon have resulted in the breakup of Nigeria.

This was in fact the goal of Sir Brian Sharwod-Smith, the governor of the Northern Region. In 1956, at a constitutional conference, he actually minuted to Lennox Boyd, the Colonial Secretary, suggesting independence for the North, to create a country like Jordan – Muslim and friendly.[10] This was surely a grave betrayal of Britain's colonial trust.

By the settlement of 1957, arising from the London conference, Nigeria at last achieved a proper federal cabinet responsible to a federal prime minister and Abubakar Tafawa Balewa assumed that role. It was fortunate that his relations with K. O. Mbadiwe, the senior NCNC (National Council of Nigeria and Cameroons) Minister at the federal level, were good and that although the NCNC ministers outnumbered the NPC by two to one, Mbadiwe recognized the position of Abubakar as the choice of the NPC and the largest party in the federal legislature and agreed to serve under him. The personal friendship between the two men helped to make the federal cabinet coalition work smoothly.

## Independence and the First Republic

Nigeria became independent in 1960 with a federal constitution which gave sufficient formal powers to the federal government to create an inward leaning federation with a federal government as strong as that of India under Nehru. Unfortunately, the political forces were such as to create an outward leaning federation, tending in practice toward confederalism. The federal government had no ability to foster a sense of national unity and could only, with increasing difficulty, mediate between the hostile claims of the regions.

Abubakar himself lacked the necessary power. He was reasonably successful in leading his coalition cabinet of NPC and NCNC but within his own party he was only the deputy leader whereas the Sardauna, the Northern Regional Premier, was the President of the party. Furthermore, membership of the party was limited to those of Northern origin. This was the total denial of all federalism, and it is significant that the framers of the 1979 Nigerian Constitution, having learned the lesson of the NPC, provided in Section 202(b) that no party could participate or be licensed by the Federal Electoral Commission unless 'its membership is open to all Nigerians, irrespective of place of origin, sex, religion or ethnic grouping'.

Abubakar's position was further weakened by the fact that he was a Prime Minister and not an Executive President. He was dependent on the serried ranks of Northerners in the Federal Parliament to remain in power from day to day. Sardauna referred to him as 'his lieutenant' and although on several important decisions, such as the appointment of Aguiyi Ironsi, an Ibo, to succeed Major-General Sir Christopher Welby-Everard as General Officer Commander of the Nigerian army in 1965, he acted in defiance of Sardauna's wishes, he suffered from undue pressures from Kaduna. There never actually was a plot among federal NPC members to remove Abubakar, but if he had quarrelled openly with Sardauna such a political plot would have been a possibility. The leader of Nigeria must not only be independent of regional pressure groups, he must also appear to be independent.

In Nigeria, as in the United States of America, pre-civil war federalism was based on an assumption that the federal tie was literally federalism depending on a 'foedus' or treaty made between equal authorities. If any region considered itself to be cheated or disadvantaged in that treaty relationship it implicitly assumed that it could withdraw from the relationship and secede. The poison of secessionism, first introduced in the thought of the North, spread to the utterances of leaders of both the other regions at times of crisis, though no secessionist action was taken. Sardauna openly regarded Lagos as an 'outpost' to which he sent his lieutenant, the Prime Minister, to look after Northern interests.[11]

A further weakness of Nigerian federalism in the First Republic (1960–6) was the fear of the South that it was being dominated by the political power of the North not only because of its tradition of 'sarauta' or assumed right to rule, but also because its share of the population (more than 50 per cent) gave it a majority in the Lower House of Parliament on which executive power depended. In federal systems the Upper House provides a way of checking this kind of threat by giving equal representation to states of unequal population size. In the Nigerian case under the First Republic, the South, with its two, and later, after the creation of the Mid-West, three regions, enjoyed a majority in the Senate, but unfortunately the Senate's powers were based on those of the British House of Lords. Only in the Second Republic (1979–83) was the model of the powerful United States Senate adopted for Nigeria.

The federal government assumed emergency powers in the Western Region in 1963 when the Action Group split between Chief Awolowo, the leader of opposition at the federal level and party leader, and Samuel Akintola the Regional Premier. The split resulted in fighting in Parliament deliberately provoked by the Akintola faction and this induced Abubakar to declare an emergency in the Western Region, to suspend the regional legislature and executive and send down his doctor, Dr Majekadummi, as the administrator. At the end of the period of emergency the federal government ignored Majekadummi's advice to hold a regional election and instead reinstalled Akintola who quickly obtained a majority in the Regional House for his new party, the NNDP (Nigerian National Democratic Party). He became more or less a client of the Northern government and this tendency of members to shift their allegiance according to where the power was seen to be, made the East feel increasingly restive that it too might one day become a client of the Northern power group.

The power of the centre to take over regions or states in an emergency which had some sanction in the wording of the Constitution of 1960, was not written into the Constitution of the Second Republic and President Shagari never made any attempt to use such a power. The right of a federal executive to take over a state government totally for a period on the decision of its own federal parliament exists elsewhere, being frequently used as 'Presidential Rule' in India. It does not, however, exist in this total form in any of the federations in the developed world. It is not clear whether or not Nigeria will need such a power for use in emergencies in the future.

The government limped from crisis to crisis, with Abubakar forced to act more as a conciliator than as a leader. Its impotence was shown in the general strike, and its inability to reach a commonly agreed basis in population statistics for the federal balance of power in Parliament was shown in the census crisis. In the universities and in the parastatals there was a fierce tribal and ethnic competition for top positions which were assumed to depend on political patronage. Finally, the federal government, which had prime responsibility for the electoral process through the Federal Electoral Commission, failed to conduct a fair federal election in 1964 while the subsequent Western Regional election of 1965 was even more blatantly rigged and led to large scale violence.

## The crisis of 1966

On the night of 14 January 1966 a group of seven army officers, all but one of whom were Ibo, co-opted a number of junior officers and private soldiers and led them out to seize power in the coup. In the course of the coup two out of six Yoruba senior officers were murdered, four out of five Northerners, (the fifth, Gowon, escaped by good luck), and one out of about ten Eastern and Mid-Western officers. Among civilians, deaths were equally one-sided. Abubakar, and Okotie-Ebo (from the Mid-West) were murdered in Lagos, Sardauna in Kaduna and Akintola in Ibadan. There was no violent coup and no deaths in Enugu and Benin and the Premiers of the East and Mid West, who were both Ibo, were unscathed. This one-sidedness may have been partly due to operational considerations, since any group from one tribe tends to trust its fellow tribesmen and not to regard them as potential enemies, but its effects were catastrophic in their effect on the trust of Northerners. General Ironsi escaped the coup makers in Lagos, put himself at the head of the loyal Northern NCOs who had rallied with Northern officers to put down the coup, and was in due course handed power by the rump of the federal cabinet in order to restore order. The present vigorous debate between publications by surviving coup makers and those of senior Northern officers, civil servants and others makes it clear that there is likely to remain a considerable element of doubt as to the exact course of events. For our analysis of federalism, however, it is enough to observe that the whole Nigerian political system received a profound shock, causing initial fear in some and rejoicing in others. Reactions to events differed profoundly between East and North. The distrust arising among Northerners and some Westerners from these events and from the failure of Ironsi, himself a Ibo, to try the Ibo conspirators who had murdered fellow officers and political leaders, made it far more difficult for him to reform the federal system.[12]

The Federal Military Government under General Ironsi as 'Supreme Commander' moved from the outward leaning federalism of the First Republic to an extreme centralization of power by way of Decree Number One, which gave the Federal Military Government power to legislate by decree anywhere at any time and on any issue at its discretion. Decree Number One contained implicitly the doctrine of unitary government, which was strongly supported by radicals and by most Ibos who stood to gain from an open job market in government service throughout Nigeria. The assumption of the military government was that they were a 'Corrective Regime',[13] whose job it was to use authoritarian means and suspend normal, democratic processes in order to correct certain specific faults in the Nigerian political system, one of which was excess regionalism and lack of national unity. Military governors were appointed to each of the four regions, and ruled with the help of the civil service. In each state the governor was an indigene, but as subordinate military officers they were intended to be 'men under authority obedient to their superior officer in Lagos'. Federalism had in effect been suspended.

In order to fulfil its task of creating greater unity in Nigeria the military government needed a common purpose and a climate of trust among Nigerians and this existed neither among the people as a whole nor in the army, where the bulk of the combatant soldiers among NCOs and other ranks were Northerners from the Middle Belt. Their sense of justice was outraged by the January events. The initial impetus of the military regime was soon dissipated and the Federal Supreme Military Council did not actually use its powers under Decree Number One to legislate for the regions. Of the many Committees of Enquiry set up by the military government to make recommendations for various aspects of the government of the Nigeria of the future, only the Commission on the future of the public services under Francis Nwokedi, an Ibo and a former Permanent Secretary of the Ministry of External Affairs, made real progress.

At regional and local level government continued much as before. All elected personnel of party political provenance were dismissed but the civil service continued to operate. In the North considerable reform took place under the dynamic guidance of Colonel Hassan Katsina, the Governor, Ali Akilu, and Liman Ciroma, the Heads of the civil Service. The Native Courts and the Native Authority police were removed from the supervision of the Native Authorities and placed under the regional judiciary and the Nigerian police; the prisons were also removed from Native Authority control and put under the federal prisons department.

In the West, Governor Fajuyi pushed ahead with the building of the University of Ife, while in the Mid-West in 1968 Governor Ogbemudia pushed ahead on his own initiative with plans to start the University of Benin. This regional activity was not something ordered from Lagos, but rather a kind of *resonance* – an energetic regional response to an ethos of activity set up by events at the federal level. This relation has been typical of much regional development in Nigeria.

Ironsi sat uneasily on his position of power caught between the revolution and the counter-revolution. Every issue came to be interpreted in regional and tribal terms of a struggle for power. The Ironsi regime came to be interpreted somewhat inaccurately as an 'Ibo power' which Northerners wished to 'topple'.[14]

The occasion of overt conflict came over the debate about federalism. An open debate on the question of whether Nigeria should remain federal or become unitary was allowed and even encouraged by the government, but half way through the process the issue was foreclosed unilaterally by the federal government in the Unification Decree Number 34 of 24 May 1966. This was based on the secret interim report of Francis Nwokedi submitted to Ironsi personally for his immediate action, without the knowledge of the other members of Nwokedi's commission.[15]

This was a classic case of the mixture of administrative and political considerations. Nwokedi presented the case for unification of all the regional and federal civil services above the rank of executive officer. In this way he hoped to bring the 'tonic of competition' to enable the civil service to exercise a role as the leaders of a unified Nigerian nation. He criticized the existing Federal Public Service Commission (PSC) headed by a Northerner, Alhaji Sule Katagum, and recommended the creation of a new one to be headed by a retired professor, judge or permanent secretary over the age of 50. Clearly, he was providing a job specification for a post which he could well fill himself. Furthermore, the civil service was to be reorganized under twelve 'super permanent secretaries'. Appointments to these posts were to be made on the recommendation of an 'administrative officer' with a temporary mandate and with the same qualifications as for the chairman of the PSC. This position would be one of supreme patronage in the federal civil service. It may well be that Nwokedi did not have tribal considerations in view in his recommendations, but they were interpreted in that light as soon as his secret report was leaked to influential Northerners and others.

The Unification Decree was launched in the worst possible circumstances, at a time of mutual distrust among the military, and in a highly secret manner in the Federal Military Council. To the Northerners it was a threat not only to their ethos and way of life at the local level, but also to their jobs in the regional civil service and to the patronage over contracts, scholarships, licences and other benefits which that service controlled. Under pressure from Northerners the Supreme Military Council delayed the full application of the decree to apply at first only to superscale posts but it was clear that this was only a first instalment. The title of 'Region' was now replaced by 'Groups of Provinces' to indicate that federalism had in principle been replaced by unitary government.

Had this decree been made in January, immediately after the coup, Ironsi might conceivably have got away with it because of the general fear then ruling among most Nigerians, but by May the North had recovered its confidence and was ready for a counter stroke. The students of Ahmadu Bello University in Zaria in the North were given permission to go out on a demonstration. They paraded with banners marked 'Down with military government' and 'A raba' – let us part. Thus did overcentralization provoke a demand for secession. The student demonstration was followed by a deliberate attack by Northern hooligans on Ibos living innocently in the North and several hundred were killed. Since the army and the police in the North consisted overwhelmingly of Northerners who had some sympathy with the motives for the riot, the Federal Military Government which had previously proclaimed the most severe penalties for infringement of the law was unable to punish any of the rioters. It contented itself with appointing a Commission of Enquiry.[16]

Ironsi had been advised to win the hearts of the Middle Belt soldiery by creating a Middle Belt state; but he refused to listen.[17] He preferred to rule by peremptory edict, but it would have been wiser for him to have strengthened the power of the federal government by creation of more states in place of the existing four regions and by taking powers and influence piecemeal for the federal government in order to create national unity. This was what the Gowon government did after his overthrow.

The May riots were followed by a period of extreme tension within the army where Northern and Ibo officers and men watched each other in a climate of unsettling rumour, each expecting the other to make a pre-emptive strike, for there was an assumption that a 'licence to kill' situation had been unleashed, where whoever struck first and killed his opponent would obtain legitimation from the mere possession of power. The Northerners struck first in July in an action which was a mixture of a deliberately prepared coup and a mutiny of Northern private soldiers and NCOs.[18] More than 200 officers and men, nearly all Ibo, were murdered by Northern other ranks. Ironsi himself was arrested in Ibadan, handed over to private soldiers and NCOs, and executed.

For a few days the whole survival of Nigeria hung in the balance as the Nigerian army exploded through its tribal tensions. Almost all Ibo soldiers were murdered or were forced to flee back to the East. Northern soldiers would obey no officer except a Northerner. Brigadier Ogundipe, a Yoruba, the next most senior officer, tried to assume command, but finding that the soldiers would not obey him, he quickly resigned. Colonel Yakubu Gowon, the senior Northern officer, a Northern Christian from a small minority tribe, the Angas in Plateau Province, was highly respected as the Chief of Staff army; he went down to Ikeja where the Northern rebels were stationed and was told by them that they wanted him to be the new head of the army and of the military government. Gowon accepted the post and delivered a speech containing the sentence, 'The basis of unity is not here'. He meant, I think, 'The basis for unitary government is not here'. He promptly prepared a decree restoring federalism.

Gowon's first battle, however, was to head off the Northern soldiers' aim of marching back to the North and breaking up the unity of Nigeria. The soldiers were clearly influenced by old politicians of the NPC with their secessionist ideas. At this, the most crucial of all the challenges to its unity, Nigeria was saved by a number of forces. The federal civil servants had established a genuine feeling for national unity; they drove down to Ikeja to seek to persuade the soldiers. Colonel Hassan flew down from Kaduna and pointed out that it would be suicidal to abandon Lagos to a potentially hostile power. Gowon himself, as a man of the Middle Belt and a soldier loyal to Nigeria, wished to preserve the federation. The British High Commissioner and the American Ambassador called again and again on Gowon to stress the need to preserve Nigerian unity. In a seminar in Keele University in 1980 Gowon explained the principle that he adopted to outside pressures. 'I only let them influence me', he said, 'if they were pushing me in the direction in which I wanted to move anyway'.

Gowon declared his intention to hand over power to civilians 'quickly, I mean quickly' and called a meeting of leaders of thought at regional levels to prepare for an *ad hoc* constitutional conference. Influential figures from among politicians, civil servants and other civilians were called together under the regional governments to discuss the future of Nigeria. It was plain that the will to unity was weak. Three contradictory forces pressed for a confederal plan. The Easterners, traumatized by the murder of Ironsi and of so many Ibo soldiers, naturally pressed for a loosening of the federal tie. The hatred of Ibos among federal soldiers was at this time so great and so irrational that Colonel Ojukwu (the Ibo Governor of the Eastern Region) could not have gone to Lagos without grave danger to his life. Awolowo had assumed the title of 'leader of the Yorubas', an unfortunately divisive role for a politician involved in preserving Nigerian unity. He and the Western delegation put forward a twofold plan. An ideal one of ethnic federalism, and a tactical one of separation of the regions into a confederal system if the first plan was unattainable. In the North the old NPC elites, who considered that the preservation of the unity of the North was more important than the preservation of the unity of Nigeria, managed to persuade the Northern leaders of thought to adopt a confederal stance based on the model of the East African Common Services. Only the Mid-West took its stand on the principle of full Nigerian federal authority.

The conference was a civilian one and Gowon exercised his influence only from a distance. After the first week of the conference a crucially important change took place in the Northern position. Under pressure from Tiv and other Middle Belt soldiers and from the political leader J. S. Tarka, the Northern delegation abandoned its confederal stance and came to support full federalism with the creation of more states. This event was at once followed by a wave of murderous attacks launched on innocent Ibo civilians living in the North. There is no doubt that this massacre was deliberately instigated by certain people including some of the old elites of the NPC. The motive was to put an end to the danger of the breakup of the North by procuring the breakup of Nigeria. The massacres were carried out in a systematic way by thugs and by mutinous soldiers of the fourth battalion, who had been responsible for the murder of Ironsi and who had been redeployed to the North.

Some eight thousand Ibos[19] were murdered in the North and the remainder, numbering between one and two million, were driven back home to the Eastern Region. This total failure of Nigeria to provide the essential defence of the safety of the citizen naturally gave rise to a furious anger in the East and a strong movement towards secession. It also broke up the *ad hoc* constitutional conference.

Gowon rebuked the murderous soldiers and slowly re-established discipline and control but the basis of trust had been fatally undermined. A last attempt at saving Nigeria by conference took place in Aburi in January 1967. Gowon intended the Aburi meeting to be the first of many to re-establish confidence between the East and the rest of Nigeria; Ojukwu intended it to be an occasion for the rewriting of Nigeria's federal constitution so that the regions could 'go apart a little in order to come together later'. Federal civil servants thought that once the regions had gone apart they would never come together again. The Aburi conference was a military affair and demonstrated the military leaders' lack of experience in constitutional matters. They signed a communiqué which was self-contradictory. One part of it provided for a confederal arrangement, with regional armies under the regional governors and the requirement of the agreement of all the regional governors for any important actions or appointments by the federal government. Another part of the Aburi communiqué spoke of returning the federal balance to its position of 14 January 1966 (before the military coup), which was clearly one of federal government. The brief euphoria of Aburi was soon dissipated. The Ibos thought that Ojukwu had gone too far towards co-operation with the federal government while the federal civil servants thought that Gowon had gone too far in reducing the powers of the Nigerian government. They produced a joint paper putting forward their case, which inevitably leaked and was taken by Ojukwu as evidence that the federal civil servants were more dangerous than any 'swash-buckling federal soldier', and that they had lost their regional roots. When the civil servants met to implement the Aburi agreement they were impeded by lack of an authentic record as to what exactly had been agreed, despite the leaking of the tapes of the meeting by both sides. In the end the sticking point was the inclusion in the federal government's decree of implementation of the old power of the federal government to take over a region in an emergency which it was given the unilateral right to declare. This induced Ojukwu to reject the decree and to proceed steadily towards secession. In a sense, secession was already inevitable from the moment when the Northern troops left the East in August 1966 and when the Eastern government began to expel civilian non-Easterners 'for their own protection', and to recall all its citizens back to the region. The federal government controlled the rest of Nigeria, but as regards the link with the East there was nothing except the Lagos–Enugu telephone line on which Gowon and Ojukwu had long conversations hoping to recreate some of the old camaraderie of the officers' mess and use it to restore Nigeria's unity. After Aburi the relation between Gowon and Ojukwu soon soured as Gowon came to believe that Ojukwu was set on secession.[20]

## Civil war

In May 1967 Gowon had incontrovertible evidence that Ojukwu had made his preparations, obtained his mandate for secession from a co-opted Eastern regional conference of notables and was about to secede as the 'Independent Republic of Biafra'. Gowon and his civil service advisers quickly brought forward their plans for creation of states in place of the overmighty regions. This, the most important change in the constitutional federal balance of Nigeria was entirely the work of the federal military government and was prepared with extreme secrecy. Even Colonel Hassan, governor of the North, was taken by surprise and at first resented the breakup of his region, though he loyally implemented the plan and sought to retain some vestige of Northern unity through the interim common services organization of the North. The federal decree created twelve states, six in the North, three in the East and gave Lagos separate statehood thus making three states in the old Western Region. This was Gowon's constitutional coup and one of his greatest achievements for in one stroke it remedied the regional imbalance and provided a structure which was bound to strengthen the federal government. At the same time he sought to win the loyalty of the minority non-Ibo tribes in the East to whom he gave the two new states of Rivers and South East, and to remove southern fear of the North. He wished it to be known that if civil war broke out it would not be a war of North against East but of the whole of Nigeria against secessionists in one state, the East Central where the vast majority of Ibos lived.

On 30 May, three days after the state creation decree, Ojukwu duly declared the secession of the East as the 'Republic of Biafra'. In July federal troops invaded the East from the North to re-establish Nigerian unity and two and a half years later forced the surrender of Biafra and the re-establishment of Nigerian unity.

In assessing the motives for Biafran secession one must take account both of the sense of injury and rejection of Nigerian authority produced by the failure of the federal government to ensure rights of citizenship to Ibos outside the Eastern Region or to protect their lives, and of the advantages which the Eastern leaders thought that they would attain if they were independent. Independence would remove the need to share the oil wealth of Nigeria, most of which came from land in the Eastern Region, with the rest of the federation. It is this fear of the need to share that has undermined so many federations in Africa. The Ivory Coast (now Côte d'Ivoire), for instance, always opposed the West African Federation of which it was a part under French colonial rule, for it was the richest member of the eight colonies of the federation.

Gabon, the richest state of Equatorial Africa, was the leader of the successful move to break up the four-nation federation of French Equatorial Africa. President Tshombe of Katanga in the quasi-federal Congo, (later Zaire), at the time of independence, naturally sought to secede from the rest of the Congo in order that his province, which had about a sixth of the Congo's population and some two-thirds of its mineral wealth, could enjoy its riches alone without having to share them with the rest of the Congo.

Faced with these powerful tendencies, one can only reiterate the truism that the existence of a nation state, whether it be federal or unitary, imposes upon the richer parts of the nation the obligation to share wealth with the poorer. If there is no sharing there is no unity, no nation.

Confronted with the challenge of the civil war, the federal government in Nigeria increased its powers in order to preserve national unity. It was possible to change the principle of revenue allocation to states in a nation-building way. Since the Rivers and Mid-West, the main oil producing areas, were reliant upon the federal army drawn from all the peoples of Nigeria to liberate them from Ojukwu's rule, it was only fair that the federal government should ask them to forgo the 50 per cent of oil revenue that had accrued to the region of origin under the First Republic and make do with 10 per cent instead. It was decided that the remaining 90 per cent should be divided among all the states through the 'Distributable Pool' according to equality and to population size as shown in the 1963 census.

## The regime of Yakubu Gowon

The magnificent reconciliation after the civil war was a great credit both to Yakubu Gowon and to the people of Nigeria. Gowon had proclaimed a doctrine of 'no victor no vanquished' and had used the famous words of Lincoln's second inaugural of the need to 'bind up the nation's wounds'. His policy was one of 'three R's – Reconciliation, Reconstruction and Rehabilitation'. In all the history of civil wars, there has hardly ever been one followed by so generous a reconciliation.

Upon this foundation of reconciliation the federal government built up the structure of federalism and national unity. Peace was easily maintained throughout Nigeria in a relaxed manner that allowed for the preservation of the freedoms associated with the open society which Nigeria had inherited and developed from British rule. Only the right to vote was still absent both at central or regional and at local government level.[21] The oil wealth of Nigeria quadrupled in a single year after the Yom Kippur war and most of it was used for capital development projects. These were provided for in a series of comprehensive five-year plans. The third five-year plan launched under Gowon was prepared with the help of a skilled group of planners and brought together both federal and state projects with many financed by both state and regional governments. The plan provided for an expenditure of 32 billion naira, (at that time about £25 billion), a huge sum by the standards to which Nigeria had been accustomed in the past.[22]

A structure of 'co-operative federalism' developed through informal channels of consultation between state and federal officials, while the state governors as men in a military hierarchy naturally discussed the economic plans of their states with Gowon as their superior. The federal government sought to inculcate a sense of service to the nation by launching a National Youth Service Corps for all Nigerian graduates; they were sent to serve for a year in states other than their state of origin. The scheme at first attracted considerable resistance from student organizations, but the federal government pushed on despite this opposition and the corps has come to be an accepted part of Nigerian life. Its political advantages outweigh its indifferent economic performance.

The regime of Yakubu Gowon which had rebuilt so well after the civil war later began to lose momentum. His post-war promise of a return to elected civilian rule in 1975 was taken back in 1974 since it was declared to be 'premature'. Issues which should have been firmly grasped and solved were swept under the carpet. A new constitution for civilian rule needed to be drawn up; a new site for the capital chosen, for Lagos is overcrowded and in the extreme South-West of the country; and the twelve states, though a great improvement on the four regions, urgently needed further subdivision for they were most unequal in size and included together in one state a number of opposing groups who could not co-operate.[23] Furthermore, the state governors were left in their jobs too long and became military princes uncontrolled by any accountability to institutions within their states and inadequately disciplined from the centre. They enjoyed an unusual position in the central federal institutions for they sat on the Supreme Military Council at federal level and comprised a majority of its membership. It is unusual and undesirable in federal systems to give the state governors or chief ministers a powerful voice in the federal governing body for it tends to make the national authority appear as the sum of the state authorities. Among federal systems it is only in Canada that the State Premiers have an inbuilt role in decisions at the national level.

The tendency for regional or state governors to become a law unto themselves was apparent before the civil war, where not only did Ojukwu, the Governor of the Eastern Region secede, but Adebayo, Governor of the West and Ejor, Governor of the Mid-West tried to assume a more or less neutral position for a time until the action of the army and the events of the civil war forced them to come off the fence. It continued through the Gowon period after the civil war at a much lower level. Governors were loyal in all federal matters but many of them were corrupt and high-handed in state matters. With the overthrow of Yakubu Gowon by a military coup in July 1975, and his replacement by General Murtala Mohammed, all the state governors were removed and after a commission of enquiry they were ordered to repay a total of ten million naira (about £8 million), and dismissed from the army. Under the new regime 'corrective government' was applied vigorously. The new governors were 'men under authority' on a military posting and were removed from the Supreme Military Council and made subject to General Obasanjo, the Chief of Staff Headquarters. They met together in a subordinate body, the Council of State.

### 'Corrective government' and the return to civilian rule

The Murtala goverment knew how to act, and its vigorous lead was followed by state governments. Murtala instituted a purge of corrupt and deadwood officers at federal level in the army, the police, the federal civil service, the parastatals and the universities. The state governments took up the purge with alacrity, and applied it to state personnel. Indeed, the problem for the state governors was often how to moderate the excess desire for purge rather than to encourage it. Some 9,000 people were dismissed in all, many of them at senior level.

The regime appointed another commission of enquiry to decide whether or not Nigeria needed a new site for its capital and to recommend that site. The commission recommended that there should be a new capital at Abuja in the more southerly part of the former Northern Region, in the territory inhabited by minority tribes near the geographical centre of the country. The government accepted the recommendation and began work. A great deal of money has been spent on this carefully planned project with great attention to what the planning document calls 'imageability'.[24] The capital territory was initially treated as a purely federal responsibility but may eventually become a state in its own right with the return to civilian rule in 1992. The construction of the capital has been characterized, during the civilian period from 1979–83, by considerable corruption in contracts, most of which were awarded with an eye to political advantage, but its symbolic value as a centre of national unity will be great.

The regime called a conference of state commissioners and permanent secretaries responsible for local government and under federal leadership produced a new and more or less uniform structure for single-tiered elected local government councils throughout Nigeria. The traditional authorities were given recognition but in a more or less advisory role. The operation of these new authorities was provided for in the 'Local Government Guidelines' issued by the federal government and great emphasis was put upon the local government councils as the 'third arm of federalism'.[25]

After the death of Murtala in February 1976 in an unsuccessful coup attempt, Obasanjo continued the work of 'corrective government' and in the process further strengthened the federal government. A process of social engineering from the centre was carried out by the federal government, much of it originating from the cabinet office, into which a number of civilian academic technocrats were co-opted to work with the civil service. The educational advance of 'universal primary education' was pushed forward, originated and partly financed and supervised by the federal government but operated by the state governments. The state secondary school system was reinforced by high quality federal high schools in each state. At university level the National Universities Commission exercised a level of supervision that offended several vice-chancellors, while the federal government set up a Joint Admission and Matriculation Board to exercise some control on university admission. The resultant tensions between the principle of admission on open competition by academic qualification and admission on more equal state quotas to seek to give 'fair shares' to each state, resulted in considerable difficulty for the federal government, and a sense of grievance among all parties.

The government also sought to prevent Nigeria from becoming too deeply divided by differences of wealth. A full capital transfer tax was introduced on the personal initiative of Obasanjo, to tax both gifts *inter vivos* and inheritance on death. Under the subsequent civilian administration this proved largely a dead letter.

The return to civilian rule was most carefully prepared by the military government and took place under a widely discussed constitution, which was adopted in 1979. The Constitutional Drafting Committee and subsequent Constituent Assembly were composed entirely of civilians; the forty-nine members of the former were appointed from notables in each state by the federal military government, while the majority of the 350 or so members of the latter were elected by the elected local government councils. The resultant constitution was based very much on the United States model with an Executive President, two houses, a Senate and House of Representatives at the federal level, and elected single Houses of Assembly and elected Governors at state level. The federal balance depended upon an exclusive legislative list and a concurrent legislative list with residual powers resting with the state governments. The supreme court had the right to exercise judicial review over any legislation of the federal government contrary to the constitution, and did so in the celebrated case of the Revenue Allocation Act which was passed by improper procedure. As in the United States constitution it was expressly provided that federal legislation should prevail over state legislation in the event of any conflict within the concurrent area.

The federal balance was now clearly an inward leaning one, for no state government was big enough or rich enough to challenge the federal government. The exclusive legislative list of the federal government did not differ very markedly from that in the Constitution of the First Republic except for a clause giving the federal government authority to 'promote and enforce the observance of the fundamental objectives and directive principles contained in the constitution'. The fundamental objectives and directive principles were not themselves justiciable but they related to the objective of national unity, common citizenship and honest government for the benefit of the people. They also included the concept of 'federal chracter' which was to become a key phrase in Nigerian government both under the civilian government of the Second Republic 1979–83 and under the subsequent military government.[26]

Section 14(3) of the 1979 Constitution reads:

The composition of the Government of the Federation or of its agencies and the conduct of its affairs shall be carried out in such a manner as to reflect the federal character of Nigeria and the need to promote national unity, and also to command national loyalty, thereby ensuring that there shall be no pre-dominance of persons from a few states or from a few ethnic or other sectional groups in that government or any of its agencies.

Section 14(4) reads:

The composition of the Government of a State, a local government council or any of the agencies of such government or council or such agencies shall be carried out in such a manner as to recognize the diversity of the peoples within its area of authority and the need to promote a sense of belonging and loyalty among all the peoples of the Federation.

This high ideal is in practice to be achieved by ensuring the spread of benefits and jobs equally among constituent states of the federation, and within a state their spread among the local government areas. It applies explicitly to ministers in the federal cabinet, at least one of whom must come from each state (Section 135(3), Presidential appointments to senior posts (Section 157(5)), commissioners of state executive councils, (173(2)), Governatorial appointments at state level, (188(4)), the composition of the Armed Forces (197(2)) and 199(b)), and the governing body of every legal political party which must have members from at least two-thirds of the states in Nigeria (203(b)). In practice the principle of equal shares has come to be applied to many other jobs and benefits. Even under the subsequent military governments of Buhari and of Babangida there has been an attempt to keep at least approximatly to this formula for appointments to military governorships and to the Supreme Military Council, (renamed Armed Forces Ruling Council), and to the Federal Executive Council.

The principle of 'federal character' clearly has considerable relevance to other situations in Africa where there is a danger of ethnic domination. Three points should be noted however. First, in the Nigerian case no mention has been made of tribe in the allocation of offices: government uses the surrogate of geography for ethnicity. Everyone knows that the cabinet member from Imo or from Anambra will be Ibo, likewise the army officer or presidential appointments; similarly, one knows that the cabinet member, army officer or presidential appointment from Oyo, Ogun, Ondo and probably Lagos and Kwara will be Yoruba and that from Kano, Katsina, Sokoto, Bauchi and perhaps Kaduna, will be Hausa – but tribe, like sex, is not to be mentioned!

The second point relates to the need to keep a sector for open competition, which is as Nwokedi described it, a 'tonic' in any service. The absence of this open competition sector has caused great frustration and grievance among people from states with high levels of educational achievement like Bendel, (the former Mid-West), Imo and Anambra. It is surely wise to make an explicit compromise between the two contradictory but attractive principles of open competition and fair shares among states or local government areas by dividing up the entry into (say) a 50 per cent open competition part and a 50 per cent federal character quota sector.

The third caveat relates to the need for the geographical areas to be roughly equal. It can easily appear unjust to give equal shares to states or to local government areas which are of very unequal size in terms of population. Nigeria is unique among federations in having deliberately sought to create regional units of roughly equal population. But even Nigeria has not been entirely successful in achieving equality among states. The most populous, Kano and Oyo, have populations, according to the 1962 census, of 5.8 and 5.2 millions whereas the least populous, Rivers and Ogon, have populations of only 1.5 and 1.6 million. Already the Ibos are discontented by a distribution which gives to their two populous states an allocation of posts and jobs only about half that of the Yoruba who have four and a half states, three of them of fairly small population. Perhaps Nigeria will have to develop a more sophisticated version of 'federal character' based on a quota of jobs corresponding to population; alternatively more surgery will be needed to state boundaries to make states equal in population.

Further power was given to the federal government by the creation of a number of autonomous bodies to which appointment was to be made by the President with approval of the Senate or of the Council of State. These bodies included the Federal Electoral Commission which not only exercised control over federal and state elections but also had great supervisory powers over parties and over candidates, who could not compete without FEDECO approval. The commission carried its supervisory role to levels which many considered excessive, even banning candidates who had not paid their tax on time in each of the last three years. There was a suspicion that it was influenced by the will of the federal military government and, after the return to civilian rule, by that of the President.

The all-important task of preventing corruption was given to two specially created bodies at federal level, the Code of Conduct Bureau and the Code of Conduct Tribunal. These bodies were required to receive statements of assets from all elected personnel, all federal and state and local government employees and all employees of parastatal bodies and to forward to the Code of Conduct Tribunal for trial any *prima facie* cases of corruption made out again any of these. Those who were found to have contravened the strict Code of Conduct laid down in the Constitution would be removed from their posts and if the Code of Conduct Tribunal so ordered, banned from the holding of any public office for up to ten years.

Unfortunately, the operation of the Code of Conduct Tribunal and Bureau required to be set in motion by an Act of the Federal Assembly and such an Act was never passed, for many members of the Assembly were guilty of breaching the Code of Conduct. Nothing whatever was done to counter corruption. Its powers should have flowed automatically from the Constitution without the need for enabling legislation.

The federal principle was incorporated into the electoral process for the presidency; the successful candidate had not merely to win the largest popular vote of any of the candidates, but also to win 'not less than one quarter of the votes cast at the election in each of at least two-thirds of the states in the Federation'. Similarly, a candidate for governorship had to win the largest vote and not less than a quarter of the votes in at least two-thirds of the local government areas in the state. As luck would have it, Shehu Shagari won the largest vote and over a quarter of the vote in twelve of the states of the Federation and a fifth of the vote in the thirteenth state. Since two-thirds of the nineteen states is twelve and two-thirds, the court had a problem. It finally ruled that in the thirteenth state Shagari only needed to get two-thirds of a quarter, i.e. a sixth, and so he was declared elected President and took power on 1 October 1979.

There is no need to recount the history of the Second Republic. Its main achievement was in the openness and tolerance of the style of government and its failing was its inability to check vast corruption or to manage the economy successfully, so that when the oil price fell, Nigeria went bankrupt, fell into debt and could not import goods. As regards the federal aspects of the regime, we find an inward leaning system. The states were dependent on the federal government both for specific grants and for authority to raise loans abroad. Shagari went out of his way to cultivate good relations with governors of other political parties. Where collisions occurred between state and federal government they were mostly about symbolic issues as where the Deputy governor of Oyo, ordered bulldozers to destroy federal dwelling houses because he had not given the federal government permission to build on that particular bit of land. These foolish battles of prestige were soon settled in the federal government's favour.[27]

In the more serious field of planning, the state governors came together under the chairmanship of the Vice-President in the National Economic Council and dealt with planning issues in a co-operative manner. A good deal of informal co-operation also occurred between federal and state officials. In Nigeria the important figure at the central level is always acutely interested in the development of his own home area and therefore would co-operate with the state authorities from that area even if they came from opposing parties.

## Military government again

With the overthrow of Shagari's government in December 1983 by a military coup, Nigeria experienced another severe dose of 'corrective government' under General Buhari. Most policies were dictated from the centre and the supposition was that 'if the medicine is going to do you any good it will have to be painful'. About a thousand of the former political leaders were arrested, and some of them were tried and sentenced to long terms of imprisonment by courts with a military president sitting in secret and assuming guilt until innocence was proved. The National Security Organisation became interfering and tyrannical under its head, ex-Ambassador Rafindadi. A strict and painful programme of structural adjustment was introduced in economic matters. State governors who were all military men and served outside their own states of origin were expected to enforce the corrective policies. Nigeria was operating more or less as a unitary state except that jobs and patronage in state affairs were administered for the benefit of the indigenes by the state government.

Buhari was in turn overthrown in a coup in 1985 and a more liberal regime succeeded under General Babangida. Serious preparations have been undertaken for a return to civilian rule. It is assumed that the basic institutions will not differ very much from those of the Second Republic and the federal balance will be roughly the same. The Constituent Assembly has been told that the federal nature of Nigeria is not subject to debate nor is the existence of an elected executive presidency. The military government have sought to obtain a higher standard of honesty by banning a very large number of former office holders by category from participating in the return to civilian rule. Some will be allowed to participate a year after the initial elections, some after ten years and some are permanently banned if they have been found guilty of corruption. A powerful National Electoral Commission has been appointed to conduct elections and to oversee the activities of parties. Only two parties are to be allowed; it is not explained how the multiplicity of parties, which will inevitably arise in so vibrant a political culture as that of Nigeria, will be forced into the narrow mould of just two parties.

There seems also to be a need for some means to prevent the corruption of state government which occurred in the Second Republic. There was also massive corruption at the federal level, but if Shagari had been able to exercise some political control over state governors of his own party, as Mrs Ghandi and Rajiv Ghandi have over Congress Party Chief Ministers, there would have been more discipline. A constitutional change would also be advantageous to enable federal audit to look at state accounts. This power did not exist in the Second Republic and the state auditors were naturally subject to being overawed by the power of the governor. A particular abuse was the use of large 'security funds' by the governors for political purposes. Audit of state finances is part of the all-India legislative list in the Indian Constitution; this is a good example for Nigeria.

The military government have created two new states to make the total number up to twenty-one, which can be exactly divided by three and thus avoid the ambiguity over the question of the quarter of the votes in two-thirds of the states required by the successful presidential candidate.

## Local government as the 'third arm of federalism'

The first electoral arena created by the military government has been that of local government councils. The elections were carried out somewhat incompetently in several states, but when held again a reasonably fair and efficient election resulted. Parties were banned. The elected local councils have been used to choose the members of the Constituent Assembly. This use of the 'third arm of federal government' is important and we will conclude by considering its significance in the Nigerian context.

The vision of Obasanjo, who took a close personal interest in the issue, was that elected local government would be a third tier in a federation. There is much good sense in this. A federal constitution is one which divides up power between two different layers of government according to a constitution so that the lower level exercises its power within its sphere by right and not subject to the arbitrary will of the superior level. This principle can perfectly well be applied to *three* levels of government so that the level closest to the people has a guaranteed autonomy to exercise power within its local sphere in local matters. This situation hardly ever exists in law in unitary states or in other federal states. In theory the central government in a unitary system or the state government in a federal system can interfere with local government at will. In practice no government in a developed country sacks the elected local government councils and replaces them with its own appointees, although it may interfere excessively by giving all manner of instructions to local governments, by abolishing a whole tier of them and by telling them how they are to raise their revenue. In the Third World, however, it is very common for holders of power at central or state level to dissolve local government councils and to replace them with its own appointees and political clients. This has happened only too frequently in Nigeria.

From the days of the old Native Authorities, local government played an important role in Nigeria, especially in the North where it had great prestige. The post-war policy of encouraging elected local government as a preparation for national independence had its effect in Nigeria, but as independence approached regional governments began to dominate local government, to overawe and to dismiss chiefs who did not support the government party and to dissolve local governments and replace the elected councils with caretaker committees or sole authorities appointed by themselves. For a brief moment General Obasanjo was able to reverse this trend through the 1976 Local Government Decree, setting up a more or less uniform system of elected single-tier local government all over Nigeria. In the elections, parties were banned and turnout was only about 10 per cent, but at least this was the beginning of local autonomy. The Constituent Assembly for the discussion of the Draft Constitution was largely drawn from these councils since they were the only elected body in Nigeria.

The 1979 Constitution Section 7 expressly guaranteed 'the system of local government by democratically elected local government councils' but unfortunately provided no constitutional means to enforce this guarantee. The return to civilian rule was soon followed by the end of all elected local government since the state governors declared that the councils' three-year term was up and that they were therefore dissolved and replaced by their own appointed caretaker committees. No new elections were held because the new Electoral Register had not been prepared nor the electoral law introduced into the Assembly.

By the time of the end of civilian rule in the coup of 1983 elected local government had still not been established and furthermore state governors had subdivided local government areas and multiplied them by about 100 per cent in order to win support from the fissiparous tendency of Nigerian politics, by which every area seeks for autonomy from its neighbour in order to increase its status. The number of local government areas has wisely been reduced again by the military government to conform with the list of local governments given in the first schedule in Section 3 Part 1 of the 1979 Constitution which corresponds to the local government areas set up in 1976. The constitutional provision allocating local governments 10 per cent of Nigeria's total revenue had often been a dead letter under the Second Republic, since the payment was made through the state governments who were short of cash and appropriated the money due for local government. The military appear to have remedied this fault. Now that local government councils are elected again, it only remains to entrench in the Constitution some practical way of guaranteeing their autonomy from state government interference and prolonged dissolution.

## Conclusion

The vicissitudes of federalism in Nigeria provide many lessons for the application of federalism elsewhere in the world, and more especially for its application in developing nations. With great labour and suffering Nigeria has gradually approached the equilibrium of a true federal balance, having experimented disastrously with the two opposing extremes of confederalism and strict unitarism. In doing so the country has experienced the need to adjust the boundaries of the constituent states to ensure that there is no overmighty region, and that smaller ethnic groups have their own political representation. It has also experienced the need to uphold the principle of 'federal character' in appointments to office, and come to appreciate the importance of building up a solid, autonomous system of local government as the 'third arm of federalism'. All these lessons deserve to be carefully digested by those who seek to establish federal systems in other areas.

## Notes

1. Apart from the ephemeral unions of Guinea, Ghana, Mali in the Nkrumah period, of Egypt and Sudan for a brief period, of Libya and various neighbours (none of which has been consummated in effective federal institutions), there have been only four real unions after independence of previous separate states or colonies. (1) British and Italian Somaliland, which were united by very strong bonds of common Somali nationalism and ethnic identity joined together in a unitary state within twenty-four hours of independence. The recent unsuccessful revolt around Hargeisa in the area of former British Somaliland in the North indicates that there are still tensions between the two areas, which are split not only by geography but by clan genealogy. (2) The Southern part of the territory of the Cameroons administered by Britain as part of Nigeria opted in 1961 in a UN plebiscite to join the French administered part of the former Cameroons which had become independent as the Cameroon Republic. The choice was between joining Nigeria, as the Northern part of the trust territory administered by Britain opted to do, or joining the Cameroon Republic. The option of independence as a separate state was not offered. (3) Six weeks after independence Zanzibar experienced a violent revolution against the rule of the Sultan and the Arab hegemony and within four months opted to join Tanganyika in the new state of Tanzania. This case is dealt with in the text. (4) The Union of Eritrea with Ethiopia in 1952 following a vote in the Eritrean parliament. Most of Eritrea is now in revolt. The case is dealt with in the text.
2. When federalism was abolished, Eritrea was placed under the direct rule of an Imperial Governor named Azrati, who was a most able and honest administrator. He was later murdered during the revolution in Ethiopia.

For a brief period after the forced abdication of the Emperor, it seemed as though peace might be found under the rule of General Aman Andom in 1974, for Andom was himself half Ethiopian. Andom, however, was murdered by the faction of Mengistu, under whose rule a fierce policy of forced unification has been followed as part of the campaign of *Ethiopia tikdem* – Ethiopia above all. It is perhaps too late now for a purely federal remedy.

3. The peace-making exercise which led to the Addis Ababa agreement between the Sudanese Government of General Numeiri and the Anyanya rebels in the South was indeed remarkable. It owed a great deal to the good offices both of the late Emperor of Ethiopia and of Canon Burgess Carr, of the World Council of Churches, who was asked to 'moderate' in the all-important early meetings between both sides. The essence of the agreement was a system of autonomy for the South as a single unit with its own elected Assembly and Vice President and with control over its own administration. It involved also a recognition that Sudan was a country of two great religions – Islam and Christianity – rather than merely an Islamic state. The process of negotiation has been analysed in detail in an unpublished work by Nelson Kasfir, presented to Politics Graduates Seminar at Manchester University. It was so successful that the civil war ended and life began to flood back to the South. Unfortunately in his later years, under the threat of Islamic fundamentalism, Numeiri undid the good work of the Addis Ababa agreement and the result has been a yet more bitter civil war.

4. It is interesting that the Fulani traditionally used the offensive word *Arna* (pagans) to describe the non-Muslim people in the North, in the same way that white South African racists used the word *Kafir* (idolatrous pagan) to describe black people in South Africa. The use of the word *Arna* in Plateau State has now been prohibited.

5. The emphasis of the colonial government of Nigeria in the early period was totally hostile to the idea of a Nigerian nation. Sir Hugh Clifford's denunciation of the National Congress of British West Africa in his speech to the Nigerian Council on 29 December 1920 revealed the government's basic attitude towards the concepts of self-government, patriotism, nationality and nation. (1) The idea of a Nigerian nation was inconceivable. (2) National self-government was a concept applicable only to 'self-contained mutually independent' Native States (based on powerful Native Authorities). (3) True patriotism and nationalism were sentiments that must be directed to these 'natural units'. (4) The question of the ultimate control of the superstructure binding these separate states together in a modern political unit was then outside the realm of permissible discussion. James Smoot Coleman, *Nigeria: the background to nationalism*, Berkeley (1958), 194. Governor Clifford's dismissal of Nigerian nationalism in favour of tribal particularism shows remarkable similarities to the attitude of P. W. Botha and other South African white leaders of the 'National Party' to the feasibility of a South African nation. History will, I believe, show the pessimism of Botha to have been as inaccurate as that of Clifford.

6. The record of these administrative quarrels has been admirably set out in the study by Jeremy White on *Public Administration in Nigeria 1914–48*,

London (1981).

7. In the 1963 census the Northern Region share of the population went down from 56 per cent to 54 per cent. It is noteworthy that no other working federation has had one unit with so large a share of the total population. The highest is New South Wales with about 35 per cent of the population of Australia. Uttar Pradesh comprises about 15 per cent of the population of India. Ontario about 34 per cent of the population of Canada, and California 10 per cent of the population of USA. The Russian Federal Republic comprises just over 50 per cent of the population of the USSR but that political system is a federation in a cultural rather than a political sense for the centralizing power of the Communist Party underlies all the institutions of government.

8. Many of the present states correspond exactly to provinces under British rule, e.g. in the former North Sokoto, Katsina, Kano, Borno, Kaduna (formerly Zaria Province), Bauchi (except for the loss of Jarawa district to Plateau), Benue (except for the loss of Keffi and Nassarawa districts and of Wukari district to Gongola and the acquisition of Igala District from Kabba), Niger (except for the loss of the capital city territory), Kwara is the old Ilorin Province (except for the acquisition of Igbirra and Kabba divisions from the old Kabba province which has not become the basis for a state). The ten states in the former Eastern and Western regions also bear a close resemblance to former British provinces.

9. Related to the author during his service in Northern Nigeria as a district officer by a British administrative officer serving in Kaduna. The text of the eight points plan is given in Ahmadu Bello, *My Life*, Cambridge (1962) 143–4.

10. Evidence of John Smith, formerly Acting Secretary of the Premier in interview with John Paden, 12 August 1983, quoted in John N. Paden, *Ahmadu Bello*, London (1986), 221 and 222.

11. See John Paden, *Ahmadu Bello*, 357, 'He relies heavily on his "gateways" or "outposts" in Lagos to mediate the question of distribution of resources and linkages at the national level.'

12. General Gowon made it clear in an interview with the author 1969 and later, that continuing distrust of Ironsi, because of his repeated failure to start the trials of the conspirators who had murdered fellow officers on the night of 14 January 1966, was the main motive for the Northern outburst after the Unification Decree. Gowon as a soldier considers that if Ironsi had tried the conspirators he could have done what he liked in constitutional matters, with impunity.

13. See chapter by M. J. Dent on 'Corrective government' in *Soldiers and Oil*, ed. K. Panter-Brick, London (1978).

14. This was the response that the author met from Tiv and other Northerners in 1967 in their comments on the January and July coups. It was unfortunate that these traumatic events were seen by a very large number of Nigerians in crude terms of tribal dominance.

15. The author was shown a copy of the report three years later. Now that Nigeria has attained secure reconciliation and a balanced view of past history, perhaps it is time that the Nwokedi report was published for the

benefit of Nigerian historians. It is a classic instance of an able administrative plan, prepared by an able but over-confident administrator, who totally ignores the political dangers involved in his policy. It also shows the damage of too much secrecy in government. The degree of Northern distrust aroused by the Nwokedi report is hard to over-estimate. It was (probably wrongly) assumed to be a tribal plot and hastened the July coup and the descent into civil war.

16. The Commission's report was only submitted at the time of the July counter coup, and was never made public.
17. Information from the late J. S. Tarka and from Professor O'Connel. Professor O'Connel warned Ironsi of the danger of discontented Tiv soldiers. Ironsi was more inclined to discuss his plans to conciliate with old Northern notables from the far North such as the ex-Emire of Kano, Sanussi, who was in exile from Kano in Katagum.
18. This description of the July coup occurs in the comments of Northern senior officers at the Aburi conference. A good account of the mood of the soldiers at this time is available in Robin Luckham, *The Nigerian Military: a sociological study of authority and revolt*, London (1971).
19. This is the estimate of Professor James O'Connel and is a reasonable figure. A much higher figure of 30,000 was used by the Biafran side in the civil war period.
20. Interview with Yakubu Gowon, 1980.
21. Party political activity was also forbidden, but politicians served by co-option in federal and state executive councils. They soon found ways of forming alliances for winning support, and used surrogates for party, e.g. business associations as informal political groupings.
22. See *Third National Development Plan 1975–80*, Central Planning Office, Federal Ministry of Economic Development, Lagos.
23. For instance, Bauchi and Bornu were hereditary enemies from the wars of the nineteenth century. Their inclusion in one state caused friction. Benue and Plateau, as the chief centre of Middle Belt feeling, should have co-operated admirably but soon developed a bitter rivalry. The whole of the Yoruba West (apart from Lagos), remained together in one extremely populous state many times bigger than Rivers, the smallest of the states.
24. See *The master plan for Abuja, the new federal capital of Nigeria*, presented for the federal government by Abran Krushov, Walter G. Hansen and Thomas A. Todd, Federal Capital Development Authority, Federal Republic of Nigeria, (1979).
25. See *Local Government Guidelines*, Federal Military Government, 1976.
26. See A. H. M. Kirk-Greene, *Federal Character, Boon of Contentment or Bone of Contention*, published privately, mimeographed edition in *Nigeria the first year of civilian rule* (Keele Conference Papers, 1980) by Ali Yahaya, Dennis Austin and Martin Dent. Kirk-Greene's article was republished in *Ethnic and Social Studies*, vol VI, no 9 October 1983, 457–76.
27. I am indebted to Joe Okoroji for information on these disputes. See his, as yet unpublished, thesis at Keele University on 'Federal-state relations in Nigeria's Second Republic. A study of conflict and co-operation'.

*Part Three*

# Federalism and contemporary problems

# 8 Nationalism, federalism and Ireland

*Richard Jay*

Federalism offers a means of securing political integration where allegiance to central institutions is at risk from contending loyalties to narrower territorial, political or communal identities. According to its proponents, it has a unique capacity to deliver unity in diversity (*e pluribus unum*). The separation of powers between a single federal/ national and a number of provincial/state (or occasionally community) governments provides institutions which can further the common interests of all, while safeguarding, through constitutional rules and 'checks and balances', the autonomy of component units in areas of vital concern to them. In our own time, federal ideas have offered a singularly attractive alternative to the orthodox nineteenth century doctrines of nationalism, the nation-state and national sovereignty. Recoiling from the excesses of these doctrines – mutually-damaging economic protectionism, world war, 'Balkanization', and the forced imposition of uniform cultural and political practices upon variegated societies – federalists can point to the triumph of the quasi-federal European Community in overcoming ancient conflicts, and of several former European colonies where federation helps contain divisive communal conflicts.

Modern Ireland appears in this light to have much to gain from federalism. The current round of troubles in Northern Ireland, now twenty years old, is permeated by contending views of national sovereignty, national identity and political integration. Out of a total population of around a million and a half, over two and a half thousand people have died, and many more have been injured, as a consequence of civil disorder, communal violence, sectarian and terrorist assassination, and military action between state security forces and revolutionary insurgents – the Provisional Irish Republican Army (IRA) and other groups – intent on forging a united Irish republic. Only massive injections of outside funds have counteracted both the direct and

209

indirect consequences of political violence in a region which, once a heartland of the industrial revolution, has for most of this century suffered from its peripheral location within the United Kingdom economy. In 1972, the system of devolved government established in 1920 was suspended, since when direct rule by the United Kingdom parliament, reinforced by exceptional security legislation, has sought to manage an inherently unstable political arena. No political alternative has yet obtained widespread consent. Nor have the troubles been of merely local significance. Their consequences have spilled over into the domestic politics of Britain and the Republic of Ireland, severely straining their mutal diplomatic relations, and complicating those with America and the EC.

The problem has also to be placed in a wider context. Their experience of colonial rule, and political integration within the United Kingdom between 1800 and 1920, has profoundly shaped both Northern Ireland and the Republic. British influence is to be found in their legal and political institutions. For many decades after independence, the economy of southern Ireland remained integrally linked to Britain's, and even today some 30 per cent of its overseas trade is conducted with the United Kingdom. Several commentators have recently noted other linkages that survived dis-Union: dual citizenship for Irish nationals in the UK and residents of Northern Ireland; a range of institutions – banks, churches, trade unions, businesses, even the system of car registration – which continued to operate on an all-Ireland basis; the 'permeability' of the border to communications, and everyday personal and commercial traffic.[1] Given the new framework provided by their membership of the EC, it would seem rational for the peoples of these offshore islands, barely fourteen miles apart at the nearest sea crossing, to subsume ancient quarrels and focus more upon what unites them rather than on what divides them.

Two obstacles are encountered, however, in approaching the 'Irish problem' from a federalist perspective. One is the marginal role played by federal ideas in the Anglo-Irish political tradition. Britain has resorted to federal options in the process of decolonization, but been less enthusiastic in the home state, not least because the core doctrine of 'parliamentary sovereignty' has appeared compatible with political variations suited to particular needs – from administrative devolution in Scotland and Wales to the feudal relations between the Crown and Britain's smaller offshore islands. The 'Westminster model' has also permeated Ireland, gelling with Jacobin conceptions of the one and indivisible republic, romantic nationalist notions of cultural uniformity, and ultramontane Catholic doctrines suspicious of pluralism. As George Boyce has noted, it was precisely *because* of Ireland's diversity that its nationalist tradition was so concerned to emphasize uniformity.[2]

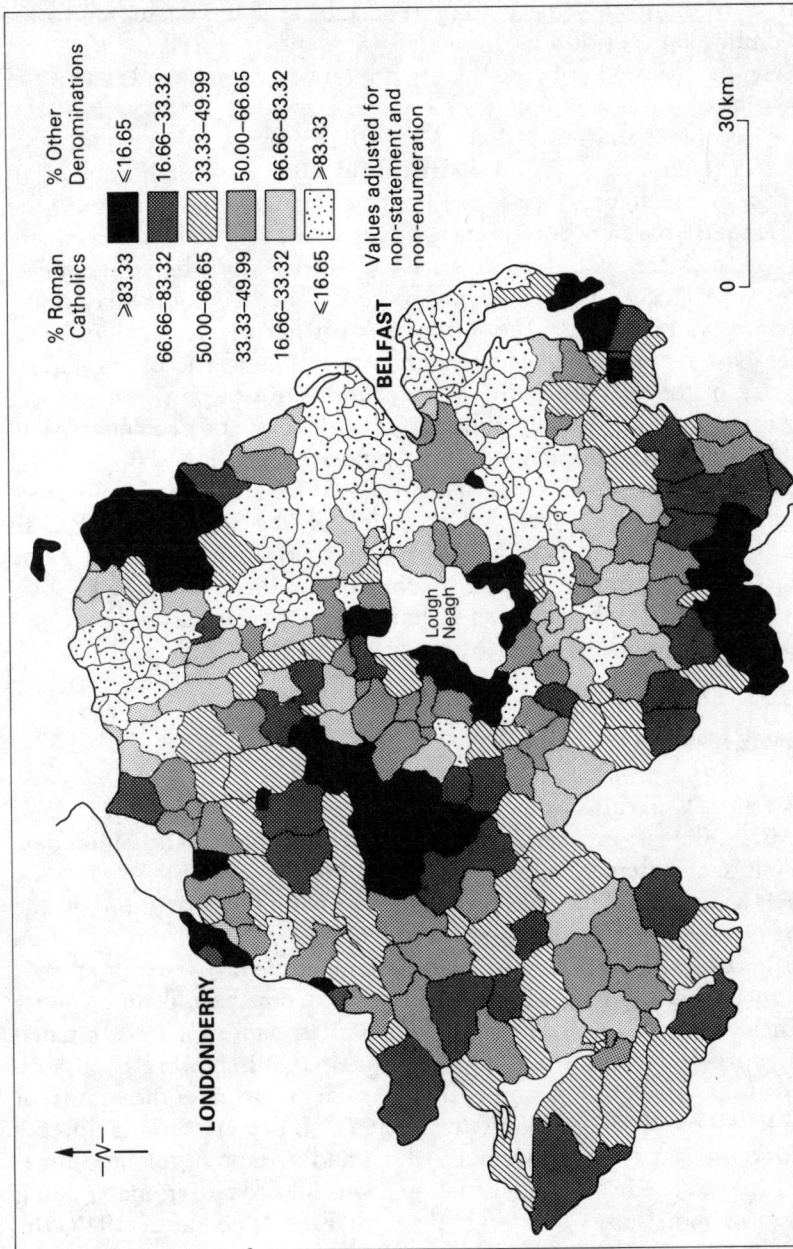

| % Roman Catholics | % Other Denominations |
|---|---|
| >83.33 | <16.65 |
| 66.66–83.32 | 16.66–33.32 |
| 50.00–66.65 | 33.33–49.99 |
| 33.33–49.99 | 50.00–66.65 |
| 16.66–33.32 | 66.66–83.32 |
| <16.65 | >83.33 |

Values adjusted for non-statement and non-enumeration

LONDONDERRY

BELFAST

Lough Neagh

0        30km

Religious distribution in Northern Ireland 1981*

Closest to federal ideas has been the powerful strand of contractarian thought inherited by northern Scots-Irish Protestants from seventeenth century covenantism; but this has reflected, and served to reinforce, their ambivalent position in the matrix of Anglo-Irish relations.[3] As we shall see, federalism has in fact played an important historical role in the Irish context, but not an entirely happy one.

The second obstacle is that, while there are many examples of successful federal constitutions in the world, all capable of adaptation to different circumstances, there are many which have failed because the initial 'federal bargain' could not be made or was subsequently broken. Lack of political will, the absence of sufficiently strong common interests, or suspicions too deeply rooted to be overcome may make integration impossible. In the context of Northern Ireland, all of these factors exist in abundance, blocking the way to political accommodation. The tone of this chapter is therefore cautious, if not pessimistic. After delineating some of the key dimensions to the current problem, I shall look briefly at past attempts to tackle Anglo-Irish relations along federal lines, examine proposals for transferring sovereignty over the province to some new Irish federal government in the event of a British withdrawal, and conclude with a discussion of possibilities offered by the Anglo-Irish Agreement, signed in November 1985, for forging new kinds of political links between Britain, the Republic of Ireland, and Northern Ireland itself.

## The Nature of the Problem

Northern Ireland came into existence under the Government of Ireland Act (1920), the last in a series of unsuccessful attempts to accommodate Irish nationalist demands through devolution ('Home Rule') within the United Kingdom. The Act provided for a unique partition of the country. A new local parliament in Dublin would exercise jurisdiction over twenty-six of the thirty-two counties, one in Belfast ('Stormont', as it came to be called) over six counties carved from the old nine-county province of Ulster. In addition, a Council of Ireland was to be created from representatives of the two parliaments with powers over both jurisdictions, available at some future time to assume the status of a single Home Rule parliament. In 1921, however, Sinn Fein, the revolutionary separatist movement which had by now supplanted nine-teenth century parliamentary nationalism, succeeded in negotiating wider dominion status, creating the Irish Free State (after 1949, the Republic of Ireland). Stormont opted to keep within the terms of the 1920 Act. The Council was effectively abandoned.

Partition reflected, but could not directly correspond to, two basic differences that had emerged between Ulster and the rest of Ireland over the previous century and a half of economic development and political mobilization. First, over most of Ireland, economic integration with Britain had blocked the establishment of a competitive manufacturing sector and encouraged complementary agricultural production, with commerce focused upon the *entrepôts* of Dublin and Cork. The north-east of Ulster, however, emerged as a growth point of Britain's industrial revolution, producing a distinct regional economy centred on Belfast and, to a lesser extent, (London)Derry. 'Uneven development' thus accentuated rather than reversed the centuries-long effect of geographical factors which had linked Ulster more closely to southern Scotland than to southern Ireland. The seventeenth century patchwork settlement in Ulster of Protestant Scottish and English tenant farmers, displacing the indigenous Catholics, was the most significant of these, and provided the second distinction. Uneven development in Ulster, rather than eroding differentials between the two communities, tended to translate them into new urban settings, sustaining the ancient fears, resentments and insecurities of a frontier society. This cleavage became sharply politicized. Though Belfast Protestants in the late eighteenth century spearheaded a non-sectarian popular republican opposition (the United Irishmen) to the Anglo-Irish ruling class and British imperial control, it lost the initiative in the nineteenth century to nationalist movements based upon the emergent native-Catholic middle class and tenantry. All the key issues of the Victorian period – land reform, state–church relations, education, commercial policy, representation, the powers of local government – functioned to sharpen political divisions in Ulster based upon perceptions of a distinction between first and second-class citizenship in the United Kingdom. The Anglo-Irish elites who sought to keep the Union intact laid down only shallow roots through most of Ireland – in Ulster, the threat of minority status within a predominantly Catholic country ('Home Rule is Rome Rule'), and of its prosperous industrialized economy being subordinated to the interests of the rural South, permitted them to acquire a mass base in popular Protestant sectarianism as British governments sought to adapt the system of direct rule to accommodate Catholic and nationalist demands.

Like most of the malformed European state creations that emerged from the First World War, the Irish settlement of 1920–1 represented an attempt to compromise essentially incompatible national-territorial claims within the security system required by the victorious powers. Weakened by the War, and unwilling to continue a costly repression in Ireland, Britain settled for the removal of contentious Irish matters from its parliamentary system; the retention of naval bases in the Free State, military industries in Ulster, and reserve constitutional controls; and handed to its successor regimes the task of repressing revolutionary republicanism. The bulk of Sinn Fein compromised their demand for a unitary Irish republic, and fought a civil war with former colleagues, anticipating that history would eventually deliver them their ultimate goal. Ulster Unionists compromised their integral status in the Union to gain a political bastion from which to resist further surrenders to nationalist demands. Like all other European boundaries drawn at the time, the border between North and South cut across communal lines, leaving minorities of some 6 per cent Anglo-Irish and Protestants in the Free State, and around half a million Catholics scattered unevenly amidst a million Protestants in Northern Ireland (see map on page 211).

Over the following decades, 'Balkanization' and the increasing marginality of Ireland to Britain's key interests had inevitable consequences. In the Free State a new nation was forged – poor; agricultural; conservative; ultimately dependent upon, but suspicious of, its powerful neighbour; aspirational towards Northern Ireland, but recognizing the limited power at its disposal to redeem its fellow-nationals. In 1937, the constitution was repatriated. Built around liberal-democratic principles, it asserted (Article 2) irredentist claims to sovereignty over the North, and legitimized a special role for the Roman Catholic Church, Catholic social and moral doctrines, and the Gaelic culture. Not until the late 1950s, with the abandonment of economic protection, did more modern values and less stereotyped attitudes towards the North begin to penetrate the political culture.[4] In Northern Ireland itself, conservative Unionist leaders tightened their grip upon the new institutions. Subjected immediately to the onset of economic depression, they faced over the following years a large Catholic minority which rejected the regime's legitimacy, periodic republican insurrections, a hostile neighbouring state, and the possible threat of British withdrawal. Any movement towards political pluralism was resisted: reliance was placed instead upon consolidating a dominant one-party state resting upon popular sectarian attitudes and practices, and an ideology parasitic upon British imperialist rhetoric. Many Catholics found a place in the regime, as did many Protestants in the South. But most of the minority, politically fragmented, vainly sought salvation in the ending of partition.[5]

The 1960s proved, as in the South, to be a time of change. Economic modernization, weakening Protestant solidarity around the old Unionist elite, Catholic familiarity with the benefits of Britain's welfare state, and unilateral disarmament by the IRA, introduced some flexibility into the system. The government opened up communications with the Republic and with the nationalist opposition. For the first time, the minority became mobilized *en bloc* for a sustained political campaign – directed, however, not against partition, but, along the model of the American civil rights movement, to obtain the status of equal citizenship in the UK, if necessary by civil disobedience. Instead of aiding the transition to a more pluralist state, however, the movement generated a reaction from the regime which precipitated the crisis of 1968–9 and reintervention by the British government.

The view taken by many Irish nationalists and republicans that today's problem is consequential upon the 'unresolved national question' has some validity. Most European states whose boundaries, set after 1917, posed national and minority problems were soon devastated by political disarray, economic depression and international war, and then re-constructed under American or Soviet tutelage. If the old problems remain, they do so in a very different form. Ireland, however, was not reshaped by these continental sea-changes. Of all European states, it best confirmed in the 1960s Lipset and Rokkan's thesis concerning the persistence of party-political cleavages established in the early 1920s.[6] In Northern Ireland, they persist still. In searching for solutions to the problem, however, it is important to isolate the various dimensions to it, and also to the way in which it is perceived by the leading actors. I shall summarise these in terms of two broad categories: exogenous and endogenous accounts.

Within the first category fall orthodox nationalist and orthodox unionist versions of the situation. The former locates the problem in partition and the continued British presence in Ireland. By frustrating the will of the Irish people (as expressed by the majority on the island) for self-determination, Britain has upheld traditions of Protestant supremacy and ancient patterns of communal conflict, blocking the transition to a 'normal' modern state. So long as unionists can rely upon the British guarantee, they lack an incentive to reach accommodation with their neighbours. The northern minority will therefore always feel threatened, alienated and frustrated, and conflict perpetuates itself. Unionists, by contrast, reject any affinity with an Irish nation. To them Northern Ireland remains legitimately a part of the UK by international norms of sovereignty, and by the express wish of the majority to remain British citizens. While resistance to this comes within the province from the minority and the Republican movement, it gains succour and legitimacy from the irredentist claims of the Irish Republic upon sovereign British territory. Without that, northern Catholics would, like their compatriots in Liverpool or London, have adapted to British citizenship. Both of these views can be located from a third, 'bird's eye', view. Northern Ireland constitutes a broad 'frontier territory' of two metropolitan nation-states, in which its members have for historic reasons come to identify themselves in terms of one or other nationality. The problem arises because both states have failed to collaborate in controlling or neutralizing the local implications of perpetuating historic territorial disputes.

Endogenous accounts, by contrast, identify the problems of nationality and sovereignty as contingent aspects of a communal conflict
generated internally. Ulster developed from its roots as a settler society
in a way which has left a serious, but not unique, problem of ethnic or
race relations differentiating it from the societies of both Britain and the
Republic. Like Cyprus, say, but unlike Holland or Switzerland, the two
parties proved unable to find a common identity in terms of which to
reach accommodation: instead, each community sought support against
the other by allying itself with 'outsiders', and they, out of sentiment,
solidarity or interest, have been sucked in to reinforce the conflict. On
this view, the problem of Ulster has to be tackled by internal reform,
compromise and conciliation. Resolving disputes between the national
governments makes this easier, but the problem remains one whatever
sovereign government(s) assume responsibility.[8]

In the main, British governments since 1968 have tended to act on this
second approach. The 'Irish dimension' to the problem has been
acknowledged, but an awareness that overexuberant initiatives in this
direction generate unionist reaction and destabilize the situation has led
them to focus upon internal reform, accommodation and security.
Unfortunately, this set of priorities severely compromises its attempt to
play the role of external mediator or 'honest broker' between the local
communities. This was a role accepted in the 1960s and early 1970s by
civil rights leaders, but it has become increasingly identified with the
failure to deliver peace and to reduce sectarianism in the province. Irish
governments, by contrast, have tended to act on non-unionist versions of
the exogenous account. So long as Britain persists in treating Northern
Ireland primarily as an internal UK matter, the northern majority will
expect all members of Northern Ireland to conform to their own view of
British citizenship, and the minority will feel its national identity and
'legitimate national aspirations' being denied and oppressed.

In practice the positions of the two governments are more complicated. Ever since 1920 British governments have been caught between a
desire to remove the troublesome 'Irish question' from domestic affairs,
while publicly acknowledging[9] that any change in Northern Ireland's
constitutional status must be with the 'consent' of its people. This is not
so much a legal or moral commitment as a reflection of the fear that,
without consent, communal violence may erupt into civil war and the
complete destabilization of its island neighbour. Precedents for this
'doomsday scenario' can be found in events surrounding the constitutional settlements of 1920–1. This imposes a majority veto – in practice,
a veto of *the* (unionist) majority – over any changes, which was only
partially circumvented when the Anglo-Irish Agreement (AIA) was
signed in November 1985 without consultation or approval in Northern
Ireland (see below, p. 244). Irish governments, *pari passu*, have been by

no means eager to assume responsibility for the North in the absence of a stable system of provincial government, and have alternated between criticizing Britain's role and collaborating in attempts to install internal institutions acceptable to both communities. Indeed, under the AIA, the Republic has accepted the principle that constitutional changes must receive majority consent. (§1A)

One feature of the internal situation which initially raises hopes of political accommodation is that neither Protestant nor Catholic communities are entirely cohesive. Opinion polls and more scholarly investigations show wide ideological variations within each, complexities in attitudes towards national identity, gaps between 'moderates' and 'ultras', and disagreements over various proposed 'options' for the province – independence, integration into the UK, a united Ireland, majoritarian and consociational forms of local self-government.[10] Each community is split politically – Protestants between the Official and Democratic Unionist Parties (OUP, DUP), Catholics between the constitutional nationalist Social Democratic and Labour Party (SDLP) and Sinn Fein, the political wing of the Provisional IRA. The small Alliance Party (APNI), Workers Party (WP) and other minor Labour groups gain cross-sectarian support. (See Table 8.1) The SDLP has always combined its long-term objective of a United Ireland with a willingness to negotiate partnership in a new provincial government within the UK: 'Reform, Reconciliation, Reunification', as its leader, John Hume, has always stated its programme. Many Unionists have recognized that failure to build such a partnership risks their eventual ejection from the UK. These differences, however, rather than permitting greater flexibility, tend to encourage political stalemate. Few options can gain unequivocal support in each community. Competitive political elites cannot rely upon their capacity to 'deliver' their voters into agreements (as Unionist leaders who participated in a power-sharing executive in 1974 found to their cost) with mass followings historically attuned to suspect both 'the other side' and the 'loyalty' of 'their own' people. Finally, the existence of paramilitary forces waiting, and frequently active, in both wings offer a disincentive to political changes which might throw the initiative for a 'final solution' into their hands.

## Anglo-Irish Federation: The Unionist reponse to Nationalism, 1870–1920

Throughout the early part of the nineteenth century, Irish political nationalism represented a demand for repeal of the Act of Union and the restoration of a parliament coequal to that at Westminster under the British Crown.[11] In this context, there were many who, believing that

**Table 8.1** Party percentage share of the vote, 1979–87

| | UK General 1979 | NI European 1979 | NI Council 1981 | NI Assembly 1982 | UK General 1983 | NI European 1984 | NI Council 1985 | UK by-election 1986 | UK General 1987 |
|---|---|---|---|---|---|---|---|---|---|
| Official Unionist Party | 36.6 | 21.9 | 26.5 | 29.7 | 34.0 | 21.5 | 29.5 | 51.7 | 37.9 |
| Democratic Unionist Party | 10.2 | 29.8 | 26.6 | 23.0 | 20.0 | 33.6 | 24.3 | 14.6 | 11.7 |
| Other Unionist | 12.2 | 7.3 | 5.2 | 5.8 | 3.1 | 2.9 | 3.1 | 5.2 | 5.3 |
| Alliance | 11.9 | 6.8 | 8.9 | 9.3 | 8.0 | 5.0 | 7.1 | 5.5 | 10.0 |
| Social Democratic and Labour | 18.2 | 24.6 | 17.5 | 18.8 | 17.9 | 22.1 | 17.8 | 12.1 | 21.1 |
| Sinn Fein | – | – | – | 10.1 | 13.4 | 13.3 | 11.8 | 6.6 | 11.4 |
| Other Nationalist | 8.1 | 5.9 | 5.3 | 0.3 | – | – | 2.4 | – | – |
| Workers' Party | 1.7 | 0.8 | 1.8 | 2.7 | 1.9 | 1.3 | 1.6 | 3.1 | 2.6 |
| Others | 1.1 | 2.9 | 8.2 | 0.3 | 1.7 | 0.3 | 2.4 | 1.2 | 0.0 |

*Notes*
1. European, Northern Ireland Assembly and Northern Ireland council elections are held under the Proportional Representation system and these figures refer to the percentage of first preference votes won by each group. UK elections use a plurality system.
2. From 1983, Northern Ireland had 17 seats instead of 12 at Westminster.
3. In 1986, by-elections were held for 15 of the 17 NI seats at Westminster. Foyle and West Belfast were the two exceptions.
4. Others includes a range of candidates of which the most prominent are various Labour candidates. It also includes Independent, Liberal, Communist and Ecology Party candidates and in 1986 the Unionists' 'dummy' candidate 'Peter Barry'.

*Source:* C. O'Leary, S. Elliott, R. Wilford, *The Northern Ireland Assembly, 1982–1986* (1988).

pure resistance was counter-productive, or sufficiently dismayed by Britain's treatment of Ireland, sought a form of local self-government which maintained the benefits of the Union. Both federation and Home Rule (devolution) offered this middle way. That neither provided a solution was not entirely due to any inevitability about the course of Anglo-Irish conflict. As much it lay in the ambivalent relationship between these two schemes, and the contradictory nature of the proposals they entailed.

This was particularly apparent in the case of Isaac Butt, a member of the Anglo-Irish professional classes, who initiated the Home Rule movement in the 1870s. Under his successor, Parnell, this became the crucial mobilizing agency of mass-based nationalism. In his *Home Government for Ireland* . . . (1870), Butt argued a case for local self-government on the expectation that this would logically entail subsequently extending the principle to Scotland, Wales and England, leaving the Imperial parliament at Westminster dealing solely with defence, colonial and foreign affairs. Though Butt characterized his scheme as a 'federation', it was not intended to provide co-ordinate powers for the central and local parliaments, nor did it explicitly present a case for constitutional guarantees of 'states' rights' on the American model.[12]

These proposals arose from a conjunction of three events: the resurgence of revolutionary Fenianism in the 1860s; Gladstone's attempt to stabilize Irish Liberalism among the Catholic and Presbyterian middle classes by disestablishing the Anglican Church in Ireland (1869) and land reform (1870); and the confederation of British North America in 1867, which provided a model of integration. Butt was no friend of England, believing that Ireland's problems originated in mismanagement by a parliament far-distant from the local scene, and by absentee landlords who failed to perform their role of social and political leadership in Ireland. A Tory unionist, rather than a nationalist, he was concerned that local self-determination should strengthen the role of Ireland's propertied classes in both Ireland and the UK as a whole. Against the advocates of Repeal, he insisted that a return to the pre-1800 constitutional relationship would deprive Ireland of its representation in Westminster, excluding her, thereby, from active participation in imperial and world affairs, and reducing her to a provincial, introverted, island. Moreover, he insisted on the re-establishment of an Irish House of Lords as a bulwark of the traditional order, on the grounds that 'There is no people on earth less disposed to democracy than the Irish'.[13]

There were manifestly paradoxical features to this proposal. While it was offered as a means of securing political integration against the dangers of separatism (indeed, compromising its ostensibly federal character by retaining the 'supremacy of the imperial parliament'), the case for it necessarily had to be fought for on anti-integrationist grounds. Butt set out to create a broad popular movement built around a nucleus of 'Tory patriots', and thereby fragment a democratic alliance of Catholics, Presbyterians and Liberals, but in highlighting national grievances and injustices to build his political movement he soon alienated Tory and Unionist supporters who, quite reasonably, came to question how the mobilization of those least sympathetic to the Union could possibly be a means of strengthening it. By 1880 when Parnell assumed control, it had already assumed a characteristically nationalist form, in which the grand strategy for a federated British Isles had given way to arguing for the special and distinctive case of Irish self-government.

These tensions over the significance of Home Rule, and between it and federation, widened when, in 1886, Gladstone adopted Home Rule to build an all-Union political alliance between liberalism and nationalism. While he claimed that this would create a 'union of hearts' reinforcing political union, opponents questioned whether it would not merely institutionalize endemic conflict and provide nationalists with leverage to pursue wider separatist goals. These different interpretations permeated all debates on clauses of the four Bills presented to the House of Commons between 1886 and 1920. Four issues in particular seemed difficult to resolve. First, if revenues were raised primarily by the Imperial Parliament, the freedom of the Irish parliament would be severely curtailed, and there might be continual skirmishing between the two over Ireland's share. If, however, the Irish parliament acquired control over taxation, customs and excise, could it arrange its economy to raise sufficient revenue without imposing internal tariffs within the UK? Secondly, if Ireland's representation at Westminster ceased because it was internally self-governing, it would have no say in Union affairs. If it remained represented, could Irish MPs legislate on internal British affairs? And could they be stopped from using their political leverage to secure further privileges for Ireland? Thirdly, could sufficient safeguards for the Irish minority (or minorities) be built into an Irish constitution? If not, could rights of appeal to the Imperial Parliament be devised which avoided a veto power and the possibility of political stalemate? Underlying all this was the fourth problem. Did nationalists see Home Rule as a final settlement, or, as many made clear, as a step towards a separate co-equal parliament?[14]

It was such problems that, in 1886, led the renegade Liberal, Joseph Chamberlain, to argue for a genuine federation of all the UK nationalities – a proposal which formed the only constructive Unionist counter to Home Rule for the next three decades. Chamberlain's case had three major components. While Home Rule entailed unequal treatment throughout the Kingdom, and would provide a lever for nationalists to prise Ireland out of the Union, a UK federation provided equal treatment, resolved the dilemma over Irish representation at Westminster, and integrated national components of the Union by giving them a greater stake in its affairs. Secondly, Home Rule represented a potential disintegration of the Empire at its very heart, while federation would provide both a model and a framework for the ultimate strengthening of the Empire through imperial federation. Thirdly, federation would resolve the growing problem of 'overload' in central government by shunting off purely local business to local assemblies and freeing the United Kingdom parliament and civil service for more effective discussion of the 'big' issues.

There is some question about whether Chamberlain himself was altogether seriously committed to such a constitutional overhaul, or whether 'federation' was merely an effective political counter for a politician seeking to display his Liberal credentials while in open conflict with mainstream Gladstonian Liberalism.[15] What is certainly clear is that, for Chamberlain and his successors, the concept of 'federalism' was extremely ill-defined and wide-ranging. Popularizing it under the slogan 'Home Rule all round' throughout the 'Celtic fringe' obscured the fact that its prime purpose was to strengthen the machinery of central government. The slogan itself was applied to schemes of very different character based variously upon the United States or Canadian constitutions, systematic legislative devolution, and more limited administrative devolution with regional councils. In general, however, one principle tended to be asserted – the 'sovereignty of the Imperial Parliament' should not be impaired. As in all unitary states contemplating an internal federation, the very existence of an operational central heart made it difficult to contemplate a new 'bargain' or 'social contract' between the nationalities which might reconstruct the nature of centre-periphery relations.

Small sections of the British governing classes continued to propagate federation over the next decades. They were not, however, primarily concerned with the problems of peripheral regions of the UK, but imperialists intent upon the federation of the British Empire. At the main points of crisis in Anglo-Irish relations – 1910, 1912–14, 1918–20 – it was individuals from the Round Table organization, members and associates of Sir Alfred Milner's South African Kindergarten, who were most effective in placing the federal option upon the political agenda. Two matters differentiated them from Chamberlain. He had directly addressed himself to the 'Ulster question', and long before the 'solution' of partition was hit upon, had seen federation as permitting the creation of regional assemblies in both Dublin and Belfast. The Round Table members, by contrast, assumed a single Irish parliament, and only belatedly acknowledged that Ulster Unionists, even under federal arrangements, might reject government from Dublin. Secondly, Chamberlain came to take imperial federation seriously through his concern with the Irish question: the Round Table's priority was to provide a coherent structure of policy-making for imperial defence through the creation of a body representative of the UK and its colonies. Only by removing internal matters from Parliament would it be possible to accommodate colonial representation and to focus upon external affairs. It would also permit, they believed, greater coherence of imperial and foreign policy-making by shifting matters into the hands of experts and away from the partisanship of popular democracy.

As with the Home Rulers, there was a great deal of 'hazy thinking'[16] in this. If there were to be regional parliaments and an Imperial Parliament with colonial representation, should there not also be a distinct UK parliament? Or were the colonial representatives to legislate for internal UK affairs? If there was to be an Imperial and UK parliament, what, on the federationists' premises, was the need for regional parliaments within the UK?

There were wider reasons, also, why the federationist case failed in this period to shape the course of Anglo-Irish affairs. Unlike the 1960s and 1970s, when reform of the British constitution assumed a high place on the political agenda, nationalism in Wales and Scotland posed only minor political challenges to the two main parties. Nor did governments have to face demands arising out of economic disparities between the English regions. Since the only pressing problem of centre-periphery relations was therefore Ireland, it was hard to explain why a complete overhaul of the constitution was necessary when it was possible to isolate the Irish problem for unique treatment. It was also hard to see parallels between the task of integrating a worldwide empire, and that of establishing forums within a small state for more extensive local self-government. Even members of the Round Table came to acknowledge after 1910 that the aesthetic symmetry of universal federation was perhaps irrelevant for coping pragmatically with individual cases. Finally, while they saw imperial federation as a way of integrating colonial diversity into the central decision-making process at Westminster, they regarded a UK federation, conversely, as a means of removing regional diversity. A federation, however, by entrenching regional representation, is just as likely to give the localities a more, rather than less, powerful voice in national affairs.

## Quasi-Federalism: Northern Ireland in the Union, 1920–72[17]

The 1920 Government of Ireland Act, under which Northern Ireland operated until 1973, enacted a limited form of devolution, under which the local parliament and executive assumed responsibility in a wide range of areas, particularly local government, health, social services, policing, agriculture, education and commerce. Powers retained at Westminster ('excepted' powers) included defence, foreign affairs and external trade, and several 'reserved' powers (taxation, land purchase, post and the supreme court) were intended to be transferred to the stillborn Council of Ireland. Stormont had limited sources of finances, most revenue being drawn as a proportion from nationally-raised taxes. The supremacy of the Imperial Parliament was asserted in §75; §5 prohibited discriminatory legislation; and §§5(1), 8(6) and 12 specified powers whose use was subject to higher review. The retention of sovereignty at Westminster was clearly shown by the suspension of the

Act in 1972, and the subsequent period of direct rule through the Secretary of State for Northern Ireland.

In practice, however, relations between London and Belfast assumed a quasi-federal nature. A ruling by the Speaker of the House of Commons in 1923 that questions concerning powers granted to Stormont could not be raised at Westminster marked the early appearance of a federalist version of the Act. In 1922 the British Cabinet withdrew the Governor's veto upon legislation changing the local electoral system when threatened with the provincial government's resignation. Thereafter the Home Secretary in London exercised only weak supervision over its internal affairs, and in 1964 declined to exercise his powers under §4 of the Act to investigate discriminatory practices. Constitutional experts came to take the view that it would be illegitimate for Westminster to legislate on devolved matters. Relations between the two systems were thus increasingly those of co-equals, rather than of super- and sub-ordination.

The basis of this new relationship was neither constitutional nor judicial, but political. Having disposed of the Irish question in 1920–2, Britain's rulers were disinclined to permit its return as a contentious national and party-political issue at Westminster. Unionists deploying their devolved powers to consolidate political control, were anxious to avert potentially destabilizing intrusions from the national level. Moreover, local nationalist politicians, unreconciled to their continued membership of the UK, only periodically sought to bypass the local system of appealing, invariably unsuccessfully, to the higher authority. This tacit bargain to leave well alone was reinforced by two factors.

One was the unique party relationship. Before 1920, Irish Unionist and nationalist parties had been closely allied to, though organizationally distinct from, the British Conservative/Liberal Unionist and Liberal parties, which in effect ceased contesting Irish elections. Thereafter, British parties, including the Labour Party, withdrew entirely from Northern Ireland, refusing to admit its residents to membership. While Unionist MPs at Westminster generally voted with the Conservatives, and the occasional nationalist MP supported Labour, the separateness of the province's party system reinforced the political autonomy of its governing structure.

The second was the distinctive financial relationships which emerged between Belfast and Whitehall. As the economic depression of the 1920s bit deep into Northern Ireland revenues, expenditure on public welfare provisions grew. To avert bankruptcy, the imperial contribution deducted from nationally-imposed revenues was commuted, and the local budget became increasingly subsidized with the growth of welfare services. The practice emerged whereby the Exchequer and the Northern Ireland Ministry of Finance negotiated annually a bloc transfer payment, which came to be calculated on the basis of maintaining 'parity of services' with the mainland with additional funding to compensate for its relatively backward economic and social infrastructure. A consequence of this was that financial accountability virtually ceased. British ministers raised revenue on a national basis, negotiations at civil service level settled the grant, Stormont ministers reported the sums and then spent them. There was always a risk that Westminster might tug at the financial purse strings as a way of dictating political directions in the province, and within the Unionist heirarchy there developed some tension between groups concerned to direct funds towards their (primarily Protestant) political clients, and those worried that 'irresponsible' expenditure would threaten financial and political links with London.[18]

In general, however, the arrangements served to stabilize government in the province. Tying local welfare provisions to mainland standards rapidly accentuated the distinctions in living standards and social benefits between the north and south of Ireland. Unionists became even more dependent upon Britain than they had been before 1920, and increasingly in the post-war world, large sections of the Catholic minority came, if not to identify with the state, at least to acknowledge the high costs entailed by a straightforward British withdrawal.

In some areas – e.g. unemployment and social security benefit – national rules made any kind of discrimination impossible; in others, however – electoral law, education, housing, industrial location – Stormont and the local authorities (mainly, but not all, under Unionist control) secured sufficient discretion and funding to underwrite sectarian distinctions.

External economic support for the local state provided, therefore, opportunities for Unionists to maintain control, eliminated some of the major distributive flashpoints of a divided society, and permitted London to keep Belfast at arm's length. Unionist politicians also secured the freedom to hold together ideological tensions in their movement. While they remained on most social and economic matters on the right wing of the Conservative Party at Westminster, they were able at home to present the fruits of social-democratic legislation as a simple consequence and advantage of the British link.

In the 1970s, when devolution became a significant issue in UK politics, the practical experience of Northern Ireland was frequently referred to as a potential model. The Report of the Commission on the Constitution, chaired by Lord Kilbrandon, claimed, for instance, that 'in the large areas of government which were unaffected or at least not dominated, by the community problem, conspicuous progress was made' under Stormont – a comment made with special reference to the economic powers widely used in the late 1950s and 1960s to modernize the run-down economic infrastructure of the province.[19]

In a divided society, however, the line between 'communal' and 'other' activities of government is, at best, a fine one. During the 1960s, for instance, the decision to locate a second university in the mainly Protestant town of Coleraine rather than in the mainly Catholic city of (London)Derry, may have been taken on non-sectarian grounds; but it was widely perceived as having sectarian implications. Grants encouraged new industries to locate in growth areas with pools of skilled labour near to cross-channel communications. New roads and housing areas were developed to support them. These areas, however, were historically the more heavily Protestant areas, while the more solidly Catholic areas away from the north-east and towards the border, received far less favourable treatment. Public housing was always a major source of contention, partly because political patronage strongly influenced allocation, but also because, with the Catholic population growing faster than the Protestant, Catholic residence areas were under more severe pressure, and their expansion threatened the sectarian balance in electoral areas. Since a great deal of 'business' in small provincial societies like Northern Ireland tends to be transacted through informal networks – Orange and Masonic Lodges, party and church committees, graduate associations, extended family networks – the fact that these networks were often communally organized consolidated social distinctions and advantages.

In general, the regime survived, not through blatant discrimination and repression (though these were intrinsic features of the system), but because its 'normal' governmental functions sustained traditional sectarian divisions rather than eroding or accentuating them. Unionist leaders had little interest in counteracting them in order to build an alternative to their sectarian-based majority. And when, in the 1960s under Prime Minister O'Neill, attempts were made to modernize the image and practices of the regime, the system proved unmalleable. Faced with the civil rights marchers in 1968 and 1969, it fell apart at the seams as sectors of the government, the Protestant masses and the local security forces combined to react as if demands for reform from the minority posed a challenge to the regime itself. As indeed, by this time, they did. In this situation, the contradictions of the quasi-federal relationship with Britain became rapidly apparent. In order to sustain a relationship which kept Northern Ireland's problems at arm's length, the Westminster government was reluctantly compelled to intervene directly by applying pressure for internal reform and sending troops to maintain civil order. While presenting itself as an external mediator, and initially welcomed by the minority as a protection against the local state, it soon, facing a declining security situation and disillusion with the pace of reform, became entangled within the factious politics of a Unionist leadership whose political base was fast disintegrating, and locked in military confrontation with civil rights marchers and resurgent physical-force republicanism emerging from within the Catholic minority. There was only one escape from these dilemmas. On 24 March 1972, Stormont was prorogued, and responsibility for the government of Northern Ireland was reassumed by London.[20]

The experiment with quasi-federalism after 1920 had two funda-mental weaknesses. Because it rested upon the presumption that some kind of balance of power between nationalism and unionism existed on the island as a whole, which might one day usher in a shared pluralist state, no attempt was made to create a balance of power within the North's divided society. And since Britain's purpose was to shunt the problems of its turbulent Irish province on to local elites, it was willing to abandon its supervisory responsibilities in Northern Ireland so long as Unionist leaders were able to neutralize the local conflict and avert its intrusion into British politics. National effort thus went into ensuring that the regime had means at its disposal to remain stable, rather than into compelling its adaptation beyond the politics of 1920.

Both these weaknesses have been acknowledged in the fitful attempts since 1972 to return to some form of local self-government. The Northern Ireland Constitution Act (1973), technically still in force, led to the brief experiment in devolution in January–May 1974 before it was brought down by a loyalist general strike. It had three crucial innova-tions. First, it required the Executive to include political representatives of both the Protestant and Catholic communities. This power-sharing or 'grand coalition' basis represented a limited application of consociational principles. Secondly, the role of the Governor as representative of the Crown under the old regime was now assumed by the Secretary of State for Northern Ireland, with powers to appoint the Executive, scrutinize legislation, and exercise responsibility for 'reserved' powers. This represented direct political, rather than previously nominal, supervision of the local system. Thirdly, controversial political and security matters were excepted or temporarily reserved to the UK government – elections, emergency powers, policing, and the administration of justice.

It has so far proved impossible to secure consensus around these principles, though implementing them remains the ostensible object of British policy, and, indeed, provides the only basis for an internal settlement with any hope of long-term stability. Opinion polls also show that it is still the preferred option of the electorate. Many Unionist politicians would undoubtedly prefer a return to the 'Westminster system' of majoritarianism, some might prefer complete reintegration into the UK, but most have in recent years turned their attention back to the experimental principles of 1974. Two fundamental difficulties remain. Can Unionist leaders woo their electorate into accepting power-sharing? And could the SDLP accept a purely internal settlement? For what is crucially clear is that they have increasingly in recent years regarded any internal settlement as a transitional agreement on the way to a wider all-Ireland framework. It is in this context that we can examine proposals designed to achieve this on different, federal lines.

## Irish Federation – The Nationalist Response to Unionism

In the last days of Stormont, Northern Ireland showed every sign of being a 'failed political entity'. The prospect existed that, having failed to stabilize it, Britain would seek a way of abandoning its commitments, and of building new relations between north and south. Indeed, by accepting a Council of Ireland as part of the political package worked out in 1973 to establish a local power-sharing executive, Britain appeared to be contemplating a re-run of the stillborn experiment of 1920. In this situation, those who believed that Northern Ireland's problems could be resolved only in an all-Ireland context needed both to find a means of easing the suspicions of northern unionists and to provide Britain with a mechanism of bypassing its own guarantee on the constitutional status of the North by offering other kinds of guarantee. Federation played a major role in this new orientation. It was advocated in 1972 by, amongst others, the Provisional IRA in its revised *Eire Nua* ('New Ireland') programme;[21] the SDLP in its first major policy document, *Towards a New Ireland*; and in a substantial study of Ireland's current problems and opportunities by the up-and-coming Fine Gael politician, later Taoiseach (Prime Minister) of the Republic, Dr Garret Fitzgerald.[22] In 1979, Fine Gael published federal proposals in a pamphlet *Ireland – Our Future Together*, and the Forum for a New Ireland, convened by representatives of the main southern parties and the SDLP in Dublin during 1983–4, saw a variety of schemes offered up for consideration. The Forum Report (1984) put forward three proposals: a unitary Irish state; a federal state; and joint British-Irish sovereignty over Northern Ireland. And it was widely held that federation would be its main recommendation until, at the last minute, Charles Haughey, then leader of the Opposition, declined to sign the document unless preference was shown for the first, more traditional, option.

In fact, however, the idea of a federated Ireland goes back to the foundation of the state. During 1921, sections of the Sinn Fein leadership became acutely aware that the immediate prospects of a unitary republic were slim, but were reluctant to concede Britain's continued tutelage over the North. A 'think-tank' led by Professor O'Rahilly of Cork University, for instance, offered Switzerland as a possible model. More significantly, Eamonn de Valera, the Sinn Fein leader who led political opposition to the Treaty of 1921, founded Fianna Fail and later became Prime Minister and President of the Republic, has recently been revealed as a convert to federal principles.[23] Qualifications, however, have to be made to this view, which reveal some of the limitations of the nationalist perspective.

First, like British unionists responding to nationalism, de Valera clearly saw federation, not as a union of equal partners, but as a means of drawing a political entity of dubious legitimacy under the aegis of the only truly legitimate state formation. To accommodate unionist fears, he contemplated devolution of powers from a central state to Ulster, or to assemblies corresponding to the four 'historic provinces' of Ireland, but this was a granting of powers, not a bargain over the structure of the central state. Secondly, his prime interest was to limit the national territory over which unionists could exercise jurisdiction. His only systematic statement of a federal proposal was made in 1921. It entailed a plebiscite in the North, based upon pre-1920 parliamentary constit-uencies or smaller adminstrative regions of District Councils or Poor Law Boards, to determine membership of the two regions: Unionists 'could demand no more'. This was, in effect, a proposal for repartition, rather than federation; it would have produced a truncated, possibly fragmented, and certainly unviable northern political unit; and no attention was paid to safeguarding the position of minorities trapped on the 'wrong' side of these borders.[24] Thirdly, despite his aspiration for a reunited Ireland, de Valera's principal concern came to be the stability and identity of the southern state. In the course of his career, he was compelled to suppress his former colleagues of the IRA, limit his commitments to the northern minority primarily to rhetorical support, and, by drawing up a new constitution in 1937, settle for a form of 'republicanism in one country'. Northern unionism was discounted as essentially unredeemable.

No greater success could be expected from the Provisional IRA's revival in 1971/2 of the scheme for a federal Ireland based upon the four historical provinces of Ulster, Leinster, Munster and Connaught. Although the relevance of these provinces for a modern state was not explained, the intentions behind the schemes were clear. By re-creating the old 'nine-county' Ulster in place of the present 'six-county' Northern Ireland, and providing it with a *Dail Uladh* (Ulster assembly), unionists would retain their regional identity, the Protestant minorities in the three border counties of the Republic would return to the fold, and the sectarian head-count would be much more evenly balanced. From the Republican viewpoint, it was a significant concession. From the unionist, it was limited, since the demographic balance and trends in a reformed Ulster, as well as the possible fragmentation of party allegiances, would have limited its electoral safeguards. Essentially the burden of the scheme, like de Valera's, rested upon repartition within a basically majoritarian conception of popular sovereignty, rather than upon federation. Having gained little support outside the republican movement itself, the proposal was eventually removed from the constitution of Provisional Sinn Fein in 1981.

*Eire Nua*, as the language of its title suggests, was written from within the framework of traditional republican values, not least in its preference for small-scale community organizations and economic enterprises rather than the centralizing, cosmopolitan character of the modern state. These themes were prevalent in Ireland, as throughout the Western world, during the late 1960s and 1970s, and gave added impetus to a revival of the O'Rahilly proposal for adopting Switzerland as the model of a federated Ireland. Widely canvassed, it aroused considerable interest at the Forum when presented by the veteran republican and civil liberties campaigner, Sean MacBride. The concept of a thirty-two canton Ireland represented one extreme of federalist thinking, less concerned, perhaps, with forging the instruments of political integration than with retrieving the supposed virtues of face-to-face societies. Certainly, the Swiss analogy was not convincing. There seems little point in artificially imitating, through legislative fiat or some popular convention, the long and painful process by which Switzerland's isolated mediaeval communes were welded into a modern state. Insofar as the proposal is directly addressed to the problem of Northern Ireland, its function, like the four-province federation, seems designed primarily to create institutions that will dissolve political cleavages and the structure of party-politics in some amorphous conception of 'popular self-government'. Like all such schemes for the 'artificial' redrawing of political boundaries, it is largely abstracted from the kind of context in which a 'federal bargain' could be struck between unionists and other parties on the island.

The dominant view of a federation is one incorporating the two existing entities with their defined areas of jurisdiction, administrative machinery, and identifiable regional allegiances. This appears to have been the option considered by the SDLP, by the Fine Gael leadership under Garret Fitzgerald, and by most of those who favoured federation at the Forum. Though far and away the most plausible option, it raises considerable problems which I shall now explore. Three things have to be kept in mind if the proposal is to be convincing: Unionists must see some benefits from throwing in their lot with the Republic: federation has to offer something not available in a unitary state; and there has to be some prospect that the institutions will not lead to deadlock or instability.

## Number of components

Federations of *two* or *three* component units have a very poor track record. Rarely have they been attempted, and the experience of Pakistan, the UAR, Malaysia (technically more than two units, but in practice a union of Malaya and Singapore) and the 'communal federation' of Cyprus with two units, Nigeria, the Central African Federation, and the aborted East African Federation, with three units, does not bode well. Framers of the Canadian constitution, intent primarily on uniting Ontario and Quebec, took great pains to induce the maritime states also to join in as a counterweight. Constitutional changes in Belgium over the last two decades appear to offer a counter-example. Here, however, the arrangements arose from devolution, not integration; other political cleavages cut across that of linguistic regionalism; the question of national sovereignty has not had the same divisive significance; and, finally, it is not at all clear that current arrangements have produced a stable solution.

Reasons for the vulnerability of two/three unit federations are not hard to find. Since federations must embody a number of veto arrangements at the federal level, as well as autonomy at the local, viability depends upon the capacity of the parties to reach decisions by bargaining, coalescence and, indeed, 'logrolling'. Multi-state systems make shifting coalitions of the various units possible – two-state federations necessarily begin with a confrontation/veto relationship, and three-state ones are prone to unstable rotating coalitions of two against one. Such considerations lend some credibility to schemes for a more extensive partition of Ireland ('cantonization', 'four historic provinces'), and many federal states (e.g. Pakistan, Nigeria) have redrawn their federal maps for these reasons. All, however, have been reconstructions of existing federations, not products of the original federal bargain.

All federations face the problem of imbalances between the states in terms of population, wealth, natural resources, size of territory, degree of industrialization, etc. An Irish federation would comprise two units of one and a half and three and a half million people respectively. Although the historic disparity between the South as a poor, under-developed agricultural economy, and the North as a relatively wealthy and industrialized one, has, in recent years, been partly bridged, there remain major incongruities. The Republic has long experience of economic self-management, but has only recently experienced economic development; the North, by contrast, has passed through a long, if erratic, period of de-industrialization, with standards of living tied to those of the mainland through subventions from the British taxpayer (see Table 8.2).

Two points can be made here. First, in terms of the representation of

**Table 8.2** Some comparisons, Northern Ireland and Republic of Ireland

|  | Year | Units | North | South |
|---|---|---|---|---|
| Population | 1981 | 000s | 1562 | 3443 |
| av. per sq. mile. | 1981 | nos | 111 | 49 |
| Labour force | 1982 | 000s | 631 | 1283 |
| GDP at factor cost (current prices) | 1981 | IR£bns | 4229 | 9352 |
| Agriculture | 1980 | %GDP | 6 | 11 |
| Industry | 1980 | %GDP | 30 | 33 |
| Services | 1980 | %GDP | 64 | 56 |
| GDP per head | 1981 | IR£ | 2707 | 2716 |
| Personal income per head | 1981 | IR£ | 3102 | 2975 |
| Central government current expenditure | 1981 | %GDP | 70 | 53 |
| Social welfare expenditure | 1981/2 | mill. | £805.8 | IR£1277.1 |
| Calculated British subvention to NI Exchequer | 1963/4 | £m | 48 | |
|  | 1974/5 | £m | 653 | |
|  | 1982/3 | £m | 1312 | |

*Source:* New Ireland Forum *A Comparative Description of the Economic Structure and Situation, North and South*, Dublin, 15 December 1983 (adapted)

the component units, all federations must devise rules which both express, and run counter to, relative population sizes. It is imperative to avoid both domination by larger units, and undue preponderance for the smaller. In the proposed Irish federation, such rules would be difficult to draw up. Northern Ireland might require, for instance, the right to veto federal legislation, weighted voting in a federal chamber, equality within a second chamber, or a permanent 'power-sharing' executive (safeguards, after all, which the northern minority have demanded within Northern Ireland). It is unlikely that this would be acceptable in the South except as the most short-term transitional arrangement. Inability to reconcile majoritarian and minority-rights considerations virtually destroyed the consociational system in Cyprus within three years. Secondly, federal systems necessarily end up developing allocatory or redistributive mechanisms at the national level to equalize burdens and benefits among the states. In the Irish case, particularly where bloc grants received from outside the state (viz., the British subvention, American aid, EC regional fund) are likely to be a continuing feature, allocation may very easily become a zero-sum game, continually threatening the cohesion of national governments.

If we were to look to local precedents for the likely relationship between the two states, it would not be wholly appropriate to think in terms of the fairly stable relationship between Stormont and Westminster after 1920. As we noted, this depended upon the fact that the local majority inherently favoured the Union, and Westminster had little interest in the province. Quite the reverse would be true of a federated Ireland. A much better analogy could be drawn with the failed attempts before 1920 to devise an acceptable relationship between Britain and Ireland within the UK.

## Cultural diversity

Much has been made in recent years of the 'two traditions' ('identities', 'cultures', 'ethos', 'ways of life') in Ireland, and the way in which historic 'differences' have solidified as malignant 'divisions'.[25] The central virtue of federation, it is claimed, is that within its two states each 'tradition' can be assured of effective representation and security, leading thereby to greater tolerance, understanding and harmony. Given the orthodox view within Irish nationalism of northern unionism as either an essentially alien phenomenon, or a form of false consciousness, such legitimation of its distinctive character has been a major step forward. Indeed, it was precisely to publicize this revisionist account that the Forum for a New Ireland was established. Whether it offers a more coherent perspective is questionable.

The two 'traditions' of 'Irish Catholic nationalism' and 'British Protestant unionism' were, after all, not forged *independently* of each other, but, if we may use this terminology, in dialectical opposition. They emerged as countervailing forces during the nineteenth century mobilization of mass publics, and in part still retain their 'meaning' because each is a rejection of the other. The two 'cultures' do not simply represent variations and diversities, but symbolize ethnic and political solidarities of mutual self-defence and self-assertion. The Orange Order and its Catholic counterparts are not merely social clubs, but modes of political integration: the parades, bonfires and other celebrations of ancient historical events are not akin to the jollities of November 5th in Britain, but displays of communal solidarity, political commitment and opposition to the 'other'. Likewise, the use of the Irish language in public forums or on street signs, the opening or closing of shops and public places on Sunday, the proliferation of wall paintings showing 'King Billy' or dead republican heroes, create annoyance, not because of intolerance of different values and identities, but because they are public representations of the ability to control political or geographical space against the historic enemy.

Categorizing fairly unpleasant forms of ethnic conflict and political ideology under the somewhat anodyne label of 'differing cultures' has the effect, and probably also the intention, of understating the scale of the problem which has to be tackled. While it acknowledges contrasts between the conflicting 'cultures' of Ireland, and the diverse, pluralist cultures of most other modern liberal-democratic states which provide a model for some future Irish state, it it not clear how mere 'recognition of diversity' can translate one into the other.

But there are also other fundamental problems with the language of the 'two traditions'. In Northern Ireland, the confrontation of 'Catholic/ Irish/nationalist' versus 'Protestant/British/unionist' obscures subtle variations. While religious background, perceived nationality and political ideology are closely correlated, they are by no means identical, and each is itself ambiguous. Many Catholics by background reject the values and culture of the Catholic church, as many 'Protestants' reject fundamentalist Protestant values. Many Catholics from the 'nationalist tradition' have little interest in the traditional symbols of cultural nationalism, and those concerned to defend their British identity have found it hard to define essential components of 'the British way of life'. Many 'nationalists' reveal little faith in the virtues of a united Ireland, and the complexities and ambiguities of unionism have been the subject of many an academic study. Party alignments reflect splits within the two communities, and some cut across them. In general, the idea of securing equal recognition for the 'two traditions' leaves in the air precisely what is to be recognized. For all its concern to get to grips with these matters, the Forum was undoubtedly reluctant to accept the view that the basic 'identity' of unionism is defined, not by what it is for, but by what it is against, i.e., Irish reunification.

It is also questionable whether much sense can be made of the 'two traditions' as an all-Ireland phenomenon. In the Republic, the old clash between the Anglo-Irish Protestant Ascendancy culture and the subordinate popular native Catholic culture has virtually disappeared. In its place has appeared one between the (still-dominant) conservative, rural, quasi-Gaelic, ultra-montane Catholic culture, and a modern, materialistic, secular, youthful culture intent on reform of the old order. This conflict has been in the 1980s fought out over such issues as divorce, abortion, the role of the Catholic Church, and economic priorities between agriculture and industry, rural and urban areas. Indeed, the interest of many 'modernizers' such as Garret Fitzgerald in some form of reconciliation with the North originated as much from a desire to use the prospect of integration as a weapon in the reform of southern society as to resolve the northern problem itself. To this end, there has been a tendency to underestimate the extent to which the North retains the old cultural clash. And although a major part in unionist ideology is played by the defence of 'Protestant liberties' against 'Catholic authoritarianism', communal conflict has made it difficult for such principles of individual freedom to be translated into values of political pluralism.

The kind of federal arrangements proposed correspond to what writers have called an 'asymmetric' or 'incongruent' federation, rather than a 'symmetrical' or 'congruent' one.[26] That is, cultural variations are not evenly spread among the different states and across the system as a whole (as, according to Lijphart, occurs in Australia, Austria, Germany and the USA), but different cultural identities are 'bunched' in the different components (as in Belgium, Canada, Switzerland,[27] and, it should be added, Yugoslavia and India). Which kind of arrangement is more conducive to long-term viability is a matter of some dispute. Aspects of federalist theory, which appear to be followed by Irish federationists, suggest the latter. Asymmetric systems offer different cultural groups the opportunity to express their unique identity at the local level, and hence defuse conflict at the national level. Unfortunately, this runs counter to practical experience. As Maurice Vile observes, '. . . it is clear that where the boundaries of the member-states are drawn so as to coincide with communal divisions the likelihood is that the problems of operating the machinery of federalism will be exacerbated.[28] If, for instance, it is claimed that partition blocked Ireland's path towards a modern pluralist state by permitting the creation of a Catholic state for Catholic people, and a corresponding Protestant state for Protestant people, federating the two does not necessarily undermine the division: rather, it is embedded in a new framework, can be safeguarded by possible vetoes at the federal level, and defended by the threat of secession if challenged.

But the federation would not, of course, be completely asymmetrical. The problem of the northern Catholic minority would still remain. The extent to which they themselves share a 'common culture' with members of the Republic is, as I have noted, problematic, and under a two-state federation minority safeguards would necessarily be demanded. But this adds to the complications of the proposals. For northern Unionists are not being offered the option of a state to protect their cultural identity, but one in which two cultures are to co-exist on broadly equal terms. If, however, this is both necessary and possible in one portion of a federal state, what precisely is the rationale of federalism? Why could comparable guarantees not be given to the minority 'unionist' culture within a unitary Irish state – as the current Taoiseach, Charles Haughey, might argue – or to the 'nationalist' culture within an essentially 'British' state?

Overall, the language of the 'two traditions' or 'two identities', and the need for each to be given political 'recognition', tends to lead to obfuscation. It is not at all clear that they can be satisfactorily defined.

Acknowledging and institutionalizing them is not necessarily the most appropriate way of eliminating their divisive significance. And the language of cultural differences obscures the underlying conflict over political power – the northern minority's struggle to get access to it, the northern majority's determination that the means of access shall not be through the political reunification of Ireland.

If the problem could be reduced to one of securing tolerance and equality of treatment for the two traditions, another federal alternative offers itself to that based on territorial units, particularly since any geographically-based divisions necessarily cut across communal lines (see map on page 211). This would be some form of *communal* ('corporate' or 'personal')[29] federal arrangement. Under such a system, communal identities would be defined, individuals assigned either by fiat or personal choice to membership of one or other community, and each community would acquire political autonomy in relation to matters of communal concern – education, religion, cultural institutions, etc. Such practices are familiar from imperial states (e.g. the *milets* of the Ottoman Empire), and were offered by the Austro-marxists as a solution to Austro-Hungary's ethnic problems. Modern examples might be inter-war Estonia, Cyprus after independence, Lebanon after 1943, and contemporary Belgium. Whether such arrangements can genuinely be called 'federal' or not is open to question. In Northern Ireland, such arrangements would probably correspond more closely to the 'segmental autonomy' component of a 'consociational democracy' as characterized by Lijphart.

Erecting such a system on an all-Ireland basis has little to commend it. To introduce such options into an increasingly secular, pluralist society would be retrogressive indeed. It is highly unlikely that even Trinity College Dublin would today wish to reassociate itself with such 'non-Irish' cultural values as raising the Union Flag over its buildings.

Even in Northern Ireland such a scheme smacks of perversity. Communal federations (as indeed consociations) seem best suited to pre- or neo-democratic states – where non-elective traditionalist community leaders retain authority to speak on behalf of 'their' people – and to pre-modern or modernizing societies, where communal isolation and self-sufficiency may be high. Modern adminstrative states are inherently territorial (to be 'of no fixed abode' or have 'no place of work' puts one at a permanent disadvantage); communal isolation and self-sufficiency are impossible; and potential communal leaders have to bid for electoral support. It is perhaps significant that, in Belgium, the communal-based federal arrangements were paralleled by territorially-based ones, and the two have partially merged.

Northern Ireland is, in this respect, a modern society. Though communalism is endemic, the legal and institutional underpinnings of communal distinctions were removed long ago. The universities are mixed. TV and radio target audiences on a regional and national, not communal, basis. Newspapers have their distinct audiences, but few are institutionally linked to specific communal or party organizations. Many residential areas are self-segregated, but the patterns are complex. Schools, too, are self-segregated, between a state sector that is growing out of its purely Protestant past, and a subsidised voluntary, mainly Catholic, sector. Educationalists, teachers and administrators are working to break down these barriers, rather than consolidate them, not least by encouraging integrated educational and recreational facilities.

There is no reason in principle why communal councils should not be established to finance and oversee facilities and activities favoured exclusively by one or other community. However, there has been no political demand for such a scheme, and it would run completely counter to the thrust of recent policy which is to undermine segregated practices. Moreover, such councils would be unsuited to tackling the key contentious issues, which are not linguistic and cultural, as we noted earlier, but relate to economic opportunities, security, and political relations outside the province.

## Motives for federation

While federation can be offered as a means of safeguarding the unionist minority in a united Ireland, the basic question remains: why should they sacrifice the undoubted benefits of membership of the UK for such an uncertain future? The premise, as we noted earlier, is that Britain has no particular interest in retaining sovereignty over Northern Ireland and that withdrawal is frustrated by the problem of delivering a stable, and not unfriendly, successor regime. Unionists, in the long run, simply *have* to come to terms with their own minority and the Irish majority as a whole. Independence, though possibly attractive in the short-term, will prove economically and politically unviable. In addition to this, however, there are two basic gains which it has been suggested unionists will make: greater security; and better economic prospects.

Mutual protection against common enemies – security – (along with the prospect of mutually advantageous imperialist ventures), is, according to William Riker,[30] the central motive behind all federations. And all federal systems empower the central government with control over defence, foreign policy and last-resort internal security. Neither political entity in Ireland, however, faces a common external threat. The Republic is a neutral power which declined to join NATO in 1949. This policy has largely been conditioned in the past by a determination to dissociate itself from British foreign policy, and has been made possible by geographical isolation and knowledge that Britain would never permit a hostile power to establish itself in Ireland. From its membership of the UK and, through it, NATO, Northern Ireland is externally secure except against threats from its traditional unfriendly neighbour, the Republic. Nationalists occasionally attempt to interpret hostile gestures between the British government and unionists as signs of the latter's recognition that they cannot rely upon Britain's protection. This view glosses over the fact that unionists tend to fall out with Britain when British governments attempt to drive them towards accommodations with the minority or the South.

According to A.H. Birch,[31] there are precedents for federations being forged on grounds of internal, rather than external, security; and both parts of Ireland clearly face a destabilizing threat from armed republican organizations. Throughout the troubles, security forces on both sides of the border have collaborated against this challenge, and since the signing of the Anglo-Irish Agreement this has increased further. Would a federal Ireland increase the effectiveness of the security operation?

Rather than being an incentive for federation, this prospect brings to the fore the most controversial aspects of the current situation. To the southern elites and the SDLP in the North, the roots of republican violence lie mainly in Unionist intransigence towards legitimate political aspirations, a history of sectarianism and excessive use of force within the police and army, and of partiality in the legal system. Co-operation in the security operation from nationalists will invariably be qualified if it is conducted by British troops, a locally-raised Ulster Defence Regiment almost 100 per cent Protestant in composition, and the Royal Ulster Constabulary which is able to attract a Catholic membership of little over 10 per cent. Nor can support be expected if it appears impossible to suppress the vigilantism of Protestant paramilitary organizations. On this analysis, the obvious purpose in transferring security to a federal government is not just to improve operational efficiency, but also, by ensuring greater impartiality and accountability, to enhance the legitimacy of the operation as a whole.

To most unionists, however, and, in part, the British government, the roots of the problem lie in the nationalist aspiration itself. Pressing the case for Irish unity itself provides tacit legitimation for republican violence. It also means that 'the battle against terrorism' is supported in a half-hearted manner, with suspects and criminals finding safe-havens in nationalist areas or across the border, and constant criticisms being levelled at the British security forces and judicial system. On this view, any proposed transfer of security is suspect since it appears to imply that the battle will not be conducted effectively, nor will the community presently threatened by violence be guaranteed protection.

The obvious counter to this is that satisfying the aspiration for Irish unity will remove the source of violence, either by satisfying the IRA, or by undermining its political support. Both of these are unlikely, at least in the short run. The IRA's political aspirations for a new republic, though imprecise, go far beyond what might be delivered in an agreement made between unionists and constitutional nationalists. Even were it accepted by some members, there would be the possibility of a split like that which led to civil war in the Free State in 1922–3. Depriving it of communal support, moreover, would require a massive long-term reconstruction of the deprived urban ghettoes of Belfast and (London)Derry, and poor border areas, which provide its base. In the meantime, a new state would have to face the fact that political agreement might regenerate Loyalist paramilitary activity on a massive scale. The security problem, therefore, cannot simply be wished away.

There are practical problems to striking a federal bargain in these circumstances. Currently, security in Northern Ireland is under Westminster rather than local control, and would probably remain so if any future return to local self-government failed to produce a dramatic decline in violence. (If it did decline, the case and the incentive for Irish unity would presumably also decline.) A federal state, lacking British forces, would have to rely on the far-smaller and less well-trained Irish Army, in whom unionists would have much less faith. Catholic distrust of the UDR is so deep that it would almost certainly have to be stood down or wholly reconstructed, possibly releasing large numbers of Protestant military personnel whose allegiances would be uncertain. This problem would apply also to reconstruction of the RUC. If control over the northern and southern police forces were retained in the hands of the provincial, rather than federal, governments, it is not clear that distrust among the northern minority would be assuaged, or that operational efficiency would rise – if they were merged into a federal force, would unionists trust it any more than they would the Irish Army? And would the expectation be that the sectarian imbalance within the current RUC could be rectified by transfers of personnel, with northern police patrolling the streets of the South, southern police those of the North? All of these practical difficulties could be overcome with trust and goodwill: but it is precisely these qualities which are lacking.

Equally problematic is the economic case. This has been heavily emphasized in recent years. The Fine Gael proposals devoted eight out of 126 paragraphs to institutional arrangements within Northern Ireland, eighteen to the economic aspects of Irish integration – the Forum Report was accompanied by five research documents, three on economic interrelationships, one on the economic costs of the troubles. Wooing unionism on economic grounds has traditionally seemed a lost cause. As we noted earlier, the economic differences between Ulster and the rest of Ireland, compounded by years of financial support from the British taxpayer, always suggested that the North had far more to lose than gain from separation. Though it is often claimed that both parts of Ireland, particularly the border areas, suffered economic damage from partition, it is difficult to estimate the precise costs compared with those resulting from the general economic depression of the inter-war period.

In recent decades, these arguments have not had the same force. Protectionist policies were abandoned by the Republic in the late 1950s, and both states found themselves attempting to modernize their economies through outside investment, trying to increase tourism, and looking to the EC as a source of regional and agricultural support. Since an historic meeting between the two Prime Ministers in 1965, cross-border co-operation has had a high place on the agenda. (Many Unionists, it should be said, were at odds with the 'official' policy on these issues.) Rapid development in the Republic pointed, not merely to a bridging of the old economic differentials (*Ireland – Our Future Together* §23ff; Forum *Report* §3.8), but to the prospect of it becoming economically dominant. In the Republic, the EC was seen as a means of finally liberating itself from economic dependence on Britain, and moving from under the cultural and political shadow thrown by its neighbour to play an independent role in a wider arena. In many of the comments on Northern Ireland, the point was made that, as a region of the UK, its ability to share in this new future was constrained since 'British' interests would invariably be placed higher on the agenda. Linked together, the Irish states would be in a much stronger position to pursue interests they shared in common as peripheral areas of the Market.

In the late 1980s, one of the central assumptions on which this case for federation rested has come badly unstuck. Economic mismanagement in the late 1970s, failure to adapt old priorities in taxation and public expenditure, and unstable policy-making in the early 1980s brought a halt to the economic miracle in the Republic. Massive overseas debts, arrested growth, expenditure cuts, price rises and the ancient tell-tale sign of rising emigration reduce its attractive power for the North. By contrast, investment in Northern Ireland has remained buoyant, if still inadequate for its most deprived areas. But there were other assumptions made at the time about the economic benefits accruing from reunification that were questionable: that, by 'normalizing' the situation in the North, wasteful expenditure on security would cease, and its battered economy could be reconstructed; that there would be 'dynamic effects' on growth (Forum *Report*, §4.9.3); and that Britain would continue its financial support to Northern Ireland for an interim period.

As I noted above, there is no reason to believe that the security situation would instantly become less precarious after a British withdrawal, and the costs of the operation would thus fall on a relatively small Irish budget rather than a large British one. So, too, would the costs of 'reconstuction', though there would be expectations of large injections of international funds as has followed the Anglo-Irish Agreement. Whether transfer payments would still come from the Westminster government is problematic. No Chancellor is likely to be happy with transfers to Northern Ireland (or would it be a federal government?) being a first charge on his budget when he had no control over their disbursement. Moreover, either annual payments would have to be defined in advance by Treaty, when they would be unrelated to the actual financial needs of the province, or fixed annually on an *ad hoc* basis given that traditional criteria for determining Northern Ireland's share of the UK budget would no longer apply. In all cases, it cannot be expected that there will be a simple, linear adaptation of economic expectations within Northern Ireland to living standards and welfare provisions in the Republic. Were integration to have 'dynamic effects' on growth, the transition might be easier. But this view represents a simplistic interpretation of the gains from economies of scale. Now that both parts of Ireland belong to the European Community, benefits of scale can already be enjoyed. The approach of the Single European Market in 1992 makes much of the argument redundant.

In general, the whole economic case for federation possesses an air of unreality. Insofar as it has a basis, it derives very much from misconceptions about the way in which state formations such as the German Empire and the EC grew out of the Zollverein and early European experiments in economic co-operation – a misconception once shared by those who believed that a British imperial federation could grow out of imperial tariff preference. The modern world, particularly the European one, makes possible all kinds of economic linkages between states without requiring that the political boundaries between them should be altered to fit speculative views of what constitutes an appropriate 'national economy'.

## Political Parties

In sustaining the political integrity of federations, constitutional rules and formal institutions provide only half of the story. The other half, as has convincingly been argued is provided by the structure of political parties which operate within them.[32] At one extreme, the early Nigerian federation fell apart because parties had only regional, not national, bases: at the other, India, the Soviet Union and Yugoslavia have been crucially dependent upon the existence of a single dominant party capable of containing divisions. The main problem of Anglo-Irish relations began with the destruction in Ireland during the 1870s and 1880s of a union-based party system, and the emergence of one shaped primarily by local cleavages.

An Irish federation is likely, as we have suggested, to contain strong centrifugal, if not outright divisive, forces. And it is hard to conceptualize the countervailing centripetal forces which might hold them together. The various unionist and nationalist parties of the North, and the Fine Gael and Fianna Fail parties in the South, which have dominated each region since partition, reflect fundamentally different alignments, and no clear-cut alliances have been built by any across the border. The various labour, republican and centre parties which already, or might be expected to, contest elections in both states currently do not receive widespread support. Given the record of the last few decades, only Fianna Fail possesses the size of electoral support and 'governing passion' to play the role of, say, the Christian Democrats in Italy as the lynch-pin of the system. It is, however, also the party which has shown the least sympathy for a federal system and safeguarding Unionist interests.

The initial period of federation would probably have to work with a contrived executive, based on some complex power-sharing formula involving the major parties (e.g., *Ireland – Our Future Together* §114), especially if such an arrangement existed in Northern Ireland. This would be continually under pressure. Collaboration between the southern-based parties would be threatened by the competitive relationship in their own province. Representatives of the minority from a northern government would be torn between loyalty to policies agreed with their local partners, and allying with the southern representatives to outvote them. Without artificial constitutional constraints (which could well crack under the strain), the system could well open out into a whole series of unstable coalitions formed from minority parties. Secessionist threats would undoubtedly play a major part in the proceedings, as in all new federations.

Nothing about this is inevitable. Irish politics could well move towards Switzerland's conservative, coalescent system of government, loose two-party politics on the American model, or even old-fashioned British class politics. But nothing in a federal constitution could guarantee such benign outcomes as opposed to the less attractive alternatives.

## The Stabilization of Anglo-Irish Relations

It is clear that the quasi-federal relationship between Northern Ireland and Britain after 1920 proved unsatisfactory, and that there are profound difficulties associated with any simple transfer of sovereignty to an Irish federation. This points to a third approach – that of defusing the contentious issue of national sovereignty by recognizing Northern Ireland's location at the interstices of two sovereign states, a border area for which both might assume joint responsibility. Such an approach entails focusing, not so much on federation as a constitutional form, but federalism as a broad process of building institutional links across exclusive areas of sovereignty.

The proposed Irish Councils of 1920 and 1973 can partly be seen in this light, designed as they were to provide a forum for collaboration between North and South within a wider political framework. Yet they possessed the endemic weakness of requiring unionist participation in political relations with what, to them, was a hostile state on a unique basis not shared by the rest of the UK, and hence were subject to instant boycott.

An obvious way of avoiding this prospect is through institutions linking London and Dublin directly. While Northern Ireland has provided a major bone of contention in the past, both countries have common interests in its stabilization, reducing diplomatic disagreements, and, on the wider front, pursuing joint action in the European context. Unlike the Turkish and Greek governments during Cyprus's most troubled period, more unites than divides them. The foundations of such an approach were laid in the late 1970s with collaborative ventures at civil service level on energy, customs, transport and economic planning – matters intimately related to mutual membership of the EC. In 1980, this turned into a remarkable series of summit meetings between the two Prime Ministers addressed to the 'totality of relations' between the islands, the creation of an Anglo-Irish Council, joint adminstrative committees to service the Council, and regular meetings at ministerial level. 'Megaphone diplomacy', as it came to be called, still persisted. But at least the Republic had acknowledged that the unresolved problem of Northern Ireland could no longer be a barrier to normal relations between the two states, and Britain had recognized the true significance of the 'Irish dimension'. This process culminated in the Anglo-Irish Agreement of November 1985, which currently governs relations between the two states with respect to Northern Ireland. In order to clarify the significance of this innovation, it is necessary to look at the process of 'federalizing' from a number of different standpoints.[33]

Many proponents of a federal Irish state have hypothesized that resolving Northern Ireland's constitutional status could be a prelude to a future confederation of the British Isles – even, perhaps, a Federation of the WISE (Wales, Ireland, Scotland, England) or IONA (Islands of the North Atlantic). Though broader reasons could be adduced to support a reconstruction of the old Union, the special one is that northern Unionists would be travelling along the road, not to separation, but to a wider form of integration. The problem with this set of priorities is that it risks putting the cart before the horse. Federating Ireland within a broader (con)federal structure might prove possible; if the second presupposes the first, it is open to all the problems raised in the last section.

An alternative path towards confederation was sketched out by the SDP/Liberal Alliance Commission Report of July 1985, one of the most sophisticated pamphlets on the constitutional issue.[34] It strongly emphasized the need to distinguish between 'East–West' and 'North–South' dimensions to the problem. The latter (the 'nationalist/unionist' dimension) it proposed dealing with on orthodox British lines – a devolved provincial assembly and power-sharing executive within the UK, though one less rigid in its consociational features than the 1974 experiment. The long-term process towards confederation on the East-West axis, was to be advanced by creating a 'British-Irish Parliamentary Council', comprising representatives of the Dail, Westminster and the Northern Ireland Assembly, linked to the work of the Anglo-Irish Ministerial Council. It would sit irrespective of any attempted unionist boycott. The model for this was provided by the Nordic Council; and its functions, though necessarily incorporating Northern Ireland, would primarily be directed towards economic collaboration and relations with the EC, and avoid institutionalizing the 'Irish dimension' solely within the province.

Working towards confederation along such 'unionist' lines has much to commend it in preference to working along 'nationalist' ones, since it minimizes the destablizing consequences of changing Northern Ireland's constitutional status. But both raise two questions. What precise contribution does progress towards a British-Irish confederation make to the internal politics of Northern Ireland? And are there any particular benefits to be found in confederation otherwise? In relation to the first, it might certainly help reinforce an existing internal accommodation. Were this absent, however, the central institutions would face a choice between avoiding sensitive Northern Ireland issues, or focusing more closely upon them. This could well soon turn into a form of 'joint sovereignty', the third option suggested in the Forum Report. As the SDP/Liberal Alliance Commission notes, there are serious difficulties with this option. It smacks of a return to a colonial form of rule, and could just as well perpetuate as reduce the divisions in Northern Ireland. Beyond this issue, the case for confederation presumes that each country has interests in common with each other which are, of their nature, stronger than those which divide them in relation to external affairs. Traditionally, their views on international relations, as pointed out earlier (p. 236), by no means coincide. And in the flux of political relations within the EC, there could be positive disadvantages for each in having to develop common strategies over the whole range of affairs. Much of the case for confederation rests upon two factors: that the countries once belonged to the same political unit; and that it would be valuable to follow the example of the smaller European democracies (Scandinavia, Benelux) in forging wider areas of co-operation. Whether, however, these considerations outweigh the fact that Britain and Ireland once parted amidst civil war and repression, and that partnerships between a once-overbearing imperial state and a small resentful neighbour may always be fraught, remains an open question.

In the process of normalizing Anglo-Irish relations during the 1980s, the New Ireland Forum of 1983–4 was, in many respects, a gigantic red herring. Though ostensibly open-ended in its remit, the purpose of the Forum was to defend constitutional nationalism in Northern Ireland against the electoral onslaught launched by Sinn Fein in the wake of the 1981 hunger strikes of republican prisoners. At the time, Anglo-Irish relations had not recovered from public disagreements over the Falklands War; the electoral threat to the SDLP had prevented its participation in a new consultative Northern Ireland Assembly, designed as the first stage of 'rolling devolution' but now disbanded; economic crisis in the Republic had accentuated party disputes, and generated increasingly unstable and rhetorical pronouncements on the North. While the Forum Report reconsolidated a coherent nationalist position, its proposals for altering sovereignty in the North were unacceptable both to unionists and to Britain. At the same time, the Report, along with pressure from American public opinion, proved a highly effective bludgeon forcing Britain to accelerate its exploration of the 'Irish dimension'. The product of this was the Ango-Irish ('Hillsborough') Agreement of November 1985.

This has been presented, not as a 'solution' to the problem of Northern Ireland, but as a framework in which the problem can be more satisfactorily tackled. It contained four significant elements. First, it recognized the existing position of Northern Ireland as an integral part of the UK, and stated that no change could take place in its constitutional position without the consent of a majority of the people there. Secondly, it established an Inter-governmental Conference, chaired by the Secretary of State for Northern Ireland and the Irish Foreign Minister, with a Secretariat in Belfast drawn from officials of the Northern Ireland Office, and the Irish Foreign Office. This was empowered to discuss a wide range of policy matters relating to Northern Ireland – economic, social, cultural, security, the administration of justice – in which the role of the Irish representatives was 'advisory', while British ministers and their officials remained responsible for taking and enacting the decisions. The Agreement came to be backed up by an International Fund, financed particularly by

American and Canadian money, to be disbursed for projects on both sides of the border. Thirdly, it drew heavily upon the language of the Forum Report in identifying the crucial task of reconciling the 'two traditions' and ensuring their parity within Northern Ireland. Fourthly, it had the status of an international treaty, approved by the two parliaments, and lodged at the UN. Its terms were to last, initially, for three years, with the possibility of annual reviews. However, one important development could allow substantial revision – if, in the meantime, agreement was reached on an 'acceptable' form of return to local self-government in the province.

The Agreement undoubtedly had basic weaknesses. It was formulated in strict secrecy, without the participation of unionists or the southern opposition party. It was deliberately imprecise about the specific issues that would come within its remit. It assumed that the Republic could reform sectarian features of its own constitution, an assumption immediately disabused by the defeat of the referendum to permit divorce (1986). It was manifestly inspired by political considerations relating to the electoral fortunes of the SDLP and the Fine Gael government, and the British government's need to defuse international criticism. And it was presented by the two sides in very different terms –by British politicians as a guarantee of Northern Ireland's place within the UK so long as the majority wished, and as a major contribution to the security situation, by the Irish government and the SDLP as an innovation which acknowledged that the problem had to be seen from an all-Ireland perspective. (Indeed, the versions published in Britain and the Republic contain significant verbal differences.)

Despite these limitations, the Agreement had considerable virtues over previous initiatives. Not the least of these is its very open-endedness. For, rather than being an option which blocks off other options, it makes available, I would suggest, four possible 'scenarios'.

The first is that unionists appalled by this intrusion, however minimal, by the Irish government into Northern Ireland's affairs, might take up the option of revising the Agreement by initiating discussions on a return to devolved, power-sharing government. In the early days, this seemed unlikely. The Official Unionist Party appeared to respond by demanding closer integration in the UK, and the Democratic Unionist Party was hinting at a Unilateral Declaration of Independence. Both collaborated on a campaign of protest and boycotting of political bodies. However, the institutions of direct rule meant that government carried on; committed by an international agreement, the British government was prepared to 'face down' the protesters; and the workings of the Conference were not susceptible to boycott. Recognizing their isolation, unionist leaders began in 1987 to reconsider their options. While still demanding repeal of the Agreement, they proved more willing during

1988 to explore the prospects of devolution. Since the Agreement is ostensibly premised upon the fact that, in the absence of consensus within Northern Ireland the two sovereign governments act as 'proxies' for the two sides within the province, a return to devolution might permit a reduction in the scope of the Conference into a general guarantor of the internal arrangements.

Secondly, if devolved government returned, the place of the British Secretary of State might be taken by a Northern Ireland Prime Minister. A permanent forum of North–South discussions might thereby emerge which, with the later addition of a parliamentary tier, could evolve in the direction of a Council of Ireland like that proposed in 1973–4. Whether the reconstituted Conference would remain purely consultative, or gradually assume the form of a confederal arrangement, would depend upon many contingencies. The key factor, however, is that the ground-work for North–South collaboration would have been laid by *British* Ministers, and, entering the process late-on, a re-established Northern Ireland government would not be confronted with the same political pressures as it was in 1974.

The third possibility is that, if an acceptable form of devolved government did not emerge, the Conference might evolve towards joint sovereignty, joint authority, or at least *de facto* joint control. We have noted the difficulties of this option; but, at least, it would emerge as a gradual process, not an imposed solution. If it did so, and local politicians still found it impossible to operate a devolved system, membership of the Conference might be widened, or bodies attached to it, in order to provide a direct local input into decision making. At the present moment (mid 1988), while unionists are exploring the devolution option, the SDLP appears to be drawing further away from an internal settlement that might reduce the role of the Irish govern-ment. Direct access to the Conference might appeal more to them; and this, in turn, might be an incentive for other parties to participate so as not to be left out in the cold.

The final possibility is that the Conference might evolve towards the 'Nordic Council' option of the SDP/Liberal Alliance programme if a parliamentary tier were added made up of Westminster MPs (some of whom might be Northern Ireland representatives) and deputies from the Dail. The scope of issues covered by the Conference, and its membership, would have to widen, but in many respects this would resolve an endemic ambivalence in the current Agreement. For, as we noted, the key to the Alliance proposal was a clear separation of the North/South and East/West dimensions. This was necessary, it was argued, to assuage unionist fears and avoid placing Northern Ireland in a unique, and potentially confusing, position *vis-à-vis* sovereignty. The current Agreement is subject to precisely these criticisms. It covers, not

the 'totality' of Anglo-Irish relations, but matters related to N
Ireland, and there is incongruity in the fact that the Co
chairmen are the Irish Foreign Minister and the British Secretary of
State for Northern Ireland. This framework appears to support claims,
from both local Unionists and local nationalist politicians, that its prime
function is to lever Northern Ireland into joint authority or federal
arrangements with the Republic, and we have noted that these are
certainly possible developments. Events over the last three years,
however, suggest that this is far from the interpretation of the British
government. Britain's prime interest in 1985 was better security
relations with the South – co-operation against the movement of IRA
personnel and material across the border, and simplified procedures
for extradition – and defusing international and local criticism of its
wholly negative reaction to the Forum Report. Under the aegis of the
Agreement, it is legislating against a number of sectarian aspects of
Northern Ireland's life though these initiatives were already in the
pipeline. But in a series of well-publicized and highly-charged disagreements, it has, while accepting the Conference as a forum for
discussing and possibly ironing out Anglo-Irish disputes, rejected any
interpretation of the Agreement as providing any special standing for
the Republic in internal UK matters. Pressures from the Republic to
influence sensitive policing issues, the administration of justice, and
security operations have been resisted; and the current Fianna Fail
government under Charles Haughey, whose commitment to the AIA
has always been heavily qualified, has responded by erecting difficulties
over extradition. In that respect it encourages the two governments to
moralize about each other's actions in 'megaphone diplomacy', while
denying the Republic real influence or responsibility.

At the moment, the Agreement is being sustained by both governments despite such difficulties. Contrary to expectations, the main threat
has come, not from open unionist opposition, but from internal contradictions arising out of the generality of its terms and its deliberately
unspecified purpose. It has both virtues as a foundation for new political
relations, and basic defects. To parody Vice-President Nixon's incau-
tious remark upon President Eisenhower, it is the best agreement we
have. It is, after all, the only one we have.


## Conclusion

In this chapter I have not attempted to construct a hypothetical federal
constitution which might resolve the Irish problem, but have sought to
determine whether the political situation there lends itself to federalization as a solution. The overall conclusion is clear: no federation,

between whatever parties, of itself resolves the disputed claims over territory, nationality and sovereignty associated with the internal communal problem. Federal or confederal arrangements may emerge at some future time out of institutionalized forms of co-operation developed in the battle against the IRA's attempt to subvert the existing political order, the stabilization of relations between the two sovereign governments, or the development of accommodationist practices within Northern Ireland. But they are likely to lie at the end of a process that develops piecemeal and pragmatically, rather than being the product of a bargain or treaty accepted by the key actors as a novel framework for resolving the conflict.

## Notes

1. J. Whyte, 'The permeability of the United Kingdom–Irish Border', *Administration*, 31, 3 (1983): *Anglo-Irish Joint Study*, Nov. 1981.
2. D.G. Boyce, *Nationalism in Ireland*, London, (1982), 387.
3. D. Miller, *Queen's Rebels: Ulster Loyalism in Historical Perspective*, Dublin (1978).
4. See B. Chubb, *The Government and Politics of Ireland*, London, 2nd ed, (1982).
5. M. Farrell, *Northern Ireland: The Orange State*, London, (1976); P. Bew, P. Gibbon and H. Patterson, *The State in Northern Ireland*, Manchester (1979).
6. S.M. Lipset and S. Rokkan (eds), *Party Systems and Voter Alignments*, New York (1967).
7. In the lower case, I use 'unionist' (occasionally 'loyalist') to characterize the (mainly protestant) opponents of a united Irish state. Capitalized, it refers to political parties of that name.
8. See generally F. Wright, *Northern Ireland: A Comparative Analysis*, Dublin (1987).
9. The Ireland Act (1949) made any change in the constitutional position of Northern Ireland conditional upon the approval of the Northern Ireland Parliament. Under the Northern Ireland Constitution Act (1973) the consent of the majority was required. A referendum on the border conducted in 1973 showed a clear majority for continued membership of the UK.
10. See R. Rose, *Governing Without Consensus*, London (1971); E. Moxon-Browne, *Nation, Class and Creed in Northern Ireland*, Aldershot (1983).
11. Alternatives to Repeal were canvassed in the early part of the century – a federal scheme was proposed by Sharman Crawford, for instance. But the issue only becomes clarified in the 1870s.
12. D. Thornley, *Isaac Butt and Home Rule*, London (1964).
13. Ibid., 101.
14. See A.V. Dicey, *England's Case Against Home Rule*, (1886) republished Richmond Publication Co. 1973, and V. Bogdanor, *Devolution*, Oxford (1979) Ch. 2.

15. See R. Jay, *Joseph Chamberlain: A Political Study*, Oxford (1981).
16. J.E. Kendle, 'Federalism and the Irish Problem in 1918', *History*, **56** (1971), and 'The Round Table Movement and "Home Rule all round" ', *Historical Journal*, 11, 2 (1968).
17. See R. Lawrence, *The Government of Northern Ireland*, Oxford (1965); and D. Birrell and A. Murie, *Policy and Government in Northern Ireland: Lessons of Devolution*, Dublin (1980).
18. P. Bew, P. Gibbon and H. Patterson, op. cit., ch.3.
19. Quoted in V. Bogdanor, op. cit. (note 14), 73.
20. P. Bew and H. Patterson, *The British State and the Ulster Crisis from Wilson to Thatcher*, London (1985).
21. Provisional IRA, *Eire Nua*, 1971, republished with Appendix 1972.
22. G. Fitzgerald, *Towards a New Ireland*, London (1972).
23. J. Bowman, *De Valera and the Ulster Question*, 1917–73, Oxford (1982).
24. Ibid., 310.
25. For example, G. Fitzgerald, *Irish Identities*, BBC, 1982.
26. A. Lijphart, *Democracies*, London (1984), 179: C.D. Tarlton, 'Symmetry and asymmetry as elements of federalism', *Journal of Politics*, 27 (1965).
27. A. Lijphart, op. cit. (note 26), 181.
28. M. Vile, 'Federation and confederation: the experience of the United States and the British Commonwealth', in D. Rea, ed., *Political Co-operation in Divided Societies*, Dublin (1982).
29. A. Lijphart, op. cit. (note 26), 183: A.-P. Frognier, 'Federal and partly federal systems, institutions and conflict management', in D. Rea, op. cit.
30. W.H. Riker, *Federalism*, Boston (1964).
31. A.H. Birch, 'Approaches to the study of federalism', *Political Studies*, 14, 1 (1966).
32. W.H. Riker, op. cit. (note 30).
33. See A. Guelke, *Northern ireland: The International Perspective*, Dublin (1988).
34. *What Future for Northern Ireland?* SDP/Liberal Alliance publication, 18 July 1985.
*    The map of Northern Ireland which appears on p 211 is from: P.A. Compton, 'Population', in R.H. Buchanan and B.M. Walker (eds), *Province, City and People: Belfast and its Region* (1987).

# 9 Federalism and the problem of South Africa

## David Welsh

Advocates of federalism have long contended that South Africa's unique racial and ethnic problems and its sheer geographical size would be best accommodated by the adoption of a federal form of government. Many federalists have been liberals, whose prime concern was the securing of the rights of the black South Africans; another significant strand in federalist thought derives from Natal, the single region of South Africa in which English-speakers have historically been a majority of the white population. Natal federalism, as this essay will show, was anything but liberal, being an attempt by highly conservative segregationists to avoid being dominated by Afrikaners who, it was assumed, would soon threaten the British connection.

That the unification of South Africa occurred only seven years after the termination of the Anglo-Boer war in 1902 was in itself a remarkable achievement. By what at the time seemed like a miraculous alchemy, the white political leaderships of the Cape Colony, Natal, the Transvaal and the Orange River Colony were able, apparently, to transcend the bitter political divisions of the recent past and agree, at a National Convention, upon unification. That agreement was enacted as the South Africa Act in 1909 by the British Government, and in 1910 the Union of South Africa came into existence as a British Dominion.

The Convention's explicit rejection of federalism (save for a few supposedly federal elements) as a constitutional option for South Africa derived primarily from the efforts of the two dominant figures at the Convention – John X. Merriman, Prime Minister of the Cape, and Jan Christian Smuts, the Colonial Secretary in the Transvaal Government. Both spoke powerfully for a unitary system of government and attacked federalism as an inefficient, wasteful system that was inappropriate to South Africa's needs. Federalist proposals advanced by the Natal delegates to the Convention were dismissed virtually out of hand.

Opting for a unitary system with a flexible constitution was a momentous decision that set South Africa on the course that led to a highly centralized political system. It also facilitated the attack on the political rights of African and Coloured South Africans. Whether the adoption of federalism in 1909 would have made any difference to the course of South Africa's subsequent political evolution is a moot point. Those who might be called 'wistful federalists' believe that it would have. Thus L.M. Thompson concludes his major work *The Unification of South Africa* with the following lament:

A division of powers, territorially between the centre and the regions, and within the centre between the Legislature, the Executive and the Judiciary, would have provided the only sound basis for concord in South Africa. The Constitution of the United States of America would have been a better model than the British Constitution.[1]

On the other hand, Merriman's biographer, Phyllis Lewsen, says that '[a] federal constitution could not have resisted the spread of Afrikaner nationalist ideology or saved the Cape franchise.'[2]

Notwithstanding the inevitable inconclusiveness of this debate it is worthwhile reviewing the arguments that were used for and against federalism. Not only does the issue have an intrinsic historical interest for the student of federalism, but it may also have significance for the political and constitutional engineers who seek an accommodation for the racial conflict in present-day South Africa. As will be shown, most of the delegates to the National Convention were profoundly affected by the 'Convention spirit', a euphoric sense that at last white unity was attainable because Boer and Briton were prepared to put aside the intense conflicts of the recent past and together build 'a new white nation'.

Wildly optimistic expectations about the new unity were generated, while detailed consideration of the black/white issue (the 'native question', as it was then called) was deferred to the future. Expressions of this optimism parallel in interesting ways some of the hopeful expectations voiced by proponents of a post-apartheid non-racial democracy. These latter-day expectations similarly play down the possibilities of racial and ethnic conflict and the abuse of power in a future fully democratic system. An orientation towards politics which sees the struggle for power in zero-sum terms has become part of South Africa's political culture. The concluding section of this chapter, which reviews some black attitudes towards federalism, will make this point clearer (see page 264).

## The Making of Union

Unsuccessful attempts had been made to federate the South African territories in the 1850s (by Sir George Grey, Governor of the Cape) and in the 1870s (by Lord Carnarvon, the British Colonial Secretary). In the period after the termination of the Anglo-Boer War in 1902 the assumption was also that if South Africa were to become a political unit it would require a federal form of government.

Early in 1907 publication of a Memorandum by the British High Commissioner for South Africa, Lord Selborne, was a crucial spur to the growing movement for 'Closer Union'. The Memorandum dwelt extensively on the conflict-ridden relationships among the four South African colonies. Ferociously competitive railway systems and mutually punitive customs barriers could be tenuously contained by *ad hoc* measures, but it was clear that what Smuts called 'that patch-work system' was a debilitating and paralysing constraint on South Africa's potential development. Moreover, its collapse could occur at any time.

No less than the economic issues, the 'native question' and the associated problem of a coherent approach to the exploitation of African labour pointed to the need for 'Closer Union' on a federal basis. The Selborne Memorandum assumed a federal system along Canadian lines,[3] but offered no precise institutional details.

By the time the National Convention first met in October 1908, white public opinion, at least outside Natal, had not crystallized decisively either for or against federation.[4] But powerful forces were ranging up against the federal idea. There appeared, on the eve of the Convention, a book entitled *The Government of South Africa*, which had been inspired by Lionel Curtis, a member of Lord Milner's Kindergarten, who had also been the principal drafter of the Selborne Memorandum and one of the most ardent proponents of Closer Union. The authors of the book acknowledged that they had begun the task of writing it with federalist assumptions, but that the logic of the facts about federalism in general, and South Africa's circumstances in particular, had caused them to change their minds in favour of a unitary system.

For them, the fundamental problem with federalism was that it created 'hard and fast divisions' between the different functions of federal and regional governments, thereby imposing a straitjacket on the development of national life and causing 'ceaseless litigation' as the lines of division were challenged:

Our survey . . . of the actual work of government in South Africa points to the conclusion that hard and fast vertical lines dividing national from local functions are a mistake, and that we should be rash to schedule any function as one which a national government should be forbidden to touch . . . We are led to think that the functions of government cannot be divided into two lists, one national and the other local. Most, if not all of these functions, have their national aspect on the one hand and their local aspect on the other. We cannot say that the nation is solely responsible for defence and the locality for education. The true division of functions is one which assigns to the national government such duties of administration as should be performed irrespective of internal boundaries, while delegating to local agencies all such duties as can be carried out effectively within limited areas. But an arrangement which gives each kind of work to the appropriate machine cannot be fixed for all time by the rigid provisions of a constitution. Its essential principle is adaptation to the facts, and, unless society is to stand still, the facts will change, and the methods of administration must be changed as well. The apportionment of duties must not be fixed by a document, but regulated by an intelligence, which can see the necessities of the time and meet them as they arise. That determining intelligence must necessarily be the government answerable for the national well-being as a whole.[5]

There is little doubt that this line of reasoning gave a fillip to the thinking of Smuts and Merriman, whose ideas were already firmly on the unitary track. On the second day of the Convention Merriman led off with a motion proposing 'legislative union' with provision for provinces 'with power of local legislation and adminstration'.[6]

In speaking to the motion he began by noting that South Africa was part of an Empire which meant that all its external relations and defence were in the hands of the Imperial Power. 'We miss the great binding force' of common danger, and, therefore South Africa had to proceed along different lines from those adopted by independent states. In the case of the United States of America, Merriman claimed, the sovereignty of the individual state remained unimpaired, leaving it with 'absolute control' and 'free to make its own laws for its own government'. The consequence was 'lawlessness' in certain states and a variety of law on matters of vital common concern with which the federal government could not cope. Moreover, he went on, 'the people were bound to the terms of the Constitution which they were almost powerless to alter, and the principle had led to one of the greatest civil wars on record.'

Canada's federal constitution, Merriman went on, had avoided some of the errors of the American constitution, but it retained blemishes which South Africa should avoid. Canadian unity was impaired throuh 'local jealousies and differences of race and religion'. These obstacles, however, were not present in South Africa, averred Merriman, in words that, with the wisdom of hindsight, appear astonishingly naive or optimistic:

In religion there was no dividing line for the great bulk of the European population belonged to Protestant Churches. In race [the reference is to the two white linguistic groups] the people were essentially the same and experience proved to us that the race difference was superficial and would disappear. We were therefore free from the causes which led the Canadians to secure independence to certain provinces because the Provinces differed from each other in race and religion.

Further alleged drawbacks to federalism were advanced by Merriman. Corruption was said to flourish more vigorously under federalism than under unitary systems: 'pure government' necessitated central control. Federalism, as in the Australian case, caused friction among the different levels of government, and Merriman claimed, without citing any evidence, that public opinion in Australia was probably now in favour of a unitary system. He warned that it was extremely difficult to amend federal constitutions.

Merriman argued that under 'a supreme central power' far larger powers could be given to localities, and he expressed himself in favour of local self-government; which had been introduced into the Cape Colony with some success. He advocated creating provincial governments under an executive officer as president appointed by the central government.

As a senior South African statesman who enjoyed immense respect in both white communities, and who would be a strong contender for the prime ministership of the new South Africa, Merriman's speech created a powerful impression on the assembled delegates. Its strong (and highly misleading) anti-federal bias was consolidated and compounded by General J.C. Smuts, who followed Merriman with another onslaught on the federal idea. Like Merriman Smuts was a highly influential figure who dominated the Transvaal delegation. Smuts had prepared himself carefully, and, given the rather limited extent of knowledge of comparative constitutional law among the delegates, his highly tendentious views on federalism could be presented without substantial challenge.

Smuts's speech complemented and buttressed Merriman's case for a unitary system.[7] Federalism, he argued, was inappropriate for South Africa because it was essentially 'a treaty or a pact, an agreement between independent powers'. In South Africa, he claimed, 'they were not independent powers but brothers'. He warned against adopting a constitution like that of the United States, which had caused 'grave trouble' by so dispersing the sovereign power 'as to be ineffective for the essential purposes of civilised government'.

A significant part of Smuts's speech was devoted to the powers that the courts would have to exercise under a federal constitution. If federalism was essentially a contract then the courts would have to be empowered to interpret the contract, and to decide whether laws passed by the central or state legislatures were constitutional. Did South Africa, Smuts asked, want to leave the supreme power of government in the hands of so unrepresentative a body as a court, and should it be made possible for a court to override an act of parliament?

The natural result of such a system, Smuts continued, was that judicial appointments would become political, 'for a political party was likely to take such precautions as were possible to ensure itself and its measures against adverse judgements'. (Smuts could not have known at the time that a unitary system, such as South Africa was to adopt, would not render the judiciary immune to political appointments.)

A further objection to federalism, in Smuts's view, was that federal constitutions were 'practically unalterable by nature', so that the United States Constitution had only been twice amended, with the result that a constitution drawn up in the eighteenth century was being required to operate in times that were entirely different. It would be entirely wrong to tie down South Africa by means of a constitution that was virtually impossible to amend.

In rejecting federation Smuts proposed instead a 'middle course' which embodied a central sovereign parliament while permitting 'local legislatures with delegated and defined powers and of course subject to the Central Parliament'. This proposal was flexible, since the powers of the local legislatures could be extended or curtailed as circumstances demanded and would therefore create the least possible occasion for friction.

Merriman and Smuts were the most influential of all the delegates at the National Convention, representing as they did the most influential of the four colonies as well as possessing great prestige as individuals. E.H. Walton, the Convention's unofficial scribe, records that the speeches of both made a deep impression on the delegates and, in Smuts's case, 'an impression which will never be effaced from the minds of those who heard it'.

Subsequent speakers who favoured federation were to face an impossible task in seeking to convert the delegates to their point of view. The Natal delegates had gone to some trouble to prepare a federal brief and they even circulated the draft of a possible federal constitution to the Convention. But in vain did Sir Frederick Moor, Prime Minister of Natal, try to undo the anti-federal propaganda that Merriman and Smuts had voiced.[8] Moor was essentially correct in pointing out how misleading it was to suppose that federation was a failure as a technique of government. Could one seriously believe that the United States had not progressed enormously under federation, and did its history not provide 'a sufficient reply to those who sought to persuade them that the federal system was an evil and that it hampered and hindered the growth of a nation?' Moor's argument was that South Africa was too large a country for a central government to perform its task effectively without neglecting local interests. For Moor, as for the other Natal federalists, the underlying fear was that Natal, the only colony with a white population in which English-speakers predominated, would be swallowed up by a rampant Afrikaner majority in a unitary state.

Moor, however, did not reject outright Merriman's proposals. Instead, he pressed for greater powers to be vested in local councils and for Natal to retain its name as 'the Colony of Natal'. His fellow-Natalian W.B. Morcom invoked far more robust language, insisting that 'the people of Natal would absolutely refuse to surrender their independent powers of legislation'.[9] Another Natal delegate, Colonel E.M. Greene, a cabinet minister in the Natal colonial government, opened up, in the context of federalism, one of the thorniest issues facing the Convention, namely the Cape's non-racial franchise system. Greene demanded to know whether equality between black and white was to be imposed on a unitary South Africa. He insisted that under no circumstances should this be permitted: if union were established Africans could vote for the local Cape assembly but they could never be allowed to vote for representatives in the central government.[10]

Perhaps surprisingly the delegates from the other small colony, the Orange River Colony did not strongly resist the principle of a unitary state. Apart from disagreeing with Smuts's contention that it would be ill-advised to leave the power of interpreting the constitution in the hands of the courts, the Free State's Prime Minister, Abraham Fischer, accepted the idea of union – on condition that it embodied Smuts's notion of the 'middle course' and did not entail the elimination or absorption of the smaller states. Language, he said, was something that should be left to local legislatures.[11]

His fellow Free Stater ex-President M.T. Steyn, who enjoyed immense prestige among Afrikaners, spoke out strongly for unification: why tolerate boundaries that were not natural, but artificial, he asked? And would federation not lead to friction and ultimately to dissolution?[12]

In the course of the debates further arguments against federation were invoked: federation meant separate governments and separate parliaments and, therefore, extra cost and heavier taxation; the (white) population was too small and they had too few statesmen for both central and local parliaments; and how could you effectively tackle the 'native question' without a strong and unified central authority?

Several delegates who had come to the Convention as convinced federalists changed their minds in the course of the debate. Among the converts was Leander Starr Jameson (of Jameson Raid notoriety) who stood up to renounce his belief that the ideal of unification was impossible:

He believed the difficulties could be surmounted by a determination on the part of people to sink local feeling and prejudice and grasp the greater destiny which awaited them. He had no fear of injury to any locality, no fear of any neglect of any local interest and he believed that any South African Parliament would regard the whole country and the whole of the interests concerned as its duty.[13]

By the end of the debate it was clear that the federalists had only small support. Indeed, the federalist amendment to Merriman's resolution was not even voted upon.[14]

How is the decisive victory for the unitary principle to be explained? Clearly the explanation is not to be found solely in the poor presentation of the federalist case by the Natal delegates nor in the limited leverage that Natal, as the colony with the smallest white population, could wield. Indeed, popular white sentiment for federation in Natal had been greatly exaggerated, as the outcome of the referendum in June 1909 showed. While the referendum was fought on the National Convention's draft constitution for a Union of South Africa, the issue turned largely on the federation/union question, and on how Natal's distinctive identity might fare under Union. The pro-Union forces won by an overwhelming margin of three to one.[15]

Several factors explain the ease with which the case for a unitary system prevailed. First, it seems plausible to suppose that Smuts's notion of the 'middle course' and its ready acceptance of what were to become Provincial Councils gulled many wavering federalists into believing that this was an acceptable safeguard against encroachments by the central government. In defending the draft constitution F.R. Moor told the Natal Legislative Council:

I am a federalist now, and I say that . . . in that draft Constitution of ours, we leave the federal principle conserved in the provinces. My name would never have been inscribed by me upon that draft Constitution had no provision been made for provincial Councils which are to attend to local requirements. For I hold that in an absolutely united system, or by the adoption of the unification principle, it would have been impossible for our local interests, industries, and wants to have been attended to by a parliament or government located, say, at Cape Town.[16]

Elsewhere Moor denied that Provincial Council powers were vulnerable:

It is part of the Constitution, and our central Parliament would not dare to interfere with those provincial rights unless it was the will of the people that that should come about; and instead of the powers of these Provincial Councils being limited in the future, I honestly believe that these powers will be increased by the central Parliament.[17]

Another quasi-federal element in the Union Constitution also served to still federalist apprehensions. This was the provision for equal representation of the four provinces (eight senators each) in the Senate. Abraham Fischer told the Legislative Assembly of the Orange River

Colony (soon to have its name restored as the Province of the Orange Free State) that thereby 'smaller states would be safeguarded as against the bigger and larger states'.[18]

The reality, however, was that these were pseudo-federal provisions, fig-leaves that sought to hide the essential unitary character of the new state. The South Africa Act of 1909 made it clear that sovereignty resided in Parliament, and that any ordinance passed by a provincial council had to be assented to by the Governor-General in Council (effectively the cabinet of the central government). Moreover, a provincial council ordinance could have effect for the province 'as long and as far only as it is not repugnant to any Act of Parliament' (Clause 86 of the South Africa Act). In any case, the powers vested in the Provincial Councils were not great: as enumerated in Clause 85 of the Constitution they included power to make ordinances in relation to education (other than higher education), aspects of agriculture, hospitals, municipal and other local institutions, roads, and generally 'all matters which, in the opinion of the Governor-General in Council are of a merely local or private nature in the province'.

It was little wonder that the liberal Cape federalist W.P. Schreiner (whose legal commitments had prevented him from attending the National Convention) could snort that 'no decent, respectable Mayor of the smallest municipality and no chairman of a Village Management Board . . . would consent to hold the sort of position that was designed for the Provincial Councils. Why? Because they would be tied hand and foot'.[19]

Even strong protagonists of the Union Constitution like R.H. Brand, a member of Milner's Kindergarten and secretary to the Transvaal delegation at the Convention, acknowledged that the Provincial Councils were 'experimental' and predicted, accurately, that not only was it unlikely that their powers would be extended, but 'in all likelihood they will be diminished'.[20]

A second set of reasons for rejecting federation lay complexly buried in the racial and ethnic imbroglio of South Africa. There was widespread agreement among whites that South Africa needed a common 'native policy'. As Merriman told the Cape Parliament, it was vitally necessary 'to go forward as one people to combat the forces of barbarism which surround us in South Africa'.[21] Prior to Union each colony had had its own policy, and among them were significant differences, notably in relation to the franchise. Briefly, the Cape had institutionalized a qualified, non-racial franchise system, which by 1909, had enabled 21,000 African and Coloured voters (or 14.8 per cent of the total electorate) to get on to the common voters' roll.[22] Natal's original non-franchise provisions had been modelled on the Cape's, but legislation had effectively destroyed the ability of Africans and Indians to qualify for the vote, so that by 1909 only a handful of Africans were voters. No such rights, real or theoretical, had ever been granted in the Transvaal or the Orange Free State.

Federation, it was widely assumed, would perpetuate divided control over Africans, and leave Natal free to continue its reactionary and disastrous form of segregation which had provoked a serious rebellion in 1906. Severe criticism of the Natal Government's brutal handling of the rebellion came not only from Britain, but also from leading South African statesmen like Merriman, Smuts, Steyn and Louis Botha.[23] The episode strengthened the case for a common (and thus centralized) control over African affairs, and drastically undercut Natal's federalist claims.

Nevertheless, as Sir Thomas Hyslop reminded the Natal Legislative Assembly, union brought advantages to colonials who lived in a 'powder magazine':

We have a small white population, and one of the greatest benefits we shall get by Unification will be having the whole of the forces of South Africa at our back if a rebellion occurs here.[24]

Divided control over Africans also meant weaker control, and the growth among whites of the 'tacit understanding that in the last resort British troops and money can be called into action to enforce the policy of the white communities . . .'[25] Centralized control would eliminate the disturbing effect on the African population 'by the different and confusing ideals held up before it' as well as the discord among white communities fostered by different policies.

A citizen of the northern colonies resents the privileges and position accorded to the native in the Cape, and foretells the time when the coloured vote will outnumber the white. The Cape colonial retorts by contrasting his own progressive ideas with the policy of negation adopted by his neighbours, and the tranquillity of his own native territories with the recurring unrest in Natal. The wider the difference in the native policies the more does the sense of kinship decline.[26]

The issue pointed to a problem that the protagonists of federalism still have to contend with today. Federalism is most suited to societies in which diversities are territorially based. If conflicting groups are geographically interspersed the appeal of federalism as a mechanism for regulating conflict declines, and a case for federalism must be sought among some of its other advantages. In explaining why white South Africa had opted for union a contemporary observer, Hugh Edward Egerton, noted the vital point that 'the distinction in the past has been racial, not territorial'.[27] He was referring to the relationship between Dutch- and English-speaking whites. Afrikaners had a narrow demographic edge over the substantial English-speaking communities in the Cape and Transvaal and a large preponderance in the Orange Free State.

Although Afrikaners were then largely rural and English-speakers urban, the point was that their geographical interspersal was substantial.

Much the same applied in the case of Africans. The problem for a federalist was acutely summed up by a Canadian scholar, Alexander Brady, whose fine study shows a sensitivity to the distinction between a 'federal' and a 'non-federal' society:[28]

> No rigid division of power on the federal principle, however skilful, could ensure that decisive authority over all the changing ramifications of the native issue would dwell with the central government. In its larger aspects native policy was indivisible, and could not safely be left to individual provinces. From north to south an interrupted line of native peoples lived in contact. Tribe was joined to tribe. A poll-tax in Natal might cause, as in 1906, a native uprising the repercussions of which would travel swiftly to the Cape and elsewhere. Conflicting policies at the same time in different parts of the country would create irritations and unrest.[29]

Gathering political forces also served to consolidate a unitary view of South Africa. By the time of Union in 1909 Afrikaner nationalism was burgeoning. While Smuts and Louis Botha were genuine in their espousal of 'conciliation' and wished to see the development of a 'new (white) South Africanism', more radical nationalists believed that Union provided a framework within which Afrikaners could unite and capture control of the political system.[30] Federation might have hindered this process and, moreover, could have placed undue power in the hands of 'British' Natal, whose imperial sentiments were despised by republican Afrikaners. Moreover, as Andrew Duminy has suggested:

> If Natal were allowed a loose rein, she could become the cause of considerable embarrassment in future relations between Britain and the South African Dominion ... The British government might be encouraged to intervene in Natal's affairs because she believed herself to be dealing there with 'loyal' British colonists and not with Afrikaners, whose hatred would be further increased by imperial interference, to the detriment of British influence throughout southern Africa. There was also the danger that, if disputes were to arise between Natal and the future Union government, or between the Union government and the Imperial government, then Britain might be tempted to intervene in South African affairs via 'loyal Natal'.[31]

On the other hand, many English-speaking whites anticipated the day when they would constitute a majority of the white population. The forming of such a majority by means of encouraging immigration, had been at the heart of Lord Milner's policy. The same hope animated many of the English-speaking delegates at the National Convention,[32] but by the time of Union the aim was nowhere near being realized. Their hopes ultimately proved chimerical and by 1919 the core party of pro-imperial sentiment, the Unionists, recognized that English-speaking whites could not govern unaided. Their only hope of power lay in alliance with what a leading Unionist called 'the moderate Dutch'.[33]

Unification promoted also a coming together of the incipient forces of African nationalism, with its roots in a common sense of oppression by white rule. As early in 1851 Theophilus Shepstone, the most famous of South Africa's nineteenth century 'native' adminstrators, had warned of 'the evident sympathy of colour that exists among the Black nations.'[34] Unification provided the impetus for the first national gathering, the South African Native Convention, held in Bloemfontein in March 1909, to protest against the colour-bar provisions in the Union Constitution. The Convention was a significant forerunner of the South African Native National Congress (later to be called the African National Congress) which was established in 1912.

## The Growth of the Leviathan

As succeeding decades would show, South Africa's unitary, Westminster system provided scant safeguards against the power-drives of a rampant majority in Parliament. Parliament was sovereign, the Constitution was flexible (as Smuts and Merriman had explicitly desired), and no bill of rights nor strong entrenchment of the Rule of Law could stem the spate of discriminatory legislation that poured forth after 1910 to consolidate and unify the different systems of racial inequality that had existed before Union.

The Constitution had entrenched two clauses, one providing for equality between the English and Dutch (subsequently Afrikaans) languages, and the other supposedly safeguarding the rights of qualified African and Coloured males to vote on the common voters' rolls of the Cape Province. Only by a two-thirds majority of both Houses of Parliament sitting together in the third reading of a Bill could such clauses be amended or repealed. By something of an historical irony both the doughtiest opponents *and* supporters of the Cape's non-racial franchise were federalists. Natal's delegates to the National Convention took the hardest line of all in seeking to terminate the Cape's system, with Moor telling the Convention that 'the black man was incapable of civilization'.[35] While the Cape delegates insisted on the retention of the Cape system, they compromised and gave way on what had been admittedly only a hypothetical right in the Cape Parliament, namely the right of people of colour to become members of either House. To the liberal federalist W.P. Schreiner the clause restricting membership of the Union Parliament to British subjects of 'European descent' was a 'blot on the Constitution'. In Schreiner's view federalism was more supportive of liberty than a unitary system, but even more importantly he prophesied that ultimately the drive for a common 'native policy' would endanger the Cape's tradition: 'Just because our natives were more advanced than the natives of other parts of South Africa, were they going to tear up the policy of insurance which we now had?'[36] For this reason alone, he believed, the Cape should insist on federalism – or stay out of Union.

As was shown by the successful assault on the Cape African vote in 1936, and on the Cape Coloured vote in 1956 (after grotesque manipulation of a constitution whose flexibility facilitated such abuse), Schreiner's forebodings were vindicated.[37]

Today South Africa is a highly centralized state. While space does not permit a detailed account of the centralization process,[38] that process itself offers certain lessons that are instructive in considering possible future federal alternatives.

First, by creating a strongly unitary state (notwithstanding the quasi-federal fig leaves), a single, decisive site of power was established. With a sovereign Parliament patterned on a Westminster-style model (though lacking in the democratic context of the true modern Westminster system), it was highly likely, if not inevitable, that the conduct of politics would be of a zero-sum or 'winner-takes-all' character. Such a character does not necessarily affect the democratic quality of the political system in relatively homogeneous societies where swings of the electoral pendulum occur with reasonable regularity and governments alternate.

The effect of South Africa's Westminster system *manqué* had been to enable a mobilized ethnic movement to capture power in 1948 – lawfully – and thereafter to control the political system for the next 40 years. That governments have since 1910 changed only twice, in 1924 and 1948, as a result of defeats of the ruling party in elections is another indication of the rigidity of electoral politics in a Westminster-style system that has been dominated by ethnic politics. Where ethnic mobilization can secure total control by simple numerical preponderance within the (white) electorate, and where voter allegiance is more tightly sewn into the ethnic party than, say, into a class-based party in a more homogeneous society, minorities face the prospect of exclusion from a share of power in perpetuity.

The phenomenon of the crystallized ethnic majority is, of course, not unique to the operation of oligarchical politics in South Africa. It is one of the recurrent difficult problems of many deeply divided societies. Nor can it be ascribed to the peculiarities of the unitary state, although in a federal system territorially-based minorities may have better chances of enjoying some effective power at the regional level if they are unable to capture the centre.

A second lesson follows closely from the first. Was it realistic to suppose that 'a new South Africanism' would be forged in the crucible of the unitary state which swept away 'artificial and historical boundaries'; and was the Anglo-Afrikaner conflict 'a very little question'?[39] Would fusion of the white 'races' result in 'one compact nationality inspired by one common pervading spirit'?[40] Smuts, Botha and others who preached 'conciliation' confidently anticipated that a new era had been born in which the bloody quarrels of the past could be forgotten and the task of nation-building commenced. Smuts's biographer Sir Keith Hancock relates how he and Merriman expected South Africa's political evolution to conform to a Canadian pattern of growth, including the continuance of a party system cutting across the linguistic and cultural barrier.[41] R.H. Brand hoped that there would be 'opportunities in future for parties to form themselves on lines which will blur and may eventually obliterate the racial cleavage.'[42] This was optimistic thinking, given the extent to which the linguistic cleavage between whites had dominated party systems in the past. Yet in the Transvaal Botha and Smuts's *Het Volk* enjoyed significant minority support from English-speakers as well as almost universal Afrikaner support. After 1910 the South African party, for a brief period until the rise of the National party in 1915, conformed to the same model.

With the wisdom of hindsight one may claim that any talk of a 'new South Africanism' was wishful thinking which ignored the passions that ethnic mobilization could ignite and the ruthlessness with which an ethnic nationalism could subvert the spirit and the letter of a constitution for its own ends. Perhaps the casting of politics in an ethnic mould was not inevitable, but given the South African background it was at least always a strong possibility. The prognostications of some of the crusty Natal federalists, even if animated by an ethnocentric anti-Afrikaner spirit rather than sociological insight, at least had the virtue of substantial accuracy. Thus C.A.S. Yonge told the Natal Legislative Assembly in 1909:

... you have to see why people are in favour of Unification, and why the other side are in favour of Federal Union. The one under Unification can obtain what, in other ways, they have been unsuccessful in obtaining. Under that they become predominant, without let or hindrance, and at a very early date in our history. It is not so much that one is a Dutch race, and the other is an English one. It is not that so much, but their habits, their breeding, their bringing up [sic], are not identical. Their ideas of literature, their ideas of Government, are not in touch with ours, and they want Unification because by that means alone can they secure at once and for all time that prestige and dominance in South Africa which, from the Cape to the Zambesi, it has ever been their ideal to attain to.[43]

It has been no part of the argument in this section to suggest that a federal South Africa would have developed along politically more

benign lines, as some latterday federalists have wistfully supposed. Few
if any constitutions are strong enough to withstand the onslaught of
mobilized ethnic passion – and that is perhaps the most important
lesson that the post-Union experience can teach political engineers who
confront the challenge of a post-apartheid order. Perhaps only when
they have put down deep roots of legitimacy can constitutions provide a
durable framework for the regulation of political life, one that is capable
of standing up to the stresses of conflict that deeply divided societies
must regularly manifest.

That the major black opposition movements have set their sights
firmly on taking over total power ('we will negotiate only about the terms
on which power is transferred') should come as little surprise. They have
learned the lesson of South Africa's past constitutional experience that
power at the centre is the big prize. To accept anything less, they believe,
is to be fobbed off with shadow rather than substance.

Contemporary South Africa, however, exemplifies the situation of an
irresistible force coming up against an immovable object. Politically the
society is deadlocked: black nationalism cannot be repressed out of
existence, but it cannot prevail against deeply entrenched and exceed-
ingly tough white obstinacy – other than perhaps at horrendous cost
and over a long period of time. If South Africa is to have any hope of
attaining some kind of racial accommodation it will probably be based
upon a compromise whose institutional embodiment will have to transcend much of its past constitutional and political experience. Whether
South Africans have the capacity to proceed along such a learning curve
must remain in doubt. Federalism *may* be part of a possible national
compromise, but the onus will be on its advocates to show its compati-
bility with democratic non-racialism.

**Recent federal thinking**

As Murray Forsyth points out federal ideas have undergone a resurgence in South Africa since 1960.[44] Partly the impetus has come from a
reaction to the overweening centralization of the South African state,
and, far more significantly, from a search for a more equitable alternative to apartheid. In the latter respect, federalism somehow seemed an
acceptable *via media* between apartheid and universal suffrage in a
unitary state, which is the policy advocated by most of the more militant
black opposition groups. All but a handful of radical whites, however,
reject this option.

Federalism, as such, had never attracted a mass following in South
Africa. As previous sections have shown, it was historically associated
with relatively marginal groups such as the Natal 'isolationists' and

a handful of white liberals. What might be described as 'federalist mutterings' were kept alive as a political undercurrent in Natal, but the last embodiment of this phenomenon, the Union Federal Party, faded away very soon after its formation in 1953.

A renewed impetus to liberal federal thinking was given by the formation of the Progressive Party in 1959. Today its lineal descendant, the Progressive Federal Party, is the most explicitly federal of all South African political parties. Its constitutional policy proposes a federation composed of a number of self-governing federal units and a federal government linked together through a constitution agreed upon at a national convention. The federal government is to have jurisdiction over matters that are essentially national in character, such as finance, foreign affairs and defence, while, in keeping with the Party's belief that power should not be concentrated in a single site of government, significant powers should be decentralized to federal regional units.[45]

Several individual writers have advanced what might be called 'variations on a theme of federation', in terms of which different regions of the country would be designated as white-controlled or black-controlled, while some would be 'non-racial'. It is perhaps not without significance that the three most prominent advocates of this approach, Arthur Keppel-Jones, Jordan K. Ngubane and Chief M. Gatsha Buthelezi, all hail from Natal.[46] Since Buthelezi is Chief Minister of the KwaZulu homeland and leader of a significant black opposition movement, Inkatha, his views, as expressed in 1974, are worth mentioning. Buthelezi's obvious concern was to move away from a conception of politics that focused exclusively on the battle for exclusive possession of the central site of power:

The distribution or devolution of power from a unitary centre to a number of autonomous states would greatly reduce or even eliminate altogether for a long time the obsession of all groups with central power or control thereof, which at the moment threatens the country with unrest and revolution ... All states, whether a specific group has paramountcy or not, will have the same legislative and executive powers and functions. There will, obviously, be no first and second-class states. Far-reaching change of this nature entails the abolition of the present provincial system as it exists under the present unitary form of government. Parliament in its present form would also cease to exist. Its place would be taken by a federal parliament composed of representatives of all the constituent states. It would be empowered to carry out those functions which by agreement have been vested in it. The establishment of central and state parliaments would mean a shift of political attention from the single all-powerful parliament which we have in South Africa at present. The advantage of the federal concept is that the federal principle ensures that the states and their legislatures will not be subordinate to a central parliament.[47]

Buthelezi's preparedness to compromise on the one-man-one-vote-in-a-unitary-state issue, the demand of all radical black activists, his acquiescence in working within apartheid structures like homeland governments, his opposition to economic sanctions and his championing of the private enterprise system have made him a hated figure among the radicals. Inkatha, which claims a membership of 1.5 million, is nevertheless a powerful organization in the KwaZulu–Natal region and, although its membership is not exclusively Zulu, serves as a potentially powerful vehicle of Zulu ethnic nationalism. (The serious violence in the Pietermaritzburg area since August 1988 is essentially a struggle between Inkatha and more radical black movements who are contesting Inkatha's claims to hegemony in the region.[48])

Buthelezi's most recent initiative has been his involvement in the KwaZulu–Natal Indaba in 1986. From the perspective of this essay the Indaba's constitutional proposals for a single legislative body for the joint areas of Natal and KwaZulu are significant not only because they embody significant elements of corporative federalism for the region but also because their adoption by the central government would *de facto* involve their taking an important step towards the federalizing of South Africa.

Delegates to the Indaba, which met in Durban over an eight-month period in 1986, represented much of the white, English-speaking business, agricultural and political 'establishment' of Natal as well as, of course, Inkatha and the leading 'intra-system' (i.e. prepared to participate in the Tri-Cameral parliamentary system initiated in 1984) Coloured and Indian political parties. The fact that key segments of the white and black 'establishments' in the region were prepared to negotiate, and that a powerful body like Inkatha exerted significant control over Africans goes a long way towards explaining why the Indaba was able to get off the ground. The absence of a similar mix in other regions makes the replication of Indaba-like negotiations elsewhere improbable for the foreseeable future. Comparable initiatives in the Western Cape have so far failed to get off the ground.

Of significance were those organizations which either declined to participate or did not respond to the invitation. The National Party of Natal (the provincial wing of the ruling National Party) requested only observer status, while the more radical black political and trade union movements, like the United Democratic Front, the Natal Indian Congress and the Congress of South African Trade Unions declined to participate. In other words, major actors on the national political scene were not involved. Moreover, three organizations representing Afrikaner nationalist interests, the *Afrikaanse Handelsinstituut*, the *Federasie van Afrikaanse Kultuurverenigings* and the *Junior Rapportryerbeweging*, although enjoying delegate status, in the end declined to sign the Indaba proposals.[49]

The Constitutional Proposals are too lengthy and complex to sum-marise adequately here.[50] Briefly they provide for an extensive degree of regional self-government by a bi-cameral provincial legislature. The first chamber is to consist of 100 members elected by proportional representation on a basis of universal (i.e. all races) franchise. The second chamber is to consist of fifty elected members composed of representatives of the following groups:

| | |
|---|---|
| African background group | 10 |
| Afrikaans background group | 10 |
| Asian background group | 10 |
| English background group | 10 |
| South African group | 10 |

The principle is that voters may vote for their 'group' representatives or, should they decline to be associated with a group, they may vote for representatives of the inclusive 'South African group'. The deliberate over-weighting of racial/ethnic minorities in the second chamber can be inferred from the region's population profile in 1987: 5.5 million Africans, 1 million Indians, 0.8 million whites and 0.2 million Coloureds.

The proposals provide that all legislation, including money bills, must be passed by both chambers. Provision for 'group' protection is contained in a sub-clause which reads:

In the case of legislation which affects the religious, language, cultural or other rights of the members of a background group or the South African group, such legislation will require in addition to majorities in both chambers, a majority of the representatives of that group in the second chamber.

Further protective devices are provided for by constitutionally recognized and entrenched Cultural Councils, which are to have the right to invoke the judicial review of legislation and executive orders that are 'likely to infringe or affect any right or cultural interest of the group concerned or its members generally'. In addition, a justiciable bill of rights entrenches civil liberties and the Rule of Law (thereby outlawing racial discrimination), as well as explicitly protecting 'ethnic, religious, linguistic, cultural and educational rights'.

Predictably the Indaba proposals have met with a mixed response. Initially the Natal National Party rejected them outright, claiming that minority rights were insufficiently protected. According to Dr Johan Steenkamp (originally a delegate to the Indaba and presently a National Party MP) the proposals 'represent an unequal division of power, with minorities being given the booby prize of representation in a second chamber'.[51] The Government, however, has not yet formally and finally rejected the proposals and it remains in communication with the Indaba organization. Reports suggest that while the Nationalist leadership in Natal is implacably opposed to the proposals, many rank and file Nationalists in Natal and elsewhere in the country favour them. According to a poll conducted by *Market and Opinion Surveys* and released in March 1988 49 per cent of Nationalists countrywide supported the proposals, 11 per cent rejected them, and 40 per cent were undecided.[52] Other survey data indicate substantial support among all races in Natal for regional power-sharing along the lines recommended by the Indaba.[53]

The survey data, however, must be regarded as inconclusive, since the referendum in the region requested by the Indaba organization has not yet been agreed to by the Government. At the time of writing (mid 1988) negotiations on this issue were still being conducted. Even a referendum would not be a satisfactory test of public opinion should the present State of Emergency (in terms of which many of the most vocal anti-Indaba organizations have been effectively banned) continues – which is highly likely.

Critics from the left have viewed the Indaba as a cabal among conservative pro-capitalist groupings, as a move by Buthelezi to strengthen himself regionally to compensate for his weakness at the national level, and as a step in the process of 'balkanizing' South Africa.[54]

The Indaba experiment has been treated at some length, not only because of its federalist implications but also because it raises crucial questions for any effort at constitutional and political innovation in contemporary South Africa. The widely differing reactions of right and left illustrate the highly polarized nature of the society, and the daunting task of securing a viable basis of legitimacy for a new dispensation. Can *any* political/constitutional formula be found whereby black aspirations and white fears may be reconciled? Furthermore, what place, if any, should 'group rights' be accorded in a future constitution, and on what basis should putative groups be identified?

The issues identified in the preceding paragraph go to the heart of South Africa's political deadlock. On the one hand, the South African government, while committing itself to 'broadening the basis of demo-cracy' and ensuring that 'population groups of colour shall have the right to vote and be represented at the highest level of decision-making', nevertheless insists, as a non-negotiable condition, that the building blocks of any new constitution shall be the statutorily-recognized groups into which all South Africans are classified in terms of the Population Registration Act of 1950. 'Groups', in other words, do not reflect natural, voluntary or organic processes of association so much as legislated or compulsory association. It is this principle that lies at the core of apartheid, and upon which stands the entire edifice of Group

Areas, separate schooling, the homelands policy and the Tri-Cameral Parliament (to name only some major manifestations).

That this 'group approach' is intimately tied in with considerations of power will be readily apparent.[55] It is a fundamental part of a policy that has both absolutized and manipulated a version of ethnicity for purposes of maintaining racial domination. As a black leader once put it, 'Ethnicity for the government means that an Afrikaner and a Greek can be a member of one nation but a Zulu and a Xhosa cannot'.[56]

In a recent speech Dr D.J. de Villiers, a Minister in the House of Assembly and a leading *verligte* in the National Party, made the following statement:

What then is the real issue in South Africa? The real issue concerns the question of how to protect the rights of minorities . . . We are a divided society. That is a fact. The division of our society into a multiplicity of greatly diverse ethnic groups or minorities is a reality that not one of us can deny. In such a society majority rule does not protect the rights of minorities; on the contrary, majoritarianism in any deeply divided society will inevitably lead to the violation of the rights of minorities, both Black and White. It will lead to ethnic strife and racial polarisation, and even to civil war and/or a dictatorship.[57]

As an abstract statement of the crucial problem of the divided society the Minister's statement is unexceptionable; but when it is translated into his Party's 'group approach' it becomes vitiated for the reasons that have been advanced above.

Given South Africa's legacy of racial and ethnic conflict, it is naive to believe that it could easily be transformed into a 'non-racial democracy', in the sense that racial and ethnic factors played no part in shaping such things as people's political affiliations, friendship networks, choice of spouse and place of residence. At the same time, however, it is not possible to predict in advance what configuration of groupings would crystallize from the complex amalgam of racial, ethnic, regional, class and ideological factors that would surely be highly significant voting determinants in a hypothetical fully inclusive election. To set a bogus notion of 'group' in constitutional concrete, as the Nationalists do, is to ensure that no initiative proceeding from this premise has much chance of building up legitimacy.

On the other hand, the refusal to recognize the reality of ethnicity equally confounds the search for a political accommodation. One may readily sympathize with this refusal by movements whose followers have been the victims of enforced (and bogus) ethnicity, but such sympathy should not carry over into a blindness to the realities of every divided society on earth. To do so would be to repeat on a wider canvas the errors made in naiveté and optimism at the National Convention in 1908. Speaking for the African National Congress Oliver Tambo has said:

The opposition to the idea of one person one vote by those in the West who call themselves democrats, derives exactly from the attempt to define the population of our country as a conglomerate of racial groups. Universal adult suffrage is therefore seen as something that is dangerous because it would result in the black majority swamping the white majority, as the saying goes.

Similarly, the idea of power-sharing as well as that of federation or confederation is based on the notion of racial groups, each one of which must be treated as an organic political bloc which must bargain for a modus vivendi with other racial political blocs.

Tambo went on to underline the African National Congress's commitment to democracy, based upon the principle that:

Every person has a right to be considered as an individual, with unfettered liberty to live and do as they wish, to develop themselves as persons freely, provided they do not infringe on the liberty of others . . . the first question that anybody with only a modicum of anti-racist feeling should raise is exactly that question of the rights of the majority. The approach to the solution of the South African question should be – what would meet the aspirations of the majority and not, what will be accepted or tolerated by the minority![58]

Before considering the implications of this statement, it is worth recording that the African National Congress's commitment to non-racialism is both genuine and long-standing. It has never assumed that Africans are the only category entitled to rights in a democratic South Africa, and it has forthrightly rejected the counter-racism advocated by some other black opposition movements. In the same speech Tambo says:

The leadership and the members of the ANC are drawn from all the racial groups of our country. They deal with one another as equals and political bloc [sic] because they are united in the resolve to transform South Africa into a united democratic non-racial entity.[59]

While the claims about inter-racial membership, including that of the highest councils, are correct, support for the African National Congress among whites at large is minuscule. There is considerably more support among the Coloured and Indian categories, but whether it amounts in either case to majority support cannot be established with certainty. It is, however, highly likely that in the hypothetical event of a free election among Africans, the African National Congress would win majority support. It represents, therefore, a factor that will have to be involved in any future settlement of the South African problem.

Tambo's rejection of federation reflects a common African nationalist sentiment. Federalism has been widely viewed in Africa as some kind of 'imperialist plot', and in South Africa its image has been tarnished by the belief that it was little more than a sophisticated variant of the homelands policy, tailored specifically to thwart African nationalist aspirations and secure white power. As Douglas Irvine has noted 'the federal option has also been endorsed by homeland leaders from time to time – a dubious accolade, since this may weaken its legitimacy in the African view'.[60]

Some survey data purport to confirm this view. In a poll undertaken by Mark Orkin a sample of urban blacks decisively rejected the federal option: 80 per cent wanted a 'unitary non-racial democracy'. The survey claimed also that the minority prepared to accept federation:

Tend to be older, less educated, Zulu-speaking, resident in Natal, and proponents of investment. On the other hand, support for the policy of one-person, one-vote, in one state was higher than average among the young, the better-educated, non-Zulu speakers, residents of the Pretoria–Witwatersrand–Vereeniging Triangle [South Africa's industrial hub], and proponents of conditional or total disinvestment.[61]

The questions, however, were deliberately loaded to link federation with homelands, some members of the National Party, many businessmen and Inkatha, while the unitary option ('in which all blacks and whites vote together for their leaders, to participate without regard to race or group in one central government') was linked to the African National Congress, the United Democratic Front and other more radical organizations. The loading was said to reflect the political contexts in which the two options are canvassed.

No doubt there is an element of veracity in these findings, as Irvine's comment (quoted above) suggests. Yet they need not necessarily be the decisive knock-out blow for the federal idea. It would be virtually impossible to mobilize mass support among Africans for federation *per se*, but if it offered promise as part of a compromise accommodation to which the alternative was perpetuating a mutually destructive conflict, it might well be broadly acceptable. Nothing more definite can be said at this stage.

On the white side the setback suffered by the Progressive Federal Party in the election of May 1987, when it lost its status as the official opposition, was also a setback for support of democratic federalism. Yet there is possibly more support for a federal approach in the white electorate than those results might suggest. A fragment of evidence indicating this was provided by a survey of white policy preferences that was carried out in October 1986. Four options were listed, but in no case was an option identified with a particular party in the questionnaire, although it would not have been difficult for moderately well-informed respondents to make the appropriate connections. Only 5 per cent of the sample (of 1984 people) favoured a 'unitary state with *one* parliament and majority rule on the basis of "one man, one vote" '; 37 per cent favoured a 'new constitution on a (non-ethnic) regional basis drawn up by negotiation among representatives of *all* citizens. A federal or confederal central government, consisting of regional representatives, will guarantee the rights and privileges of the individual through a bill of rights'. This option identifies most closely with the Progressive Federal Party's policy. Only 20 per cent and 27 per cent respectively of the sample favoured the 'separate freedoms' for each ethnic population group (the far-right Conservative Party) and the 'group-based', 'group-autonomy' plus 'power-sharing' policy (National Party). The same showed that among National Party supporters only 43 per cent favoured the Party's policy, as expressed in the questionnaire, while 31 per cent favoured the Progressive Federal Party option.[62]

As mentioned above, these data, like those on African attitudes to federalism, are only suggestive, and by no means conclusive. If one assumes, as this writer does, that neither side in the South African struggle is likely to find itself in a position in which it can impose its constitutional views on a political *tabula rasa*, some form of negotiated accommodation seems the most desirable (if not necessarily the most likely) outcome. In general, a substantial majority of the white electorate is prepared to accept 'reform' of a circumscribed kind, provided that reformist measures do not jeopardize their security nor lead to 'black majority rule'.

In the 1987 election roughly 30 per cent of the white electorate supported the parties of the ultra-right which exploited racial fears as much as they could. Whether there is a ceiling on the potential extent of support for the Conservative Party, as many analysts have supposed, is a crucial question. A fanatical, Ku Klux Klan-like section of the ultra-right, the *Afrikaner Weerstandsbeweging* (literally 'the Afrikaner Resistance Movement'), is active and vocal, especially in the Transvaal, in demanding restoration to Afrikaners of '*die Boerestaat*' ('the Boer State'), by which they mean the Transvaal, the Orange Free State and northern Natal.

Continuing violence and economic contraction (exacerbated by sanctions) will strengthen the forces of extreme reaction, making any kind of accommodation, whether federal or otherwise, an even remoter prospect than it presently is. It is by no means inconceivable that some future transitional South African government might have to acquiesce partially at least, in the *Boerestaat*/partitionist notion, be it only as a means of extruding or buying off a dangerous fifth-column.

## Can federal juice be extracted from apartheid's bitter lemons?

Several authors have made ingenious proposals for adapting and transforming apartheid structures into federal and confederal ones.[63]

Others of more radical persuasion see in recent government moves on the constitutional front and in the implementation of regional policies a shift towards federalism which 'is seen by the ruling groups as a solution to the problem of incorporating Africans politically, while retaining and strengthening a capitalist system.'[64]

Officially the ruling National Party completely rejects a non-racial, geographical form of federation. Its chief constitutional planner, Chris Heunis, Minister of Constitutional Planning and Development, has stated categorically in a recent interview that universal suffrage in a unitary system would not be mitigated by a federal system:

If you do that, you multiply the national problem by the numbers of component states of that federation . . . if we believe that one-man, one-vote would lead to the destruction of the values we have on a national basis, there is no reason why the same result should not emanate on a federal basis.[65]

In some respects the neo-apartheid policy of the South African government appears to lend itself to a federalizing process for the society as a whole. The four 'independent' states of Bophuthatswana, Ciskei, Transkei and Venda, as well as the remaining six 'self-governing' black national states (the official term for what are commonly referred to as 'homelands'), are potential candidates as regions of a future federal South Africa. Even at present the various multilateral ties that bind the independent states and South Africa might be described as 'confederal' in nature. Critics would argue, however, that the federal possibilities are more illusion than reality, given the extremely asymmetrical dependence of all ten of these territories on the Republic for revenues and security, together with their geographically fragmented nature. Moreover, to a substantial number of Africans coupling the homelands to a federalizing process would probably do more damage to the federal idea than contribute to the accommodation of the racial problem.

Official policy remains committed to granting independence to those homelands whose leadership requests it, but in recent years it has been recognized by policy-makers that the homelands can provide for the political rights of only the people who live in them and that as many as 60 per cent of the African population 'will not be able to be accommodated physically or politically in the homelands, and will, therefore, have to exercize their political rights in South Africa'.[66] It is also recognized that the political linkage of Africans to their (supposed) homelands will not satisfy the majority. How are rights to be accorded to non-homeland Africans 'in such a way that they will not destroy the established rights of the Whites, Coloureds and Indians'?

In response to this question the Information Service of the National Party offered the following answer in 1985:

There are several possibilities: The national states might obtain powers over some of the areas outside their borders; local authorities might be given considerably wider powers; local authorities might be linked together in authoritative structures encompassing larger areas; new bodies comparable to the White provincial councils might be established; a national assembly of Black people outside the national states might be brought into being; some of these bodies might be involved in decision-making at the highest level in conjunction with the South African parliament and the governments of the national and possibly even the independent states.[67]

The answer was tentative because the eventual constitutional framework is to be worked out 'in close co-operation with the leaders of as many Black interest groups as possible'. So far, however, the Government has been unsuccessful in drawing any significant African leaders into its negotiating structures, and legislation to create a bargaining forum has not yet been enacted.

In spite of (or perhaps because of) the deadlock at the national level the Government has been busy with an extensive restructuring of the second and third tier levels of government.[68] The new structures are complex and a detailed analysis of them is beyond the scope of this essay. Their most salient features, however, must be noted. Elected (white) Provincial Councils have been abolished and replaced by multi-racial Provincial Executive Committees whose members are nominated by the State President. These Committees are chaired by the Provincial Administrator who is also (as previously) a central government appointee.

In terms of legislation enacted in 1985 the entire country (outside of the homelands) is to be divided up into areas of jurisdiction under Regional Services Councils consisting of nominated representatives from groupings of local authorities of all racial groups, including Africans. While the process of demarcation of these areas is by no means complete there will eventually be well over 50 RSCs. Conforming to the official view that affairs can be divided into 'own' (i.e. pertaining specifically to a particular population group) and 'general', RSCs will be concerned with 'general', affairs of a local nature, such as water supplies, transport, electricity and sewage disposal. They are designed also to ensure that infrastructure, facilities and services are provided in those areas where they are needed most – in practice those will be in the black urban townships. They have been given substantial revenue-raising powers to exact levies on employers and companies within each RSC area.[69]

As comparatively few Regional Services Councils are yet functioning it is premature to comment on their operation. It is true that they involve African local authorities in a limited way with regional decision-making, but, on the other hand, the 'group' basis of African, as well as Coloured and Indian, local authorities has in practice ensured that their legitimacy is strictly limited. In fact, the violence of the past few years, sparked in many cases by local issues such as rent increases, has meant that many African local authorities have been targeted by protesters and consequently forced to cease operating.

From the perspective of this essay the critical issue is whether these new structures, either at provincial or regional level, actually involve devolution of power – as the Government claims – and might thereby warrant description as 'proto-federalist' moves. Most analysts conclude that, in fact, they centralize power. Pierre du Toit concludes a sober review with the following comment:

Regional services councils represent an elaborate system of control whereby powerholders at central level will gain crucial influence at local level. The system relies ultimately on co-opting subordinate elites into new multi-racial decision-making structures. These elites will have to comply with the rules of the political game dictated by the ruling group at national level – which is politically represented by the National Party.[70]

Since the advent of the National Party Government in 1948 the trend has been to regard lower tiers of government as mere executants of centrally-determined policies. The new dispensation for provinces and RSCs confirms, indeed strengthens, this approach.

Analysts have scented possible confederal implications in a policy initiated in 1982 to promote industrial development on a regional basis.[71] The rationale for this was to address the highly uneven spatial basis of previous economic development and its concentration in the four main metropolitan conurbations of South Africa, especially in the Pretoria–Witwatersrand–Vereeniging Triangle, which contributes some 60 per cent of the Gross Domestic Product. In line with this approach initially eight, and subsequently, nine regions were identified for purposes of regional development planning. What is significant about the designated regions is that their boundaries cut across political boundaries, including those of homelands, both independent and non-independent. Region H, for example, includes the PWV Triangle, KwaNdebele (a non-independent homeland) and a part of Bophuthatswana.

Apart from the suggestion in a Government White Paper that effective decentralization efforts in this regional development programme would ensure greater co-operation across political boundaries,[72] there is, however, no evidence to suggest that these regions are intended as potential or experimental units in a future confederation. Indeed, official spokesmen have been at pains to emphasize that the sovereignty of the independent homelands will not be infringed.

## Conclusion

It will be clear from this chapter that the protagonist of a federal South Africa faces an uphill battle. The state is more centralized than it has ever been in its existence, and genuine devolution of power is not occurring, notwithstanding official claims to the contrary. Security concerns (whether justified or not is irrelevant) have placed immense power in very few hands, eclipsing even Parliament and the Cabinet in the process. It is not impossible to decentralize power after it has been centralized, just as it is not impossible to federalize states that were formerly unitary. Arguably, though, it is more difficult, since the 'zero-sum' view of policies becomes entrenched in the political culture.

Federal thinking, after its renaissance in the 1960s and 1970s, appears to be on the decline. Apart from black and white supporters of the Indaba, and the Progressive Federal Party, which has been electorally marginalized, there are no significant mobilized bodies of pro-federal opinion, as distinct from possible latent sources of potential support. Much black opinion, as the evidence has shown, views federalism as a 'second-best' option whose basic thrust is to abridge majority rule. To the extent that it would incorporate the principle of statutorily designated racial groups 'corporative' federalism that took such groups as its component units, would have no chance of putting down roots of legitimacy.

To this writer, a piecemeal process of federalization, broadly similar to the suggestions advocated by Murray Forsyth,[73] would be acceptable strategy – perhaps the only hopeful one in South Africa's constrained circumstances. As Indaba supporters have argued, if a national accommodation is for the time being (and this may be a very long time) impossible, regional accommodations should be attempted – not as potential secessionist moves but as living demonstrations of equitable and democratic systems that could be replicated regionally and, eventually, nationally. This strategy may also have been foreclosed by the violence between Inkatha and United Democratic Front supporters.

Much black nationalist thinking favours a unitary state with a strongly centralized government. In the hypothetical case of a future African National Congress government extensive redistributive measures, possible nationalization of industry and reallocation of land would probably necessitate a strong central government – or, more accurately, such a government, would be perceived as necessary.

In the late 1980s the prospects for an accommodation in South Africa look bleak. The antagonists appear still to be convinced that victory on their own terms can be achieved. A bargaining or negotiating situation has not yet developed because neither recognizes the strength and staying power of its adversary.

# Notes

1. L.M. Thompson, *The Unification of South Africa*, Oxford (1960), 483.
2. Phyllis Lewsen, *John X. Merriman: Paradoxical South African Statesman*, Johannesburg (1982) 315.
3 Thompson, op. cit., 66.
4. Edgar J. Walton, *The Inner History of the National Convention of South Africa*, Cape Town (1912) 53.
5. Anonymous, *The Government of South Africa*, Cape Town (1908), 1, 264–5.
6. Walton, op. cit., 53 ff.
7. Ibid., 57–64.
8. Ibid., 64–7.
9. Ibid., 73.
10. Ibid., 86.
11. Ibid., 68–9.
12. Ibid., 70–2.
13. Ibid., 88–9.
14. Ibid., 96.
15. Edgar H. Brookes and Colin de B. Webb, *A History of Natal*, Pietermaritzburg (1965) 244.
16. *Debates of the Natal Legislative Council*, 4th Special Session of the 5th Parliament (1909) 7.
17. *Debates of the Natal Legislative Assembly*, op. cit., 12.
18. *Debates of the Legislative Assembly of the Orange River Colony*, Extraordinary and Second Session of the First Parliament (1909) 11.
19. *Debates of the House of Assembly, Cape of Good Hope*, (1909) 15.
20. R.H. Brand, *The Union of South Africa*, Oxford (1909) 82–4.
21. *Debates of the House of Assembly, Cape of Good Hope*, (1909) 4.
22. L.M. Thompson, *The Cape Coloured Franchise*, Johannesburg (1949) 55.
23. Brookes & Webb, op. cit. (note 15), 229–30.
24. *Debates of the Natal Legislative Assembly*, op. cit., 84.
25. Anonymous, op. cit. (note 5), 1, 126.
26. Ibid., 140.
27. Hugh Edward Egerton, *Federation and Unions within the British Empire*, Oxford (1911) 87.
28. Michael B. Stein, 'Federal political systems and federal societies', *World Politics*, 20 (1967–8).
29. Alexander Brady, *Democracy in the Dominions – A Comparative Study in Institutions*, 2nd edn, Toronto (1952) 348–9.
30. C.M. van den Heever, *General J.B.M. Hertzog*, Johannesburg (1943) 261.
31. Andrew Duminy, 'Federation – the lost cause' in University of Natal: *Symposium on Natal – A Case for Devolution?*, Durban (1977), 2, 3–4.
32. Thompson, op. cit., 176.
33. Quoted in David Welsh, 'The politics of white supremacy', in Leonard Thompson & Jeffrey Butler (eds), *Change in Contemporary South Africa*, Berkeley (1975) 52.
34. Quoted in David Welsh, *The Roots of Segregation*, Cape Town (1971) 204.
35. Walton, op. cit. (note 4), 123.

36. Eric A. Walker, *W.P. Schreiner: A South African*, Oxford (1937) 306; Debates of the House of Assembly, Cape of Good Hope (1909) 18–9.
37. For a fuller account see D. Welsh, *The Politics of White Supremacy*, (note 5) 52–62.
38. For a fuller account see F. van Zyl Slabbert and David Welsh, *South Africa's Options: Strategies for Sharing Power*, Cape Town (1979) 77–89.
39. As Smuts claimed in *Transvaal Legislative Assembly Debates*, 2nd session, First Parliament (1909) 175.
40. Quoted in Nicholas Mansergh, *South Africa 1906–1961: The Price of Magnanimity*, London (1962) 51.
41. W.K. Hancock, *Smuts: The Sanguine Years 1870–1919*, Cambridge (1962) 1, 268.
42. Brand, op. cit (note 20), 130.
43. *Debates of the Natal Legislative Assembly*, op. cit., 43.
44. Murray Forsyth, *Federalism and the Future of South Africa*, Johannesburg (1984) 5.
45. Progressive Federal Party, *Constitutional Policy: A Realistic Plan for the Future*, Cape Town (1987) 16–17.
46. Arthur Keppel-Jones, *Friends or Foes?: A Point of View and A Programme for Racial Harmony in South Africa*, Pietermaritzburg (1949); Jordan K. Ngubane, *An African Explains Apartheid*, New York (1963); Chief M. Gatsha Buthelezi: *White and Black, Ethnicity and the Future of the Homelands*, Johannesburg (1974).
47. Buthelezi, op. cit. (note 46), 17–18.
48. David Welsh, 'The Washing of the spears', *Front File Southern Africa Brief*, II, 2, (1988).
49. Indicator Project South Africa, *New Frontiers: The KwaZulu/Natal Debates*, Durban (1987) 6.
50. KwaZulu Natal Indaba, *Constitutional Proposals Agreed to on 28 November 1986*, Durban (1986).
51. Johan Steenkamp, 'Minority Role', in Indicator Project South Africa, op. cit. (note 49), 47.
52. KwaZulu Natal Indaba, *Press Release*, 7 March 1988.
53. Indicator Project South Africa, op. cit. (note 49), 78.
54. G. Maré and G. Hamilton, *An Appetite for Power: Buthelezi's Inkatha and the Politics of 'Loyal Resistance'*, Johannesburg (1987) 171, 221–2.
55. For a further analysis see Slabbert and Welsh, op. cit. (note 38), 23–4.
56. Quoted in ibid., 6.
57. *Debates of the House of Assembly*, 24 March 1988.
58. O. Tambo, *Economic and Political Perspectives of the A.N.C. for a liberated South Africa* (mimeo of speech in Bonn, 8 April 1986).
59. Ibid.
60. D. McK. Irvine, 'South Africa: federal potentialities in current developments', *International Political Science Review*, 5 (1984) 493.
61. Mark Orkin, *Disinvestment, The Struggle and the Future: What Black South Africans Really Think*, Johannesburg (1986) 51.
62. Market and Opinion Surveys (Pty) Ltd., *Poll*, October 1986, 7.
63. For example, see: Forsyth, op. cit. (note 44); J.A. du Pisanie and

L. Kritzinger, 'The Federal Option', in D.J. van Vuuren, N.E. Wiehahn, J.A. Lombard and N.J. Rhoodie (eds), *South Africa: A Plural Society in Transition*, Durban (1985) 443–78; Irvine, op. cit. (note 60).

64. W. Cobbett, D. Glaser, D. Hindson and M. Swilling, 'South Africa's regional political economy: a critical analysis of reform strategy in the 1980s', in R. Tomlinson and M. Addleson (eds), *Regional Restructuring Under Apartheid: Urban and Regional Policies in Contemporary South Africa*, Johannesburg (1987) 19.

65. C. Heunis, interview in M. Abeldas and A. Fischer (eds), *A Question of Survival: Conversations with Key South Africans*, Johannesburg (1987) 494.

66. Federal Information Service of the National Party, *And What About the Black People?*, Cape Town (1985) 12.

67. Ibid., 13.

68. For a comprehensive analysis see the essays contained in C. Heymans and G. Tötemeyer (eds), *Government by the People?: The Politics of Local Government in South Africa*, Cape Town (1988).

69. *Financial Mail*, 13 March 1987.

70. Pierre du Toit, 'Regional services councils: control at local government level', in C. Heymans and G. Tötemeyer, op. cit. (note 68), 75.

71. Cobbett *et al.*, op. cit. (note 64), 11.

72. South African Institute of Race Relations, *Race Relations Survey 1985*, Johannesburg (1986) 112.

73. Forsyth, op. cit. (note 44).

# Index

United Arab Republic 230
United States of America 3, 6, 14, 21,
     22, 126, 127, 157, 158, 169–70,
     175, 179, 182, 183, 195, 219,
     221, 234, 241, 251, 253, 254, 255

Venezuela 12
Vicens Vives, Jaime 17
Vile, Maurice 234

Walton, E.H. 255
West African federation 172, 191

West German federalism *see*
     Germany
Wheare, Kenneth
     148, 157, 170
Whitaker, R. 163

Yonge, C.A.S. 263
Yugoslavia 4, 5, 45, 115–145, 234, 240

Zanzibar 173, 176
Zollverein 240